ON INSOM
Edgar Chías

LITTLE CERTAINTIES
Bárbara Colio

SEVEN-ELEVEN
Iván Olivares

THE SÁNCHEZ HUERTA GIRL KILLED HERSELF
Claudia Ríos

USED BLOOD JUNKYARD
Alberto Villarreal

*Modern International Plays in Translation
from Nick Hern Books*

Marcos Barbosa
ALMOST NOTHING & AT THE TABLE

Lukas Bärfuss
THE SEXUAL NEUROSES OF OUR PARENTS

Evelyne de la Chenelière
STRAWBERRIES IN JANUARY

Jean Cocteau
LES PARENTS TERRIBLES

Ulises Rodríguez Febles
THE CONCERT

David Gieselmann
MR KOLPERT

Eugène Ionesco
MACBETT

Klaus Pohl
WAITING ROOM GERMANY

The Presnyakov Brothers
PLAYING THE VICTIM
TERRORISM

Roland Schimmelpfennig
PUSH UP

Vassily Sigarev
BLACK MILK
LADYBIRD
PLASTICINE

International Anthologies

THE CRACK IN THE EMERALD: NEW IRISH PLAYS
CZECH PLAYS
DUTCH PLAYS
GERMAN PLAYS
LATIN-AMERICAN PLAYS
SCOT-FREE: NEW SCOTS PLAYS
SCOTLAND PLAYS
SPANISH PLAYS

MEXICAN PLAYS

EDGAR CHÍAS ■ ON INSOMNIA AND MIDNIGHT

Translated by David Johnston

BÁRBARA COLIO ■ LITTLE CERTAINTIES

Translated by William Gregory

IVÁN OLIVARES ■ SEVEN-ELEVEN

Translated by William Gregory

CLAUDIA RÍOS
THE SÁNCHEZ HUERTA GIRL KILLED HERSELF

Translated by Roxana Silbert

ALBERTO VILLARREAL ■ USED BLOOD JUNKYARD

Translated by Simon Scardifield

Edited and with a Foreword by Elyse Dodgson

Introduced by Luis Mario Moncada

NICK HERN BOOKS
London
www.nickhernbooks.co.uk
in association with
ROYAL COURT THEATRE

A Nick Hern Book

Mexican Plays first published in Great Britain as a paperback original in 2007 by Nick Hern Books Limited, 14 Larden Road, London W3 7ST in association with the Royal Court Theatre, London

On Insomnia and Midnight copyright © 2006, 2007 Edgar Chías
Translation copyright © 2006, 2007 David Johnston
First published in 2006 by Oberon Books, London.
Reproduced with kind permission

Little Certainties copyright © 2007 Bárbara Colio
Translation copyright © 2007 William Gregory

Seven-Eleven copyright © 2007 Iván Olivares
Translation copyright © 2007 William Gregory

The Sánchez Huerta Girl Killed Herself copyright © 2007 Claudia Ríos
Translation copyright © 2007 Roxana Silbert

Used Blood Junkyard copyright © 2007 Alberto Villarreal
Translation copyright © 2007 Simon Scardifield

Foreword copyright © 2007 Elyse Dodgson
Introduction copyright © 2007 Luis Mario Moncada

The authors and translators have asserted their moral rights

Cover designed by Ned Hoste, 2H

Typeset by Country Setting, Kingsdown, Kent CT14 8ES
Printed and bound in Great Britain by Biddles, King's Lynn

A CIP catalogue record for this book is available from the British Library

ISBN 978 1 85459 947 6

CAUTION All rights whatsoever in these plays are strictly reserved. Requests to reproduce the texts in whole or in part should be addressed to the publisher.

Amateur Performing Rights Applications for performance, including readings and excerpts, by amateurs in these English translations throughout the world should be addressed to the Performing Rights Manager, Nick Hern Books, 14 Larden Road, London W3 7ST, *tel* +44 (0)20 8749 4953, *fax* +44 (0)20 8735 0250, *e-mail* info@nickhernbooks.demon.co.uk, except as follows:

Australia: Dominie Drama, 8 Cross Street, Brookvale 2100,
fax (2) 9905 5209, *e-mail* dominie@dominie.com.au

New Zealand: Play Bureau, PO Box 420, New Plymouth,
fax (6) 753 2150, *e-mail* play.bureau.nz@xtra.co.nz

South Africa: DALRO (pty) Ltd, PO Box 31627, 2017 Braamfontein,
tel (11) 489 5065, *fax* (11) 403 9094, *e-mail* Wim.Vorster@dalro.co.za

Professional Performing Rights Applications for performance by professionals in these English translations in any medium throughout the world (including stock productions in North America) should be addressed to Nick Hern Books, 14 Larden Road, London W3 7ST,
tel +44 (0)20 8749 4953, *fax* +44 (0)20 8735 0250,
e-mail info@nickhernbooks.demon.co.uk

No performance of any kind may be given unless a licence has been obtained. Applications should be made before rehearsals begin. Publication of these plays does not necessarily indicate their availability for performance.

Contents

Acknowledgements   vi

Foreword   vii

Introduction: Arena Mexico   ix

Biographies   xiv

ON INSOMNIA AND MIDNIGHT   1

LITTLE CERTAINTIES   57

SEVEN-ELEVEN   109

THE SÁNCHEZ HUERTA GIRL KILLED HERSELF   185

USED BLOOD JUNKYARD   241

Acknowledgements

We would like to thank the following for their commitment to this project: the writers, translators, readers, directors and actors who took part in the 2006 *Arena Mexico* season at the Royal Court Theatre.

This project was supported by the Genesis Foundation and developed in collaboration with the British Council and the Centro Cultural Helénico, Mexico City. The Royal Court is also grateful to Conaculta, the Anglo Mexican Foundation, the Mexican Embassy to the United Kingdom, and the Mexico Tourism Board.

We are grateful to the following individuals for making *Arena Mexico* possible: Rocío Bermejo, Susan Chapman, April De Angelis, William Gregory, Chris James, Hettie Macdonald, Orla O'Loughlin, Indhu Rubasingham, Roxana Silbert, Simon Stephens, Tiffany Watt-Smith and Graham Whybrow. We owe a particular debt of thanks to Circe Henestrosa, Luis Mario Moncada and the entire staff of the Centro Cultural Helénico, who began and continue this project with us.

ROYAL COURT

CONACULTA · HELENICO
la CULTURA en tus manos

THE ANGLO MEXICAN FOUNDATION

BRITISH COUNCIL

Genesis
FOUNDATION

Foreword

George Devine's 1956 vision of the Royal Court was of a 'truly international theatre' and in the early years of the English Stage Company the repertoire included new plays by writers such as Samuel Beckett, Bertolt Brecht, Max Frisch, Jean Genet, Eugène Ionesco, Arthur Miller and Wole Soyinka. Over the last decade the Royal Court has placed a renewed emphasis on the development and production of new international work. A creative dialogue now exists between innovative theatre writers and practitioners in many different countries including Brazil, Cuba, France, Germany, India, Nigeria, Palestine, Romania, Russia and Syria. Most of these projects are supported by the Genesis Foundation and the British Council.

In October 2003 I visited Mexico City at the invitation of Circe Henestrosa, the Arts Manager of the British Council there. I visited theatres and had meetings with many different theatre professionals in order to explore the possibility of collaborating on a long-term playwriting project with emerging Mexican writers. I knew I had found our partner when I entered the Centro Cultural Helénico and met its artistic director, Luis Mario Moncada. I had never met an artistic director who was also a playwright and Luis Mario's knowledge, perception and passion for new writing convinced me that we had the perfect collaborator.

In May 2004, we began the project with two leading Royal Court playwrights: April De Angelis and Simon Stephens. Thirteen playwrights from all parts of the country took part in a workshop that lasted a week at Centro Cultural Helénico in Mexico City. The aim of the workshop was to support the writers in planning a first draft of a new contemporary play. The writers wanted to find tools to strengthen their work and asked that we focus on character, story, language and structure. On the fourth day of the workshop the entire group led by Luis Mario Moncada travelled to the Pyramids and Ancient City of Teotihuacán. This was certainly a breathtaking experience for the British team, but the writers were keen to use the site as a stimulus for their writing. As the workshop continued it was clear that this was one of the most positive and promising first workshops we had ever had. We were fascinated by a recent text produced by many of the young Mexican writers called *Versus Aristóteles (Against Aristotle)* which clearly showed an emphasis on experimenting with form sometimes at the expense of content. The workshop gave us an opportunity to explore our differences, and everyone, including the Royal Court team, felt that their perspective was shifted as a result of the work we did together.

All of the writers completed the first drafts of their plays and in December 2004 I returned to Mexico City with Simon Stephens and the director Roxana Silbert to continue the development of the plays. This time we took the plays on further by involving a group of local actors. More time was then given for a final draft of the plays, and a third workshop took place in June 2005 led by Roxana Silbert and director Indhu Rubasingham. This time we began working with a group of young Mexican directors eager to find ways of tackling new plays. This final workshop was attended by thirteen playwrights, six directors and eight actors. The dedication of the group was extraordinary.

As a result of this work, five of the plays were given readings in Spanish at the Centro Cultural Helénico in December 2005. And in early January 2006 the translated plays in this volume were presented as staged readings in the Jerwood Theatre Upstairs at the Royal Court, during the *Arena Mexico* season. At the heart of this project are the thirteen writers who worked with such devotion over a period of twenty months. As one of them described their experience: 'I always leave with a lot of questions. Far from being still and calm, I feel altered, and I like that.' In May 2007 a new phase of work began with a group of twelve new writers with the support of the Anglo Mexican Foundation and Centro Cultural Helénico. As the work continues I am convinced that many of these voices will be heard in Mexico, in Britain and in the rest of the world.

Elyse Dodgson
Associate Director/Head of International Department,
Royal Court Theatre

Arena Mexico

As the twenty-first century begins, Mexico has a chance to discover its own diversity. If we look back, we see a centralised culture that for a thousand years consigned even dazzling civilisations like the Maya and the Olmec to the margins, such was the dominance of the centre of power, located since the fourteenth century in the Valley of Mexico. The Spanish domination that lasted three hundred years only reinforced this centrifugal vision, causing vast stretches of Mexican territory – those where the gaze of the government did not reach – to be lost. Even the last century was marked by the iron grip of the capital, but even more by the grip of the single party state, from the autocracy of Porfirio Díaz (1876–1910) to the 'perfect dictatorship' of the PRI (Institutional Revolutionary Party, 1929–2000). Only now are we attempting to emerge from the lethargic culture of top-down power that allowed one vision – the Establishment's vision – to dominate.

For this reason the year 2000 marked a double celebration for our country: the millennium began with the electoral defeat of the old regime and, with it, the promise of a change to a more pluralist, inclusive and authentically federal system. The process has been rocky – our country is still unaccustomed to building consensus – and has had to withstand tough tests of legitimacy, such as the one faced at the recent federal elections. Despite this, the process seems irreversible and will surely consolidate itself, but only if it succeeds in establishing throughout the territory a culture of equality, justice and the rule of law, and above all if we accept that our country is made up of many discordant voices who nevertheless deserve to be included in the arena of decision-making.

For all of these reasons one of the projects implicit in this process of change has had to be the development of new artists to depict or reinvent the cultural mosaic of the country from very diverse frontiers and points of view. If one thing can characterise this moment, it is multiplicity, the lack of a preponderant discourse. Now is the time of single voices, of the destruction of the 'common interest' and the uncovering of contrasting identities.

But theatre is facing a painful paradox: having entered the twentieth century as one of the main events in social entertainment, it left it as an activity of 'public interest', protected by the State – that is to say, as an art in danger of extinction – despite there being more theatre produced now, perhaps, than ever in the nation's history. The debate surrounding the nature and purpose of theatre in times of mass, interactive communication recalls the paradox coined by Luis de Tavira:[1] it is an art of the present, made of time, whose essence is ephemeral and impossible to reproduce industrially; 'there seems to be nothing more anti-modern than theatre, and yet it seems that nothing like theatre can offer to humanity the chance to remember that once we were people; art only for today, radical present, nothing is more modern'.

In this endless search to find its role in the forming of a new society, theatre also needs to build a new audience. Before, it was commonplace for the theatre's main audience to be the State itself, if only to criticise it; theatre survived thanks to and for the amusement of the Tlatoani[2] and his intellectual elite who, like a *Philanthropic Ogre,*[3] beat and rewarded their own children before devouring them. But with the advent of a new reality the theatre has lost this intermediary and must strike up a direct dialogue with the public, a thousand-headed monster whose eyes we are barely used to looking into.

One of the strategic fronts in this search for identities has been the development of Mexican playwriting, and in this context the exchange of experiences initiated in 2004 by the Royal Court Theatre and the Centro Cultural Helénico, with the support of the British Council, has been providential. These three institutions decided to bring together a working party of thirteen writers to develop, over eighteen months, dramatic projects of very different natures. The pilot group was formed of authors under forty (an age at which, due to very Mexican cultural circumstances, one can still be a beginner), all of whom worked under the guidance of British artists who were almost their contemporaries but whose experience was much more clearly defined. These authors, from different regions of the country, although mostly from Mexico City (it should be remembered that at least seventy per cent of professional theatre in Mexico happens in the capital) completed twelve plays, each representing a different vision of our reality.

But before focusing on some of these plays it is worth explaining the premise of the workshop, as it is the cornerstone of what we will see in the pages that follow: the meeting began with a challenge to the idea that we see our reality as stable and clearly defined. If we thought that our concepts of territory, community, ideology, morality or history were clear, the initial exercises set about dismantling, at least partially, some of our most common ideological prejudices.

1. Mexican theatre director, b. Mexico City, 1948.
2. Supreme governor.
3. *El ogro filantrópico* was a 1979 essay by Mexican writer Octavio Paz.

From there, a catalogue of terms could be drawn up that characterised the reality of contemporary Mexico as seen by our writers. Once this new conceptual map had been developed – a rhetorical exercise whose function was to mark out a framework for the creative process – the stories began to emerge; but, above all, so did a wealth of singular characters, all of them a product of this breeding ground called the Mexico of the global era.

Of the plays developed, five were selected to be presented in a season of readings entitled *Arena Mexico*, in the Jerwood Theatre Upstairs at the Royal Court in January 2006; these same plays form this anthology. At the risk of excluding other works that also offer a dramatic reading of the contemporary world, we are sure that these plays embody the broad spectrum of themes and styles developed by current Mexican theatre. Nevertheless, it is worth recognising the interesting areas addressed by the other plays in the workshop: urban schizophrenia in *Tiempo sometido (Subdued Time)* by Carmina Narro; Latin American migration in *Cruces fronterizos (Border Crossings)* by Edgar Álvarez; the impact of social marginalisation on children in *Agua (Water)* by María Morett; the traces of destiny and the superstitions of the indigenous peoples in *Trato a ciegas (Dealing Blind)* by Verónica Musalem; the effects of guilt in *Exégisis (Exegesis)* by Rafael Martínez; the endless generation debate in *Y si te digo que te quiero? (What if I Tell You I Love You?)* by Francisco Reyes; or a take on Highsmithian suspense in *Los impostores (The Impostors)* by Luis Ayhllón.

One of the authors in this anthology, Claudia Ríos (b. Mexico City, 1965) is a playwright trained on the boards as an actor and director; for this reason we see in her later writing an awareness of space and time – both on- and offstage – and of the presence and positioning of the actor within them. Whilst working professionally as an actor, Ríos attended playwriting workshops. Here, she sketched out scenes that she rewrote and rewrote but never made public, until with *Las gelatinas (The Jellies*, 2000) her work finally came to the boil. Ríos writes plays whose stories simmer slowly, and *Sánchez Huerta, se mató la niña (The Sánchez Huerta Girl Killed Herself)* is no exception. A single space and time marks out our meeting with the divorced parents who have received the news of their daughter's suicide. Without further ado, the schoolroom is transformed into a cathartic confessional where relatives and teachers desperately search for a guilty party to cover up their own faults and failings. Ríos creates an asphyxiating atmosphere, with no concessions that might let the audience breathe. At the end, we expect mourning to give way to liberation, but the author refuses to release us and, instead, twists the screw once more . . .

Bárbara Colio (b. northern Baja California, 1969) is an engineer by profession, and also came to playwriting after working as an actor. The late appearance of her writing in the nation's theatres (the first performances of her plays took place in the territorial margins of the northern frontier) has made it somewhat difficult to identify her with one or other generation of writers, but her solitary work has yielded fruit, with plays that are increasingly consistent in their structure and in the drawing of their characters. Hers is not a lyrical work, but cerebral and premeditated; nevertheless, judging by the audience's reception for *Pequeñas certezas* (*Little Certainties*), the play that is included here, her writing also touches the emotions. *Pequeñas certezas* is an attempt to rebuild the scattered image of an absent being, as seen in the clear and human portrait of five complex personalities, inhabitants of this country in search of some spiritual order.

Iván Olivares (b. Mexico City, 1973) is another unique case in his professional training: having studied theatre at the Faculty of Arts and Philosophy of the National Autonomous University of Mexico (UNAM), he has worked as an actor, director, designer and writer, particularly in children's theatre. Nevertheless, in his approach to this genre he has sought to test out themes and techniques more common to theatre for adults; and vice-versa: in his play *Alicia en el país de las alcantarillas* (*Alice in Sewerland*, 2002) he employs techniques from children's theatre to present a dark and sordid drama about the underground life of Mexico City. In *Seven-Eleven*, Olivares again investigates this same theme and succeeds in profiling one of the emblematic characters of our marginal urban culture; Cabrón[4] is the name and nickname of this monstrous, charismatic being who, for all his lack of scruples, is engaging in his pragmatic vision of life.

Trained as an actor and playwright in the Faculty of Arts and Philosophy at the UNAM, Edgar Chías (b. Mexico City, 1973) took only five years to establish an oeuvre of solidity and depth. The first productions of his plays – *¿Último round?* (*Final Round?*, 2000) and *Cuando quiero llorar no lloro* (*When I Want to Cry I Don't Cry*, 2001) – already saw the emergence of a skilled writer, but it was his experience of devised playwriting with *Circo para bobos* (*Circus for Fools*, 2001) and *La mirada del sordo* (*The Deaf Man's Gaze*, 2002) that determined and defined a writing style that strips down both the scenic apparatus and traditional dramatic notation, paying greater service to the spoken word. *Telefonemas* (*Telephonemes*, 2004), *El cielo en la piel* (*The Sky in the Skin*, 2004) and above all *De insomnio y media noche* (*On Insomnia and Midnight*), included here, reveal a more daring, precise and convincing writer. In *De insomnio y media*

4. *Cabrón*, literally meaning *bastard* and derived from the Spanish for *billy goat*, is at once an insult and a compliment in Mexican Spanish.

noche, Chías takes a minutely short story by Thomas Bernhard as a base to develop nine nocturnal scenes about desire and manipulation. More charged with text than with anecdotal plot, the writer produces sensations and introduces veils that prevent the audience from too close an understanding, creating a splendid game of light and dark.

Alberto Villarreal (b. Mexico City, 1977) is the youngest of the writers anthologised here and, despite this, the one whose discourse is the most elaborate and ambitious; since his debut in 1998 each one of his works as a director and/or writer has marked a step forward in the creation of a theatrical aesthetic as yet unseen in Mexican playwriting. As he himself states, his work 'is focused on the creation and development of contemporary theatrical poetics contaminated with classical forms,' coming together in his ideas of production. Not for nothing is *Artillería producciones* (*Artillery Productions*), under his and Patricia Rozitchner's leadership, one of the most promising companies of the current national scene. The case of *Deshuesadero de sangre basura* (*Used Blood Junkyard*) is also paradigmatic of a renewed form of dramatic writing in Mexico; more linked to the experiences of German post-dramatic theatre, it alternates techniques of advertising, performance and political discourse to present a great fresco on the world's social and political moral decay, but does so with a sense of fun and theatrical daring that attracts the youngest of our country's audiences, making him one of the emblems of the new Mexican theatre.

These five authors, so dissimilar in their visions of theatre, and so representative of the contemporary forms of the Mexican stage, have in common the fact of emerging as writers in the current decade. But when presented in strict chronological order they also show us a continual sliding from anecdotal to post-dramatic forms. In the end, all of them are part of this new reality: a reality that, still without a fixed form, is moulding the cultural mosaic of our country.

It just remains for us to acknowledge the Associate Director of the Royal Court Theatre, Elyse Dodgson, a visionary and enthusiastic discoverer of new voices around the world, for guiding and contributing to the development of this project, along with each one of the workshop leaders who took part: April De Angelis, Simon Stephens, Roxana Silbert and Indhu Rubasingham. Their attention and knowledge have been key in allowing every one of these writers to hear their own voice and to make their voices heard.

Luis Mario Moncada
Artistic Director, Centro Cultural Helénico

Translated by William Gregory

Biographies

EDGAR CHÍAS (*On Insomnia and Midnight*)

Edgar Chías was born in Mexico City in 1973 and studied theatre at the UNAM. He is a playwright, actor, theatre critic and translator. His plays are performed throughout Mexico and include *Circo para bobos*, *El cielo en la piel*, *El drama Ausente*, *Telefonemos* and *Crack*. His play *De insomnio y media noche* (*On Insomnia and Midnight*) was chosen as a co-production between the Royal Court Theatre, Centro Cultural Helénico, the Festival Internacional Cervantino and was first produced in London, Guanajuato and Mexico City in September/October 2006. In 2007 he won the Oscar Liera Prize for the Best Contemporary Play for both *Crack* and *On Insomnia and Midnight*.

BÁRBARA COLIO (*Little Certainties*)

Bárbara Colio was born in the desert city of Mexicali, Baja California in 1969. She studied engineering in Baja California before studying theatre, and began working as an actress in 1988. She wrote her first play in 1996 and has written more than a dozen plays, of which eight have been produced including *La boca del lobo*, which was produced in the Festival Cervantino in 2004. In 2000 she was invited to take part in the Royal Court International Residency in London, and afterwards she became a resident writer in the The Writers Room in New York. In 2004, she became the first Mexican to win the Maria Teresa Leon International Prize for Theatre Writers in Spain for *Pequeñas certezas* (*Little Certainties*). *Little Certainties* was produced in Mexico City in 2007.

WILLIAM GREGORY (translator, *Little Certainties* and *Seven-Eleven*)

William Gregory studied at Cambridge, Drama Studio London and the Escuela Navarra de Teatro. His first theatre translation, Julio Escalada's *Springtime*, premiered at the Finborough Theatre, London, in 2003. Since then he has worked for the Royal Court on projects with playwrights from throughout the Spanish-speaking world. His translation of Ulises Rodríguez Febles's *The Concert*, performed at the Royal Court's 2004 *Cuba real* season, was later broadcast on the BBC World Service. Recent projects include translating for *Cuba* by Ulises Rodríguez Febles and Jennie Buckman for BBC Radio 4, and for Samuel Adamson's stage adaptation of Almodóvar's *All About My Mother* at the Old Vic, London.

DAVID JOHNSTON (translator, *On Insomnia and Midnight*)

David Johnston's translations include Juan Mayorga's *Way to Heaven* (Royal Court); *The Dog in the Manger* (RSC/Austin Shakespeare Festival, Texas), *Madness in Valencia* (Gate/RSC), *The Gentleman from Olmedo* (Gate/Watermill) and *The Great Pretenders* (Gate), all by Lope de Vega; Calderón's *The Painter of Dishonour* (RSC); Gil Vicente's *The Boat Plays*, Valle-Inclán's *The Barbarous Comedies*, *Bohemian Lights*, Vargas Llosa's *The Madman of the Balconies* (Gate) and *Divine Words* (BBC Radio 3). His original work includes *El Quijote* (Gate); *Hambone's Day*, *The Shadow of the Wedding*, *The Priest* (BBC); *Dark Root, Bitter Flower* (Strathclyde Theatre Group) and *The Poet in the City* (Crescent Arts Centre, Belfast).

IVÁN OLIVARES (*Seven-Eleven*)

Iván Olivares was born in Mexico City in 1973, is a graduate of the UNAM and has worked as an actor, director, teacher and designer as well as a playwright. He began as a writer of children's theatre and won the 2002 FILIJ Award for Best Children's Playwright. *Seven-Eleven* is his first play for adults. His plays for children include *From A-Z, Alice in Sewerland, Little Miss Mozart* and *Stories in Bed to Ring Bells and Reach the Moon*. He currently works as a Spanish accent coach for actors and scriptwriters for Colombian television.

CLAUDIA RÍOS (*The Sánchez Huerta Girl Killed Herself*)

Claudia Ríos was born in Mexico City in 1965. She studied at the School of Theatre Arts of INBA and at the UNAM from 1986 to 1990. She has been an actress and a director of many productions including Bárbara Colio's *Pequeñas certezas (Little Certainties)* in Mexico City in 2007. She won the prize for best director of the year for her production of *Celestina* in 1999. Her first play *Solo de cello* was written in 1994 and in 2000 she won the National Playwriting Prize for her play *Las gelatinas*. Her other work includes a play for radio *Historias de felicidad* in 2004. *Sánchez Huerta, se mató la niña (The Sánchez Huerta Girl Killed Herself)* was also produced at Foro la Gruta at the Centro Cultural Helénico in 2007.

SIMON SCARDIFIELD (translator, *Used Blood Junkyard*)

Simon Scardifield has prepared literal translations from French, German and Spanish for the Almeida, the National Theatre, the Donmar Warehouse, the Royal Shakespeare Company and the Young Vic, for writers such as Patrick Marber and David Hare. He has written the English-language versions of several Mexican plays for the Royal Court. He is also an actor in Ed Hall's Propeller company, and has worked as a dialect coach at the National Theatre.

ROXANA SILBERT (translator, *The Sánchez Huerta Girl Killed Herself*)

Roxana Silbert is Artistic Director of Paines Plough. She was Literary Director at the Traverse Theatre (2001–2004), Associate Director at the Royal Court (1998–2000), and Associate Director at West Yorkshire Playhouse (1997). She has directed productions at, amongst others, the Traverse Theatre, Shakespeare's Globe, the Royal Court, the Donmar Warehouse, the Royal Shakespeare Company, and on tour in the UK and abroad.

ALBERTO VILLARREAL (*Used Blood Junkyard*)

Alberto Villarreal was born in Mexico City in 1977. He works as a playwright and theatre director and runs his own company *Artillería producciones*, which is dedicated to contemporary theatre and finding new theatre languages. He has participated in international projects in Spain and Argentina, and his work has been presented in festivals in Chile, USA and Montreal. His play *Events with Life's Leftovers* was presented at the Lark Center in New York in 2006. As a director he has worked on more than thirty plays including his adaptation and production of *Hamletmaschine* by Heiner Müller.

ON INSOMNIA AND MIDNIGHT

(*A Tale to Frighten Chambermaids*)

A Piece for Two Voices

EDGAR CHÍAS

translated by

DAVID JOHNSTON

Je m'suis fait tout p'tit devant une poupée
Qui ferm'les yeux quand on la couche.
Je m'suis fait tout p'tit devant une poupée
Qui fait maman quand on la touche.

George Brassens

Characters

SHE

HE

On Insomnia and Midnight (*De insomnio y media noche*) was first performed in English as a rehearsed reading as part of the *Arena Mexico* season in the Jerwood Theatre Upstairs, Royal Court Theatre, London, on 10 January 2006 with the following cast:

SHE   Andrea Riseborough
HE   David Westhead

Director Roxana Silbert

On Insomnia and Midnight (*De insomnia y media noche*) was then co-produced with the Festival Internacional Cervantino and the British Council in the Jerwood Theatre Upstairs, Royal Court Theatre, London, opening on 22 September 2006, with the following cast, before transferring to the Teatro Cervantes, Guanajuato and the Centro Cultural Helénico, Mexico City:

SHE   Vanessa Bauche
HE   Nicholas Le Prevost

Director Hettie Macdonald

The action takes place in the bedroom of a large hotel in a provincial city.

The space is intimate and estranging. Estranging, because nobody who occupies it really belongs there: these are people in transit. Intimate, because we can only show our darkest depths, our weakness and our tenderness, the illuminations of our doubt and the capriciousness of our love, when we share that space with someone who is also alone.

HE is a man growing old, or at least he thinks he is. He feels ill. He probably is. But what he is suffering from is the decline of an intelligence that is implacable with all things, including with himself.

SHE is young, probably pretty, almost beautiful perhaps. She is not quick to understand. Indeed, she is ingenuous, even cruel: but vital.

The moment, like all moments, is a time out of time. Although it is worth saying that there are gaps between the unfolding of these moments, periods of time in which something has happened and all that is left for us are its residue or its effects.

Light and shadow are fundamental elements, as are silence and looks.

One

The only light comes through the door, which is ajar. SHE's standing with her back to him, holding a glass containing brandy. HE's sitting in the shadows, watching without being seen.

SHE. Nobody saw him. And nobody's seen him since.

HE. What do the papers say?

SHE. Not much. Nothing new. Just that she threw herself into the river. The girl, she threw herself in. That's what they say.

HE. Nothing else.

SHE. No.

HE. No photo of him?

SHE. No.

HE. All right. Shall we start?

Pause.

SHE. Can I turn on the light?

HE. What's the matter? . . . It's like you were frightened. Is that what it is? Are you?

SHE. I'm not frightened, no. It's . . . different.

HE. Different, how?

SHE. I don't know, because I don't know how to say it. Things feel . . . complicated. Maybe I shouldn't be here.

HE. But you are here.

SHE. Yes.

HE. Because you're young. Everything always feels complicated, but it passes. It'll pass.

SHE. The light. Do you mind? I'd like to be able to see. That's all. Just that I'd like to be able to. I think it would help.

HE. You said that yesterday, too.

SHE. I'd like to have been able to see yesterday, and I'd like to be able to today.

HE. Would you rather go?

SHE. I didn't say that.

HE. Do you want to stay, then?

SHE. I didn't say that either.

HE. You can turn round a bit.

Pause.

SHE. Like that?

HE. Yes. Come closer.

SHE. Here?

HE. Yes. Now take a deep breath. You're starting to make *me* feel nervous.

SHE. So can I turn on the light? It's just that the shadows . . .

HE. Close the door, then.

SHE. There'd be even less light.

HE. There'd be less shadows too.

SHE. No. It's OK like this.

HE. Let's start. Tell me something.

SHE. It's getting late.

HE. But you're here now.

SHE *moves towards the door.*

Stay still. Just as you are. Now relax. Tell me.

SHE. I don't know what to tell you.

HE. Tell me the same thing . . .

He is racked by a sudden cough.

SHE. Are you all right? Do you need anything?

HE. I don't need anything.

SHE. I could turn on the light . . .

HE. You've got lovely legs . . . strong . . . sturdy legs.

SHE. How do you know?

HE. Just tell me the same thing as yesterday. I don't need anything. I just want to listen.

SHE. All right. But don't look at me. Don't. Please.

HE. I'll try not to. But I can't promise.

Pause.

SHE. Reverend Mother didn't like me.

HE. Reverend Mother was an idiot. All mothers are. How could she not like you?

SHE. She didn't like me, that's all there was to it.

Pause.

HE. Go on.

SHE. That time, the time I was telling you about, it was eight o'clock. The moon was round and red, like a cheese.

HE. Red cheese?

SHE. Cheese made of blood. It was in the window. Watching . . . warm.

HE. Warm? What was? Reverend Mother, one of the sisters, you? You didn't tell me that.

SHE. The moon. The moon was warm . . . anyway, it felt warm. Reverend Mother was watching us. I felt scared. I could hear footsteps in the corridor. There was a bell somewhere . . . like an animal crying. All the sisters, just sitting there in silence, lifting their spoons up and down. Staring into space, chewing. Eating their cold soup.

HE. Cold, like your feet are?

SHE. How do you know?

HE. Because they are. Go on.

Pause.

SHE. I was trying so hard. My cheeks were all puffed out. I hate cornflour. It was slimy.

HE. How was it slimy? Like what? Tell me. Slimy like what?

SHE. I don't know. Like a guava, like a newborn baby, like a wet rat.

HE. Wet, like you?

SHE. How do you . . . ?

HE. Good. Very good. Go on.

Pause.

SHE. I was always telling them I didn't like soup, that it was disgusting, especially cornflour soup because it reminded me of my mother.

HE. That's not uncommon. My mother wasn't so much disgusting as pitiful. Go on.

SHE. It was disgusting because it reminded me of the soup my mother used to make – cold, watery soup. It was the soup that was disgusting. Not my mother. I feel pity for her sometimes but not disgust. It's different.

HE. What else?

SHE. Well, they took no notice. Every time I complained, they made me say the 'Our Father' over and over again. 'None of your whingeing,' that's what they used to say. They'd make me kneel down on thistles and recite 'Our Fathers' . . . over and over again. Under the altar. The huge, big empty altar. With its candles . . . smelling of grease, of rancid fat. The sisters stood over me. If I got the words wrong, I had to start all over again. It worked. I felt . . . Punished. That time, that time in particular, they didn't care that the soup was making me feel sick. I asked if I could go to the toilet.

HE. You needed to defecate?

SHE. No. I just needed to go to the toilet. To get out of there . . . to let things settle. I must have insisted too much because

Reverend Mother got cross and started shouting. She wouldn't let me go.

HE. What was she shouting?

SHE. I don't remember. Terrible things . . . they scared me. She tried to make me swallow. She took the spoon and filled it with soup. Up to my mouth and down to the bowl, again and again, into my mouth and back down to the bowl.

HE. How many times?

SHE. I didn't count. A lot. The sisters were staring. They weren't scared, but they were staring. My teeth hurt. I thought I was going to be sick. I could feel my eyes filling up. I wasn't crying. But the tears were streaming from my eyes. I could see the moon in the window, like a big stain in the middle of the window, filling up like I was filling up. It filled with water and I filled with soup. Me with soup and the moon with water.

Pause.

HE. What happened then?

SHE. I said something. No, I don't remember. No, I did say something. Reverend Mother got cross, then everything suddenly went dark and quiet . . . Then I remember her with her fists full of hair . . . my hair. It'd come away in her hand when she'd banged my head onto the table. A big hard wooden table.

HE. Was she very angry?

SHE. She was dirty, but she was angry too. Mostly dirty. I couldn't help it.

HE. What? What could you not help?

SHE. It's embarrassing.

HE. Tell me.

SHE. It's embarrassing.

HE. Tell me.

Pause.

SHE. The sick.

HE. Who was sick?

SHE. She was.

HE. Why?

SHE. Because it was disgusting.

HE. What was?

SHE. My face.

HE. Your face? Why?

SHE. Because it was covered in sick.

HE. She splashed you with sick?

SHE. Yes, but not really. I started it. The soup stuck in my throat, and I threw it up all over her habit. She held back for as long as she could, she was very particular, and she didn't vomit very much. That's what they told me. She blessed herself before she did. It splashed all over me, over my face and hair. The sisters were giggling. The rest isn't funny. Not that that bit was, but the rest was even less funny.

HE. What is the rest?

SHE. She did what she'd threatened to do. Please let me turn on the light.

HE. No, it's getting late. It's cold. It'll be time to go to sleep soon. There's no need to turn anything on. So what happened in the end?

SHE. I had to wash down the floors in the middle of the night. The bit before the end was what she threatened. She threatened that if I didn't swallow the soup, if I spat it out, like I did sometimes, she told me . . . she told me that . . . and that's what she did.

HE. Did what?

SHE. That.

HE. What 'that'?

SHE. That. She spooned it into me.

HE. And you let her?

Pause.

SHE. How could I stop her?

HE. You let her.

SHE. She said that what God has blessed may not be wantonly wasted. That it was for my own good. I had to learn. That's what it was about. Learning to please the Lord.

HE. Unbelievable.

SHE. She said you shouldn't take the Lord's name in vain. She said that was why she was carrying out her threat. If she hadn't have done that, she'd have had to do something far worse.

HE. She's right. God's a stunted little bully. He loves humiliating . . . punishing. That's why he makes so many demands.

SHE. Yes, and I was scared. God's fury. And the Reverend Mother's. Together. It was too much for me.

HE. As if that means anything! They're just empty words.

SHE. I was scared. I felt ashamed.

HE. That other thing – the something far worse . . . would you have told me?

SHE. I'm not sure. The bit about me having to swallow her sick was enough. Anyway I can't imagine what far worse thing she could have thought up.

HE. Tell me again.

SHE. What?

HE. One more time, please. Tell me again.

SHE. It's not a good idea. It's late. I can come tomorrow. I'll tell you again tomorrow.

HE. All right. Tomorrow. Pass me my drink . . . No, closer. Closer.

SHE *moves towards him and holds out his drink.* HE *coughs.*

SHE. You shouldn't be drinking. You don't sound well. You'll make yourself worse.

HE. What could be worse? This nothing life . . . That's God's real fury.

SHE. You're scaring me.

HE. You've lovely legs, sturdy, strong legs. Smooth skin.

SHE. How would you know? Maybe.

HE. Maybe. Cover yourself. Make sure nobody sees you on the way out.

SHE. I will.

HE. Come back tomorrow and tell me if they've found him, what people are saying. I'd like to know. Come back tomorrow. I need to know.

SHE. I do too. I'd like to.

HE. Come back tomorrow. Early. Tomorrow.

SHE. I'll be here.

Two

SHE *is standing beside the door, which is now closed, waiting, holding a tray.* HE *is sitting on the bed.* HE *becomes progressively more agitated.*

HE. At first it's like you are being rocked. A slow sleepy rocking feeling. Then nausea. Burning, like fingernails scraping down the inside of your throat. Your arm . . .

SHE. Can I do anything? Your arm, you said, señor?

HE. Shhh. My arm, always the same one.

SHE. The same arm?

HE. My left arm, like some ridiculous, useless, limp . . . rag. You can't move it. You can't breathe, then you start sweating, your head's spinning with fever, and everything, all the normal things, change . . .

SHE. Your drink, señor?

HE. You don't understand any of this. You're still young. Come over here. It's like . . . you were moving through thick air, or floating uselessly inside some dense liquid, like spit. And you feel like a fool, like one of those fish with great big staring eyes that never see enough to stop themselves from being caught. The minutes stretch out in front of you, not moving, and time drags on endlessly. Things, objects, have a sort of echo, they spill out over their own edges. Your eyes are closed and there's no darkness, your head feels hollow, like it's been scooped out, but it's not quiet inside. You look out from a place that's already deep inside your eyes. Sounds are muffled, they lose their clarity, they slow down. Everything that's happening, it's happening inside you, that's how it feels. You feel an inertia that permeates everything, that disorientates you. Then you get the feeling . . .

Pause.

You don't know what I'm talking about, do you? Do you want to know?

SHE. No. Go on.

HE. The feeling of things blurring, of terrible pressure. And then a surge of unstoppable anxiety. That's what I'm talking about. The walls close in around you, they threaten you, the light mists over. Everything becomes . . . like an enemy. Grotesque and deformed. And you're able to watch – I mean you can actually watch – how one of your eyes, usually it's your left eye, or it's always your left eye, and the whole left side of your head, they swell up and separate and are about to explode. And before that happens, they burst inside your head, in the most horrible detail: you see your arteries swirling with blood clots that could block them at any moment . . . You can feel the flow getting weaker, the flow of your polluted blood . . .

SHE. Señor . . .

HE. Your pulse pounding in your forehead, your teeth clenched, the paralysing pain, again and again and again . . . and that terrible desire to bite, to bite and beat and to break whatever it is so that you can drag it down with you, so you don't have to go on your own. Life's final useless gesture, to destroy. To keep your terror at bay, to inhabit the silence, to sink your nails into that one last moment, not to allow the light and that last flickering voice of consciousness to fade, to die. That final terror of going on your own . . . Because you disappear and . . . then there's nothing.

Pause. The rain can be seen through the window.

Look. It's still falling. It won't stop. Did you notice?

SHE. Do you mind if I go now?

HE. Answer me. I asked you a question, I believe.

SHE. Sorry . . . what was it?

HE. Whether you noticed. It hasn't stopped. Like yesterday.

SHE. Yes. It doesn't seem to have. And it won't.

HE. It won't stop. What sense is there to it? Can you tell me? Is there any?

SHE. Sorry?

HE. The rain, snow, the way trees slowly defy the law of gravity. Is there any purpose to it?

SHE. I suppose there must be.

HE. You suppose, eh? You suppose. What is it you suppose?

SHE. I don't know. There's some reason. Everything's here for a reason.

HE. What reason? Nothing changes anything. If we weren't here, things like that would just go on the same, regardless. They were here before us and there was no sense to them. Whatever sense they have now, it was us that gave it to them. We invented it because we wanted to. And we invented time. How else would we measure our failure, our decay? A yardstick for our crumbling bodies. What else are we – bags filled with flesh and fluids, that's all. And the bags get old, they rot, and they burst.

SHE. I don't understand. I don't know.

HE. So you don't understand, and you don't know and you don't worry about eternity, and why things are here for no reason. The simple things.

SHE. Simple things?

HE. Like this endless rain. Do you think it cares whether you and I are cold or frightened or don't understand? And do you know the worst thing, it's that all our willpower is focused on not wanting to lose it, on wishing our life would go on for ever, on wanting to the explain the senselessness of it. Because we're ruled by desire, animals driven by desire.

Pause.

You can close the window now.

SHE. I should be going.

HE. You haven't done what I asked.

SHE *gives him the drink and goes to close the window.* HE *follows her with his eyes, caressing her with his gaze.*

You're very young. Do you dye your hair?

SHE. What? No.

HE. So that's your real colour. Good. That would be senseless. Although if nothing has any sense, then why not? But that's your natural colour, you say. You can never account for beauty. If it's there at all, it's in spite of ourselves. There's no need to be embarrassed. What's your name?

SHE. Sorry, I'm not allowed . . .

HE. You're not allowed? To have a name? What stupid rule prevents you from having a name? Tell me your name.

SHE. Sorry.

HE. Then tell me this: do you still believe in God?

SHE. I can't . . .

HE. You can't believe?

SHE. I'm not . . .

HE. So what can you do? Just stand there fiddling with the hem of your skirt? You're nervous.

SHE. Your hands.

HE. What about them?

SHE. They're . . . very elegant.

HE. Thank you.

SHE. They're . . .

HE. What? What are they?

SHE. Nothing . . . I was just imagining . . . It's late.

HE. Have you been working here long?

SHE. No.

HE. Are you new?

SHE. No.

HE. Then?

SHE. I'm not allowed. To talk, I mean . . .

HE. Not allowed? Why not? What they pay you for making beds, is it enough to buy that too? Does their money buy every single hour of your day? Everything your hands do? Now that sounds tempting, sinful even. The silences you're so keen to keep? Everything you do with your mouth? Every word you speak, few and far between though your words are? All of that for a few notes and a handful of coins a week? That's what they bought from you when you started work here? And your name into the bargain? I could pay more.

SHE. Goodnight.

HE. No, don't go. Please. I didn't intend to cause any offence. Well, I don't think I did. I wasn't suggesting anything, and I wouldn't . . . unless you wanted me to. There's no need to be . . . worried. This would be beneficial to both of us. I would be free to ask you for whatever, and you would feel freed, released, from the oppressive conditions of your employment. So, a little space of freedom . . . for us both. What do you think? We could share my drink.

SHE. It's not allowed. I have to go.

HE. You're shivering.

SHE. I'm cold.

HE. I think it's warm.

SHE. But I'm cold.

HE. I'd like us to talk.

SHE. Some other time. Goodnight.

HE. Good morning. It's past midnight.

SHE. Good morning, then.

HE. You're beautiful and warm . . . like fruit ripening.

SHE. I don't know what you're talking about.

HE. Stay a moment. Just one moment.

SHE. I have to go.

HE. Please. You can go in a minute. I just want to look at you. Stay still.

Pause. HE *circles her, close enough to catch her scent.* HE *looks at her from behind.*

SHE. You're scaring me.

HE. Don't turn round. Wait, please. Please. There's no rush. I wouldn't do the slightest thing to make you . . . anxious. Take a look at me and you'll see for yourself. There's nothing to be scared of. I'm not asking you to have a drink to take advantage of you; I don't mind one way or another, but it'll stop you shivering. I don't want to be alone. All I'm asking you to do is listen. And talk.

SHE. Talk? I don't know how to talk.

HE. That's a lie. You may not like talking, but you can't not talk. You have to talk to say you don't know how to talk. And that makes you an object of . . . considerable fascination.

Take care, because sooner or later it'll cause you problems. Or pleasure. Naivety is perverse.

SHE. I'm not.

HE. Naive or perverse?

SHE. Neither.

HE. Another lie.

SHE. I have to go.

HE. I suppose you do. I'm going to be here for some time. Are you in every day?

SHE. I live here.

HE. All the better. I'm enjoying this drink. Will you bring me another one tomorrow?

SHE. You can order it from whoever's on tomorrow.

HE. You're on now and I'm ordering one for tomorrow.

SHE. Somebody else might bring it up.

HE. I'll ask for you; we'll say you made a good impression, and I was generous. I gave you a good tip.

SHE. There's no need.

HE. Here. Take it.

SHE. If you like.

SHE *goes to take it.* HE *catches her hand.* SHE *pulls it away immediately.*

HE. Do *you* like? That's what makes sense, makes sense of things. Me telling you to do it, which I'm not by the way, that isn't enough. I don't need some sort of object in a skirt. I want you to want to bring me the drink, to like bringing me the drink. It's wanting that makes sense; desire gives pleasure, and only pleasure makes sense, no matter what it costs.

SHE. I can bring your drink.

HE. Do you want to?

SHE. I don't know.

HE. You can't not know. I want – I need – you to.

SHE. Ninet brought it up yesterday.

HE. Now I know her name. I'm not interested in her bringing it though. I'm interested in you doing it.

SHE. Me? Why me?

HE. Because you listen.

SHE. I don't know.

HE. You've said that.

SHE. That's because I don't know. I'll think about it.

HE. No need to knock. The door'll be open.

Three

They are sitting opposite each other.

SHE. There was a man. Watching.

HE. Watching? How did that make you feel?

SHE. Hot.

HE. Because he was watching you?

SHE. Perhaps.

HE. Where was he watching from?

SHE. There was a crack in the wall.

HE. How do you know it was a man?

SHE. By the way he was looking. It was a man's look. Like dogs look when they're in heat.

HE. And you saw him?

SHE. Or I dreamt it. I could see his eye, his great green wet eye watching us. We were trying not to make any noise. My mother was suspicious.

HE. Who was it?

SHE. I don't know.

HE. What was she suspicious of?

SHE. What we'd been playing. I must have been about eleven.

HE. Very good. You didn't waste any time.

SHE. He was my cousin.

HE. Who was watching you or who was playing with you?

SHE. Playing. My cousin. I don't know who the man was. We were playing.

HE. Playing? At what?

SHE. The way everyone does. Doctors. First he was a doctor. Then he was a holy man.

HE. A holy man? Interesting choice. Are you going to tell me?

SHE. I will. If you want.

HE. I do.

SHE moves closer.

SHE. I had this awful disease. My body was covered in spots.

HE. What sort of spots?

SHE. Red and black ones. And leisures – is that what they're called?

HE. What do you mean?

SHE. When like a line opens up on your skin and blood comes out, you can get it on your back or on the bottom of your foot.

HE. Lesions.

SHE. That's right. Lesions. He said he was a miracle doctor, that he could cure my spots and les . . . lesions.

HE. And did he?

SHE. I think so. He took off my blouse. He said I had two on my chest, which was very serious.

HE. Two lesions.

SHE. Two spots. And they weren't red or black. They were pink. He told me he wasn't surprised and they seemed to be getting worse because they were getting puffy. In a year's time the puffiness would be very noticeable and I'd have problems.

HE. What sort of problems?

SHE. Everyone'd be looking at them and they'd know what I had under my blouse and I'd have to use crutches or something like that.

HE. You mean a stick?

SHE. A bra, he said.

HE. And you didn't know what that was?

SHE. No.

HE. How many years ago was this?

SHE. A few now. Not that many.

HE. And how old was your cousin?

SHE. Six years older than me.

HE. Ah . . . Tell me more.

SHE. Well, he told me they were getting puffy because they were full of poison, that he would use an old Indian trick, that he would suck them to get the badness out, and that would cure me.

HE. And what did he do?

SHE. He sucked them.

HE. Where exactly did you have the spots?

SHE. I can't say.

HE. You can't say?

SHE. No.

HE. You can't or you won't?

SHE. I can't. It's too embarrassing.

HE. Did he cure you?

SHE. At first, yes, I thought he had. But after a few months the little spots were still getting bigger and it scared me. I told my mother I was very sick. I said the spots had grown. She asked me what did I mean, 'spots'. And I told her everything. She asked me all sorts of questions. She made me take my clothes off, in the sitting room, in front of the gentleman.

HE. What gentleman, the one who'd been watching you?

SHE. No. Her new friend. She said he was my uncle. I had a new uncle every week.

HE. So what happened?

SHE. My uncle, that uncle, he tried as well one day, he tried to get the poison out. My mother found out. She wasn't pleased. To get me out of the way, she sent me to the nuns.

HE. Why?

SHE. Because of the spots and the lesions.

HE. What lesions? You didn't have any lesions.

SHE. I did. One. Between my legs.

HE. I see. And did your cousin cure that as well?

SHE. I think so. But in a different way. The first few times, though, he sucked too.

HE. And what did you feel?

SHE. Like itchy, tickly. I felt embarrassed.

HE. Did it hurt?

SHE. Not when he was sucking. It was tickly. First it was my spots, then my lesion. One time . . .

Pause.

HE. Tell me.

SHE. Can I come a bit closer?

HE. If you like.

SHE. Is it OK like this?

HE. That's very close.

SHE. It's OK like this. Well, one time, when he was curing my lesion, something went right through me.

HE. Really?

SHE. Yes. It made me feel strange, as if I'd been shaken by a flame, an electrical flame.

HE. A current.

SHE. No, a flame.

HE. All right, a flame. What else?

SHE. He got cross. He stopped curing me after that.

HE. He left your lesion alone.

SHE. More or less. Until he thought up the thing about the Devil and Hell.

HE. The Devil and Hell, what was that?

SHE. Nothing. A dirty story just.

HE. Tell me it.

SHE. I can't remember.

HE. Tell me, anyway, whatever you can remember.

SHE. There's no point.

HE. Did he make the story up?

SHE. He heard it in school. Somebody told him it in Logic, that's what he said.

HE. Well?

SHE. Well, there was this very holy girl who wanted to serve God. And someone said to her that in a village nearby, or fairly nearby, there was a holy man who knew all the best ways to serve God. He was very poor, and a very holy man, and he lived in the desert.

HE. So he lived in a village, but in the desert as well?

SHE. Yes. The thing was that the girl wanted to meet him. She told her parents and went off to the forest to find him.

HE. I thought he lived in the desert.

SHE. He did. But she had to go through the forest to get to the desert. The story has to be logical, doesn't it? And she got lost on the way. The girl got lost. And somebody sent her the wrong way a couple of times, but eventually she found him. Very thin, with a big long beard. And all he ever had to eat were green apples and roots and water. That's what he offered the girl when she arrived. Oh, and a vine leaf.

HE. A vine leaf? What for?

SHE. So that she knew what they looked like. The holy man said she had to gather piles of them to make her bed, because he didn't have another bed and he didn't want her to have to sleep on the floor and because he was holy, and a man and not a fool, he wasn't going to catch his death of cold sleeping there himself. So the girl had to hurry up because it was almost night-time . . .

HE. Vine leaves in the desert.

SHE. It was a test of faith.

HE. And what has all that, the bed made out of vine leaves and faith, what has all that got to do with the story about the Devil and Hell and your lesion that couldn't be cured?

SHE. Wait. Well, one day, after a lot of fasting, and watching the girl kneeling in the river washing his socks, the holy man had an illumination. He told her he'd been possessed by a Devil that wouldn't leave him in peace, and that God, all-seeing and good as He is, had led her there providentially to help him and to serve him. And so he explained to her where her Hell was and where his Devil was and for a week they set about trying to lock the Devil back up. But then the girl started to really like dousing the burning flames of Hell and she wanted to lock the Devil up as often as possible, but the holy man, who wasn't as young as he used to be, soon got fed up with it and he sent her home, and her parents married her off to someone else.

HE. I see. So your cousin used that story to cajole you, and he cured you with his Devil . . . until he got fed up.

SHE. He didn't have time to get fed up. That's when my mother found out what was going on with the . . .

HE. The spots.

SHE. That's right. The spots.

HE. So go on, then.

SHE. And she packed me off to the nuns.

Pause.

HE. You haven't finished. You didn't tell me what happened to the bed made out of vine leaves.

SHE. I don't know that bit.

HE *coughs.*

Are you OK?

HE. Yes. It's nothing.

SHE. Are you sure? It's a bad cough.

HE. I'm OK.

SHE. Shall we go on?

HE. No. I'm fed up now. You can go.

SHE. It's still early.

HE. I'm tired. Go on. Close the door behind you.

Four

They are both standing. After a silence, SHE *goes to take away the glass which* HE *has just drained.* SHE *puts it on the tray and walks to the door.* HE *closes it.*

HE. I have a request. Something very simple . . . very easy.

SHE. Yes.

HE. No questions.

SHE. What is it?

HE. You didn't listen.

SHE. I heard you.

HE. You and I share something. These dark times.

SHE. Bad times?

HE. No.

SHE. Then why dark?

HE. Because it's night-time. Times, at night.

SHE. I'm doing my job, that's all. Doing what I'm paid to do.

HE. And I'm barely surviving.

SHE. Do you really feel so sick?

HE. No. No sicker than usual.

SHE. It's usual to feel sick?

HE. It becomes usual. The important thing is not to waste your time weeping. Only cowards weep.

SHE. I don't cry ever. And it's not that I've never been hurt.

HE. Being with me, does that . . . hurt you? Has it?

SHE. No.

HE. Good.

SHE. Is it going to?

HE. No, of course it won't. Not much, anyway. Would it matter?

SHE. I don't know.

HE. Would you do things? Things, if I asked you to?

SHE. I don't know.

HE. I could pay.

SHE. There's no need. A normal tip's enough.

HE. I insist.

SHE. No. Don't. The others would suspect.

HE. Have they said anything?

SHE. No.

HE. Have they asked you anything?

SHE. No.

HE. What if they did?

SHE. I'd tell them.

HE. What would you tell them?

SHE. That there's nothing going on.

HE. That's the truth.

SHE. All I do is bring you up your drink.

HE. That's all.

SHE. Anything else is because I choose to.

HE. That's the dangerous bit, the bit that matters. The 'anything else'. And the way you say it.

SHE. Why?

HE. Because saying it like that makes it sound . . . suspicious. They might be suspicious about us, say things about us . . .

SHE. Suspicious? Do you think so?

HE. Yes, I do.

SHE. But nobody does ask me.

HE. Do they not?

SHE. No. They're usually asleep by this time.

HE. They know you've been here?

SHE. But they don't know how long I stayed. I'm always the last one in bed.

HE. That's good.

SHE. What was your request?

HE. Nothing important.

SHE. Tell me.

HE. Nothing. It's nothing.

SHE. You're very annoying.

HE. Why? Am I hurting you?

SHE. No, but now I want to know.

HE. I want to know too.

SHE. Want to know what?

HE. Time enough for that. But we have to get one thing clear from the start: this is our secret. We have to maintain our . . . intimacy.

SHE. You use big words.

HE. Big words?

SHE. Like . . . 'intimacy'.

HE. Big?

SHE. No, but . . . it makes me feel important. Like . . . maybe . . . sometime . . .

HE. This is sometime. Our time. And yes, you are important. Very important. To me.

SHE. Don't say things like that.

HE. You don't like . . . things like that?

SHE. I get embarrassed.

HE. There's no reason to.

SHE. They make me go red.

HE. You blush.

SHE. All right, I blush.

HE. Your eyes . . .

SHE. What about my eyes?

HE. They're . . . subtly malevolent. Light, childlike, malevolent.

SHE. They're not light.

HE. They shine.

SHE. Like a light.

HE. They electrify.

SHE. What?

HE. It doesn't matter.

SHE. I have a right to know.

HE. Yes, you do have a right. So listen. Creatures like you usually bring ruin to themselves, and to the unwary, like me.

SHE. Unwary? Like you?

HE. Like me.

SHE. I don't want to do you any harm.

HE. No. Nobody ever wants to. But one day you'll understand that love is never more sensuous than when it's doing harm. We can't avoid hurting other people. That's what desire is.

SHE. You know things.

HE. No more than you do. No more than you. You know everything you need to.

SHE. What do I know?

HE. How important you are to me. That's twice I've said it. Your advantage. The coin's in the air.

SHE. Are we . . . playing some sort of game?

HE. That's exactly what we're doing.

SHE. What are the rules?

HE. No rules.

SHE. What do I have to do to win?

HE. Nothing. Absolutely nothing.

SHE. So . . . ?

HE. Just be beautiful.

SHE. Me?

HE. Simply that.

SHE. And am I?

HE. You've no idea how much you are. Or how you are.

Pause.

SHE. That's all I have to do?

HE. That's all. That's how to win. How you've won already.

SHE. So what is the game?

HE. It's about not letting yourself be dragged down.

SHE. I don't understand.

HE. What you love the most can hurt you the most. You have to get what you want and you may get hurt but you have to keep yourself intact.

SHE. That's the game?

HE. Yes, it is. Do you understand?

SHE. So we have to love each other?

HE. That's right. But keeping ourselves intact at the same time. We balance on the ledge. Frightening, isn't it?

SHE. No. I want to play. When do we start?

Five

HE *is standing, anxiously.* SHE *is sitting in a chair, reading.*

SHE. I want to ask you something. Can I?

HE. Not now.

SHE. It's important.

HE. Later. Finish this first.

SHE. What does 'feral' mean?

HE. What else does it say?

SHE. But I want to know what it means. Feral. Is it something bad?

HE. No. Keep reading.

SHE. How am I going to understand if you won't tell me what 'feral' means? Is it an insult?

HE. No. It's not an insult.

SHE. OK. It's just that it says that the man, when he was detained . . .

HE. He was helping with enquiries.

SHE. No, it says 'detained'.

HE. Bloody fools, journalists.

SHE. 'When he was detained, he accused the woman of being an abject liar, vile and feral.' That's why I thought it was an insult. I understand all the rest of it, apart from 'abject', so I thought 'feral' and 'abject' were insults too.

HE. No. It's just a way of saying 'wild'. It's not an insult, though it may sound like one here. Feral. You talk about cats being feral. Fools, the lot of them.

SHE. Where do they find words like that?

HE. From their dictionaries. Their dictionaries make up for their lack of imagination, they expand their narrow horizons. What have cats got to do with this? What else does it say?

SHE. A whole lot. Do you want me to read it or just tell you?

HE. I'd prefer you read it.

SHE. It says: 'Suicide Plunge Chambermaid: Body Still Not Found.'

HE. Very eloquent.

SHE. 'The chambermaid, who worked in a well-known city-centre hotel, had alleged that a guest, a teacher of languages – '

HE. Journalists . . . useless, every last one of them.

SHE. ' – a teacher of languages, had made improper sexual advances when, around midnight, he summoned her to bring a triple brandy to his room. The teacher vehemently denied her allegations, but was detained and taken to the police station, where he in turn accused the woman of being an abject liar, vile and feral.'

HE. So it says he was the one who said 'feral'.

SHE. It looks like it.

HE. Well, they're wrong. If he is a teacher, even if he were a language teacher, assuming that the hacks haven't got that wrong as well, he would know what 'feral' means. Any bloody queer hairdresser would know what 'feral' means.

SHE. Will I go on?

HE. Yes.

SHE. 'The teacher, who is a worker in – '

HE. Who's a worker! What does that mean? That he makes cars? Worker . . .

SHE. ' – a worker in a prestigious foreign university, he had come here on holiday after having undertaken the translation of a book of philosophy – '

HE. This is unbelievable. He may be a philologist, or a mathematician or a philosopher, but not a 'teacher of languages'. No half-baked teacher of languages can actually manage to string more than a few words together in any language other than their own. Sometimes not even that. Never mind translate a book of philosophy.

SHE. ' – and was recovering from a severe bout of flu. He had been confined to bed for several days as a result of the sudden change of climate.'

HE. 'Confined to bed.' Wonderful. So, as well as a 'teacher of languages', he's some sort of maniac.

SHE. 'When it was concluded that the teacher of languages was in no fit state to seduce the chambermaid, let alone commit any act of sexual aggression, he was released after several hours and returned to the said hotel. But later he checked out.'

Pause.

HE. Is that it?

SHE. No. There's more.

HE. Finish it.

SHE. 'The chambermaid was sacked and when she saw a photograph of herself in the paper under the headline "Tarred with Her Own Brush", she threw herself into the river. To date, no body has been found.'

HE. Anything else?

SHE. No.

HE. Nothing about the teacher?

SHE. No. Other than what I read.

HE. No photo?

SHE. No.

HE. People, what are they saying?

SHE. Not a thing.

HE. What do you mean, 'not a thing'?

SHE. Just that. Not a thing. It's the sort of thing that happens every day.

HE. People always have something to say, even about things that happen every day. It keeps the boredom at bay. It gives them something to think about.

SHE. I don't know. I think she's not the only one.

HE. What do you mean?

SHE. What I said: I think she's not the only one. Or the first one to throw herself into the river.

HE. Where did you get that idea from?

SHE. Nowhere. Just a guess.

Pause.

I want to ask you something.

HE. I've already answered.

SHE. Don't get cross.

HE. I'm not getting cross. It's not you. It's me. I'm glad you're here.

SHE. So, can I?

HE. 'Feral' isn't an insult.

SHE. It's not about that.

HE. About what then?

SHE. I don't know if I should.

HE. I don't know if I can.

Pause. HE *stops behind her and slips his hand onto her neck. Startled,* SHE *stands up.*

SHE. I don't need to any more.

HE. Why not? What's wrong?

SHE. There's light . . . some light outside the window.

HE. What of it?

SHE. I should go and look. There might be somebody there, watching.

HE. There's no one watching. Don't worry. Stay.

SHE. No. I'm going to look.

HE. I haven't answered you.

SHE. I haven't asked you.

HE. So you don't want to know?

SHE. I'm not sure. The way you look at me, it . . .

HE. It what?

SHE. It scares me.

Pause.

HE. So you don't want me to tell you?

SHE. Tell me what?

HE. Whatever it is you want to know.

SHE. Are you shivering?

HE. I'm cold.

SHE. But it's warm . . . don't you think? I'm going to see who's out there. Maybe someone's looking for me.

SHE *leaves*.

HE. All I meant was . . .

Six

They are both sitting on the bed, looking at photographs, perhaps on a laptop.

SHE. What else?

HE. It's the idea behind it. It's always the same idea. Look at this one.

SHE. It's disgusting.

HE. No, it's not. Look more closely.

SHE. It's the same as the other one.

HE. No. It's not. It might look the same. But it's not.

SHE. I don't know what you mean.

HE. It's not just what's in the picture. It's the idea. I don't know where it comes from. And I don't know how I came to believe it. But it's there. Right from your childhood you hear things and you see things that insinuate it, the idea. All sorts of things, stupid things, trivial things, to do with men and women.

SHE. Men and women?

HE. Yes. It's in everything, all around you. In pictures. In words. In the way people talk to each other. What they say. And you end up believing it. The lie. You've no choice. The first time I did it, it hurt me more than her.

SHE. How?

HE. I don't know. Maybe it wasn't the right time.

SHE. Why not?

HE. I was too young. I wasn't ready.

SHE. Ready for what?

HE. The idea. To believe it. All the time you're growing up, people warn you, they try to get you ready, they tell you all the time. They're training you. To hurt. To cause pain. And I tried. I really did. But even though I didn't want to, in the end I'd no choice but to believe it. Look at this one.

SHE. Maybe it is hurting, but they're enjoying it.

HE. Look. We're all different, but the idea's the same, and it works the same way in all of us. It's life, it's a vision of the world.

SHE. They *are* enjoying it.

HE. Who are?

SHE. Them. The women. Look at them.

HE. Well, so they should. They're stronger. They're made for it, they're built for pain.

SHE. No. We're not.

HE. Well, of course, they like it in some sort of way.

SHE. But there's more to it than just pain.

HE. Well, why else would they do it? It's the pain they enjoy. That's the idea.

SHE. Money. That's why they do it.

HE. Just money? No. Look at them. They're hardly wasting away.

SHE. Neither are the men. Look at the muscles on them.

HE. But they hardly ever show their faces . . . you know why, don't you?

SHE. No . . . I've never seen stuff like this before.

HE. Honestly?

SHE. Honestly.

HE. Not even at school?

SHE. No.

HE. So what do you think?

SHE. It's strange. It makes me feel strange. I like it, but . . . I don't know, it repels me too.

HE. It's all about the same idea, everything has to do with that. When that feeling of aggression is thwarted or frustrated, so that instead of feeling pain the woman seems to share the pleasure, the man reacts, he rears up like a . . . wild animal. Because that's what the idea is – it's about tearing apart, bursting, ripping, pushing inside as hard and deep as you can, splitting her, pulling her apart, until you break her. Look at this one.

SHE. Wow! That's unbelievable. How's that possible?

HE. Very easy. Pure strength . . . and experience. He's . . .

SHE. I meant her, not him. That's just the way he's built. He was born like that. But she . . .

HE. I wouldn't be so sure. It's a trick shot, maybe an implant. They use all sorts of creams and potions and injections.

SHE. It looks real.

HE. It looks.

SHE. But she's . . . enormous, incredible. She's taken all of it. She's full. Run right through. So smoothly.

HE. No. That's not how it works. It's the other way round. He's dominating her, but she likes it.

SHE. I don't know.

HE. What's it like for you?

SHE. Well . . .

HE. Tell me.

SHE. My idea is different. It's how long it goes on for.

HE. How long it goes on?

SHE. Yes, until you're exhausted.

HE. Until it hurts?

SHE. Maybe.

HE. Until you feel you could die?

SHE. Maybe.

HE. Why not? Until you die . . . But men, we . . .

SHE. You?

HE. The whole experience is different for us. Look.

SHE. Why different?

HE. The feeling of invading, stretching, flooding. It's powerful. A very powerful feeling. Domination. We have different tools. The privilege of being a man.

SHE. Well, perhaps . . . But domination . . .

HE. Why 'perhaps'?

SHE. Is that what you really think?

HE. Yes. Look at this one.

SHE. No. Look at this one.

HE. What?

SHE. Look at it. He's weak . . . he looks puny. And she's strong, I mean, really strong. She's bored.

HE. She's a barrel.

SHE. No, she's beautiful. Strong.

HE. He looks strong too.

SHE. Not like her. He can't manage. His tool . . .

HE. What about it?

SHE. It's small. Hers is bigger. She's devouring him, swallowing him whole, wolfing him down. And she's got room for more.

HE. You find that sometimes; there are women like bottomless pits; it's like looking into an abyss. They're fat. They're nearly always fat.

SHE. She's not.

HE. She's on the fat side.

SHE. I don't think she is. Look at this one.

HE. What about it?

SHE. She's with three of them. You couldn't imagine one of them being with three of her.

HE. It happens.

SHE. Only in men's fantasies.

HE. No, any of them could do it . . . Look at the size of them. Some of them have got huge ones.

SHE. You can imagine somebody like her with three big men . . . but imagine three of her with just one of them, even the biggest one.

HE. What?

SHE. He couldn't cope.

HE. He couldn't? Not even him?

SHE. No, he couldn't.

HE. Bah! It's just your opinion, that's all.

SHE. That's what you think?

HE. Of course it is. So now it's not her who's been run through, ripped, and burst, and instead she's wolfing him down, devouring him, dominating him?

SHE. It looks that way.

Pause.

HE. You're wrong.

SHE. Am I?

HE. Yes, you are. You're wrong. That's what I meant, what I was telling you about when you are thwarted or frustrated, I mean as an aggressor – it builds up into a sort of crescendo and it drives you wild. Look at the photographs. Look at the men, there are more and more of them with her, taking her, doing it to her.

SHE. It doesn't sound too bad. Like in this one?

HE. I don't think you understand. Look – imagine three or four men like him, each with a thing like that, and two more waiting to have their turn with you, getting themselves worked up watching you, and imagine that you're like her . . .

SHE. The skinny one?

HE. Yes, like the skinny one. Imagine them, like rhinoceroses with their horns, goring you, each one of them again and again, for hours on end. Imagine them using you, emptying themselves into you, and they've left you broken . . . They've split you wide open and left you there, and you're half-dead and they're resting before they begin all over again.

SHE. I've got to imagine that?

HE. Yes. Look . . . like that and like that and like that.

SHE. Uh-huh.

HE. Imagine.

Pause.

SHE. Uh-huh.

HE. Now do you think you've devoured them, you've wolfed them down, you've eaten them alive? Do you think you dominated them? Do you? Really?

SHE. Yes. In a way.

HE. No, you don't. No way at all. That's plain stupidity. I don't know why you're so obstinate.

SHE. All I'm doing is looking at the pictures and imagining what you're telling me to. Señor.

HE. Why are you being so obstinate?

SHE. Do you not know the story?

HE. What story?

SHE. The one about the master and his slave.

HE. That's different. It's got nothing to do with this.

SHE. No, I suppose it doesn't. It's just that both of them create their own roles. The master and his slave. They swap roles.

HE. Exactly. You have to accept the role. And the story. These pictures all tell a story. One single story: that's why they were made, to show the splitting and the ripping and the invading, the supreme pleasure of violence, the supremacy of the aggressor, and that's why you need a tool like this.

SHE. Whose tool?

HE. A tool. Look, forget it. That's enough.

SHE. I'm sleepy.

HE. Fine.

SHE. Is it?

HE. Yes, it is. People get sleepy at night.

SHE. It's not that late. I just feel like going to bed . . .

Pause.

Do you mind?

HE. No, I don't mind.

Pause.

Well?

SHE. I'm waiting for you to . . .

HE. Goodnight, then.

SHE. Is that it?

HE. Yes, that's it.

SHE. Sorry, I thought . . .

HE. You thought what?

SHE. Just . . . that's all you're going to say?

HE. Yes.

SHE. You don't want me to tell you things?

HE. No.

SHE. You don't want to know if I'm . . .

HE. No. I'm sure you are.

SHE. All right. It's OK. Goodnight. Tomorrow . . .

HE. Yes. Tomorrow, tomorrow, tomorrow.

SHE. Tomorrow.

Seven

In the doorway, one each side, leaning against the wall.

SHE. What do you think of me?

HE. Does it matter?

SHE. It does to me. A lot.

HE. What do you want to know?

SHE. The truth.

HE. The truth. Which one?

SHE. How do I seem to you?

HE. What is it you're asking?

SHE. Do you love me?

   Pause.

HE. I'm not going to answer that.

SHE. People are saying.

HE. What do you mean?

SHE. That they're saying.

HE. What are they saying?

SHE. Nothing.

HE. Don't play with me.

SHE. I'm not. We're both playing.

HE. Tell me what people are saying.

SHE. Well, people . . . that's a very general thing.

HE. Abstract.

SHE. That's right, abstract.

HE. You mean, some people are saying?

SHE. Yes, maybe that's it. Some people are saying.

HE. And?

SHE. Others are listening.

HE. Just what are you driving at with this stupid rumour business?

SHE. I said 'saying'. Saying.

HE. Gossiping.

SHE. 'Saying' sounds better.

HE. It's not the same thing.

SHE. There's not that much difference.

HE. All right. I haven't got the energy for this.

SHE. All right. I'll tell you.

HE. Good.

SHE. A couple of men were following me. In the street, one evening. I went for a walk because I had nothing else to do. Are you listening?

HE. Yes.

SHE. And watching?

HE. No.

HE stifles a cough.

SHE. What are you doing?

HE. Nothing. Go on.

SHE. Are you sure?

HE. Yes.

SHE. They were calling after me . . . They came right up.

HE. Why were they following you?

SHE. I don't know.

HE. Did you do anything to encourage them?

SHE. Nothing. I was just walking.

HE. You were walking.

SHE. Yes, one evening, because I had nothing else to do. They whispered things at me.

HE. What things?

SHE. Things.

HE. What did you do?

SHE. Nothing. I listened. Men's things.

HE. What do you know about men's things?

SHE. Not very much, but I supposed they were men's things.

HE. What men's things did they say to you?

SHE. Can you not imagine?

HE. No.

SHE. If you saw me in the street, what things would you say?

HE. Nothing.

SHE. Nothing. Nothing at all?

HE. If I saw you in the street, parading like that, I'd think you were an idiot, but I wouldn't say anything. Not a word.

SHE. They said about my legs.

HE. Your legs?

SHE. They wanted to touch them.

HE. Did they?

SHE. No.

HE. What did they have to say about your legs?

SHE. That I'd lovely legs.

HE. Well, well.

SHE. They said about my breasts as well.

HE. Did they say you have spots, full of poison, and they'd have to suck them for you, like your cousin or your uncles?

SHE. Just one uncle. No, not exactly. They said about my backside too.

HE. And that's what people are gossiping about?

SHE. What they're saying. No. That's what the men were gossiping about. I wanted to know what you thought.

HE. I don't think anything. I don't care whether they say things or say nothing. It's your lookout.

SHE. The rain's cleared up. Nothing strange about going out for a walk. It's not as cold.

HE. No, it's not. I had noticed.

SHE. It's getting sunnier.

HE. Surprise, surprise.

SHE. It's getting warmer at night.

HE. Really. It's certainly getting harder to sleep. To breathe.

SHE. I'm wearing less clothes. Have you noticed? Have you?

HE. Even if I hadn't wanted to.

SHE. Do you know why?

HE. Because you're mad.

SHE. About . . . anyone?

HE. You're not. Don't even say it.

SHE. I put perfume on.

HE. I noticed that too.

SHE. You never say anything. But they said . . .

HE. That makes it less interesting.

SHE. Is that what you think?

HE. Absolutely.

SHE. All right.

   SHE *makes to go, but* HE *stops her brusquely.*

   Hey. You're hurting me. Let go.

HE. What's happened to you?

SHE. Nothing.

HE. You've changed.

SHE. So have you. You seem cross all the time.

HE. Just tired. Frightened.

SHE. Do you feel sick?

HE. I said tired.

SHE. And frightened?

HE. It's nothing. It doesn't matter.

SHE. Did you not sleep well?

HE. That's not why I'm tired.

SHE. Then what's wrong?

HE. Is it not obvious?

SHE. No, it's not.

HE. Use your eyes.

SHE. How? With no light . . .

HE. All right!

SHE. Yes. I can see you and I can guess.

HE. Well, then?

SHE. 'Well, then' what?

HE. You can't tell anything?

SHE. Not from your face.

HE. Can you hear my voice?

SHE. Yes.

HE. And what does it tell you?

SHE. What do you want it to tell me?

HE. How does it sound?

SHE. Hmm . . . Well . . .

Pause.

HE. I'm done . . . finished.

SHE. Done?

HE. Old.

SHE. No. You're not so old.

HE. No?

SHE. No.

HE. What would you call it?

SHE. Call what?

HE. This. Look at me.

SHE. I don't know. You're the teacher.

HE. What did you say?

Pause.

SHE. That it's you who's teaching me.

HE. No. You didn't say it's me who's teaching you.

SHE. I said . . .

HE. Don't say it again. Don't even think about saying it outside these four walls.

SHE. It's the first time.

HE. Get out of here.

SHE. Don't talk to me like that.

HE. Get out of here. Now. I'm fed up.

SHE. It's not my fault.

HE. No, it's not, but I want to be on my own. I'm tired.

SHE. Before . . .

HE. Before. Before. Before. Things are different now.

SHE. Why are they different?

HE. You went out.

SHE. What's wrong with that?

HE. What's wrong with it? You haven't understood a thing.

SHE. What should I understand?

HE. Do you not care about what you've done?

SHE. What have I done?

HE. Look at me.

SHE. What am I supposed to see?

HE. Turn on the light, if you want.

SHE. What for?

HE. For you to understand better.

SHE. Understand what?

HE. If you saw my eyes, maybe they'd tell you.

SHE. You tell me.

HE. Put on the light.

SHE. There's no need.

HE. Put on the light.

SHE. Everyone's asleep. Do you want to wake them?

HE. No.

Pause.

SHE. We're fine like this.

HE. Try to understand. I'm asking you.

SHE. Not so loud.

HE. I'm begging you.

SHE. God, what? What are you begging me for? I don't understand.

HE. Does it have to be so obvious, so lewd, so coarse?

SHE. I don't know what you're talking about. You're always stringing me along, with your strange words. Why don't you just say what you mean and we can save all this . . . agonising?

HE. Does this matter to you?

SHE. Not enough to argue about.

HE. You know what I'm talking about.

Pause.

SHE. Yes. It matters.

HE. It matters. How much?

SHE. Does it matter to you? That's what I came to ask?

HE. That's not true. You came to talk about the men. That you'd gone out looking for them.

SHE. I didn't go out looking for anyone.

HE. You showed off in front of them, like a bitch in heat. Displaying your power, your power as a huntress, so you could come crowing back to me.

SHE. You're mad.

HE. And you've just realised? Why would that be?

SHE. I want to go.

HE. Yes, of course. Go.

SHE. You're not stopping me?

HE. No.

SHE. You don't need me?

HE. No.

Pause.

SHE. You're hurting me.

HE. I didn't touch you. Not this time.

SHE. That's the problem.

HE. Very vulgar.

SHE. Will I tell you a story?

HE. No.

SHE. The last one.

HE. You've forgotten the drink.

SHE. There'll be a drink tomorrow.

HE. There won't be a tomorrow.

SHE. The story . . .

HE. Do you hear that?

Pause.

It's raining again. There's no sense to anything. Things are important only because they seem important. They might not exist, they might not happen, and nothing changes. Time just wears us down. It finishes us.

SHE. It'll pass. It'll get better.

HE. No. Leave it. Just go.

SHE. OK. I'll come back tomorrow.

HE. There won't be a tomorrow.

SHE. I'll come and look for you. You'll be here.

HE. I'll make sure I'm not.

SHE. You're frightening me.

HE. I don't believe that for a moment. Not now. Anyway, as I said, nothing matters that much. You're not worth the attention I'm paying you.

SHE. The story.

HE. I'm not interested.

SHE. It's very short.

HE. I said . . .

SHE. The woman felt lonely.

HE. Stand still.

HE *draws close to her, breathes her in, caresses her with his look, desires her.*

SHE. She went out of her cave.

HE. Why did she live in a cave – was she a woman or a fox? A vixen . . . ?

SHE. She lived in the dark. But one day she went out. The woman went out and they caught her. She was their prey. They hunted her down.

HE. Who?

SHE. They put their hands on her.

HE. Who?

SHE. They emptied themselves into her.

HE. Who?

SHE. But in the middle of the shadows she could see the face of another man. Even though she was their prey, she devoured them, thinking about another man.

HE pushes her away.

HE. I'm not interested. What were the rumours you came to tell me about?

SHE. Take care. People. They're searching.

Eight

SHE is standing behind him. HE is sitting on a chair, keeping his back to her as HE gazes into space.

HE. 'I'm sick. And you expect me to smile through my misery. Don't you? Say something. Are you listening? Are you sure you're listening? It would be worth it just for once, for this one last time, if we could tell each other everything as it is, or as we think it is. Would it not? That's how I see it. No, no, stand still; please, this time it's absolutely critical that you breathe very gently, that you don't close your eyes, that you stay still. Just this once. There's no moon. We are truly alone. Exactly like then. When I was seven. She was twice

my age. She was simple. I'm not being unkind, she really
was, she used to drool and things like that. One of her eyes,
I think it was the right one, used to wander towards the
ceiling while she was looking at you with the other one.
Her name was Rebecca. She had a beautiful name at least.
You could see Rebecca was racked by desire. I did it out of
kindness. It's no different now. I enjoy it more with you, but
deep down it's always the same thing. That night there was
no moon either. A coincidence, don't you think? There was
nobody about. It was still early. Barely nine o'clock.
Rebecca was on her own. She could feel my presence. She
knew I was watching her. Her mother was shouting for her
from the doorway. "Come on in, Rebecca, come on in."
Rebecca paid no heed. She was just staring into space, in
two different directions at the same time. Being Rebecca.
Staring blankly down the dark alley, and at the descending
darkness. It wasn't my childish appearance that made her
notice me, it was my smell, the heavy breathing, the fact
that my heart was pounding like some mad drummer. Just
a couple of steps . . . I was standing in front of her. Her
milky throat was crying out for me to bite her. She was
smelly. A bad smell. I had this boiling feeling of malice,
and I groped her under her skirt. Not her cunt. I wrapped
my arm round her waist, and I ground the palm of my hand
into her backside. Arse sounds better. The contact lasted
barely five seconds or so, but you really could call it an
eternity of the flesh. And then I kissed her, a clumsy, hot,
naive, brutal kiss. Once, twice, three times while I groped
around her buttocks. I could feel her breath coming in
shorter bursts. I knew it was risky, that if anyone happened
to glance our way, anyone at all, I would have been for it.
I knew all right. But that feeling, that possibility, of
stealing, of breaking in and taking something by force, of
destroying somebody else in such a sweet way, it made me
keep marauding around Rebecca's ridiculous tits and lumpy
waist. And then I let her go. I ran, I stopped and I looked
back. That vacant ugly leering face, her lips slightly apart,
thick wet lips, they had the word desire, in all its full
obscenity, written all over them, and they restored me
to the night, to the idea that I'd taken something, that she

would always remember it but that that was all there would
ever be. I don't think anybody ever kissed her again. She
was repulsive. I did it out of disdain, out of repugnance . . .
for myself. You can do anything when you're a child. Fresh,
firm flesh . . . The hunter game. Now there's just disgust.
Flaccidity. Despair. Loneliness. The same perverse game,
but less fun. Do you understand? It's no different now.
It's exactly like then. Do you understand? Rebecca has a
different name. Rebecca. You're Rebecca.'

Pause.

SHE. That's what you said to her?

HE. Yes.

SHE. And her name was Rebecca, like in the story.

HE. It's not a story. No. Her name wasn't Rebecca.

SHE. And what happened?

HE. She was crying.

SHE. And you?

HE. I sat and watched her cry.

SHE. But she wasn't Rebecca.

HE. No, I hardly knew her.

SHE. Did you love her?

HE. I wanted her.

SHE. What did she say, what did she do?

HE. Nothing. She threw herself into the river. So I heard.

Nine

The door is closed between them. HE *refuses to appear until the end.*

HE. Just take no for an answer.

SHE. It'll do you good.

HE. I'll be the judge of what'll do me good.

SHE. This will do you more good.

HE. I've no intention of finding out whether you're right or not.

SHE. I want to come in . . . Sorry. Would you mind opening the door, señor, please.

HE. I said no.

SHE. I've got your drink.

HE. I didn't order a drink.

SHE. It'll relax you.

HE. I don't think so. I feel worse than ever. My head's sore, I can't breathe and I feel like biting. Just stay away. And stop making so much noise. You'll wake everyone.

SHE. I don't care.

HE. Well, I care. I need to sleep.

SHE. Then open the door.

HE. What good will that do?

SHE. We can talk, sort things out.

HE. What else is there to say? You've come out of this very well. I lost. Game over.

SHE. That's not true.

HE. Oh yes it is. I was the one dragged down. It was me who fell. I lost my balance. I haven't got much time left.

SHE. That's not true.

HE. I don't want to go on like this. I'm suffocating . . . I'm exhausted. Did you hear me? I was coughing my lungs up all afternoon.

SHE. You'll get better.

HE. I won't.

SHE. Have faith.

HE. Pigs have faith. What good does it do them?

SHE. Then have faith in me.

HE. You were right. You've got the better tools. You're much better made. Your machinery works. Your flesh is intact, in a manner of speaking. I don't know. I remember the story, the woman who was a fox who was hunted. You meant something by that, didn't you? I was at a disadvantage. I'm worn out. I ended up the weak one, the one that was dragged down, broken, ripped, exposed, run through. You have very subtle claws. But sharp.

SHE. I haven't done anything.

HE. That's right. I did it myself. I lurched into the mud myself. Into your mud.

SHE. What did I know? You taught me all these things.

HE. What did I teach you? Can you tell me?

SHE. No.

HE. Don't try to get out of it. You played and you played well. I knew you would.

SHE. You taught me how to enjoy it.

HE. Enjoy what?

SHE. This.

HE. What 'this'?

SHE. I don't know.

HE. A lot of useless words. Just shut up and go to bed. Go on. It's raining again.

SHE. It hurts.

HE. What hurts?

SHE. But I like it.

HE. I don't understand.

SHE. I like it hurting you.

HE. You don't know what you're saying.

SHE. That's what the game was.

HE. No. You don't understand any of it.

SHE. So what was it you wanted?

HE. I didn't want anything. I don't want anything. I don't know who you are. I don't know your name, I don't know what you're doing here. I'd like you to go now, or I'll call the manager.

SHE. Why are you doing this?

HE. I'm not doing anything.

SHE. There's something I have to tell you: I talked.

HE. I didn't expect anything different. It was foreseeable.

SHE. I told somebody. They know who you are.

HE. I don't know what you're talking about.

SHE. Are you saying you're not?

HE. I can't say anything about something I know nothing about.

SHE. I need to talk to you. Just talk. Please.

HE. What for?

SHE. I need to.

HE. You can talk to whoever you like. Your friends, the manager, the dog on the street. Just leave me alone.

SHE. No, you don't understand me. Why don't you want to understand me?

HE. What are you shouting for? It's night-time. Who are you looking for?

SHE. I need you.

HE. And I need to sleep.

SHE. I'm leaving.

HE. I don't blame you.

SHE. Do you care about me? Do you? Answer me. Do you?

HE. Lower your voice, please.

SHE. Tell me.

HE. . . .

SHE. Please . . .

HE. . . .

SHE. Think of the consequences.

HE. Are you threatening me?

SHE. Bastard.

HE. You are threatening me.

SHE. It'll be your fault.

HE. I don't know what's wrong with you, young lady.

SHE. Bastard . . .

SHE runs away. HE opens the door and emerges. HE talks to the audience as if they were fellow guests in the hotel.

HE. What's going on? Because I have absolutely no idea. She was banging on my door. And then she ran off. She was talking about a river. We need to get help, because I couldn't make out what she was saying. I was too frightened to open the door. She said something about a river. And I was frightened . . .

End.

LITTLE CERTAINTIES

BÁRBARA COLIO

translated by

WILLIAM GREGORY

*Without at least a photo of the course of your life,
How could you be quite sure it wasn't all a dream?*

Characters

MARIO

JUAN

MOTHER

NATALIA

SOFÍA

OLGA

Written in the cafés of New York and Coyoacán, 2004.

Little Certainties (*Pequeñas certezas*) was first performed in English as a rehearsed reading as part of the *Arena Mexico* season in the Jerwood Theatre Upstairs, Royal Court Theatre, London, on 13 January 2006 with the following cast:

JUAN	Daniel Mays
NATALIA	Fiona Glascott
MOTHER	Marion Bailey
SOFÍA	Morven Christie
OLGA	Siân Brooke

Director Gordon Anderson

EXPOSURES

Mario and Juan.

Tijuana. The siblings' house. MARIO's suitcase. JUAN, furious, holds a red folder in his hands. A door is heard slamming loudly.

JUAN. Go on, then: run away! What's going on in your head, you stupid bastard? These documents aren't valid; they can't be valid. Where's the original? Answer me! I'll report you; don't think that just because I'm your brother I won't report you, you fucking idiot. You won't get away with this. You don't want to end up like me? Is that what you say? So what do you think I am? I work, I'm responsible; I've ended up being responsible for you two. It wasn't my fault we ended up living like this. It wasn't my fault! And I don't need therapy, all right? What I need is . . . is . . . Not even Sofía will be on your side this time. Hey, Mario! Mario! I'm talking to you. You're not going anywhere; tomorrow we'll go and straighten this out and then . . . you can go wherever you like. Onto the street, or to hell. I'd rather have you dead than taking the piss out of us again. It's finished! Get out of my house, *my* house. Do you hear?! I never want to see you again. Never!

JUAN's breathing quickens. A door opens.

The Mother and Natalia.

A bus stop in Mexico City. It has just stopped raining. The MOTHER looks towards one end of the street. NATALIA tries to make a mobile phone call.

NATALIA. I don't know why I listened to you.

MOTHER. What if it had been him?

NATALIA. There's no signal. Shit!

MOTHER. Why don't we take the metro?

NATALIA. No way. Not at this time of night.

Silence.

MOTHER. But he did look a bit similar.

NATALIA. He did not.

MOTHER. It was hard to tell with his face smashed up.

NATALIA. His whole body was smashed up, Mum.

MOTHER. Poor man. What must they do with all those bodies, dear? It doesn't even bear thinking about. Poor wandering souls. With no one to guide them to Heaven with a prayer. It's inhuman. Totally inhuman. He'd had his share of suffering in life; I could see it in his face. I don't believe that story about him throwing himself off that bridge. They say that so as not to have to investigate or whatever. And besides, in the end, of course, who would care? (*Pause.*) I don't mean that someone killed him, I'm not saying that, and I don't believe either that someone would have the heart to throw that poor man off a bridge. Why would they?

NATALIA. It's going to rain again.

MOTHER. I know he wasn't the one we were looking for, but I felt like saying it was him so they'd give me the body. At least so as to have a service for him. I know that you and your father don't like me doing things like that, but someone has to pity these people.

NATALIA. I'm going to look for a phone; stay here.

MOTHER. No! Don't leave me alone. There's a man over there; he keeps looking over.

NATALIA. Let's both go, then.

MOTHER. Calm down.

NATALIA. Mum, please! I want to catch a cab.

MOTHER. Relax. Sit down.

NATALIA. I am relaxed.

MOTHER. It's quite natural that you're upset after –

NATALIA. I'm not upset.

MOTHER. The attendant understood perfectly. Don't worry. You'll not be the first or the last person to feel sick at seeing those poor people. I know it's shocking to see –

NATALIA. It's shocking that I went along with your idea. It was impossible for Mario to be in that morgue.

MOTHER. Not impossible, dear. Perhaps Tijuana doesn't have any bridges.

NATALIA. Don't be ridiculous, Mum. Anyway, he's not necessarily dead.

MOTHER. The description I heard on the radio of the unidentified man fitted exactly the one on the news about Mario disappearing: tall, light skin, slim build, scar on the forehead.

NATALIA. You didn't even know Mario. You never saw him.

MOTHER. I felt I knew him; you talked about him a lot.

NATALIA. It's weird. I don't even have a photo of him.

MOTHER. We take our best photos with the memory of our hearts.

NATALIA. It stank in there.

MOTHER. We couldn't leave ourselves doubting, dear; you must see that. You had a duty to come and identify that body.

NATALIA *sees a taxi and tries to hail it. The taxi drives away.*

NATALIA. Those lumps we saw –

MOTHER. Corpses, dear. Corpses.

NATALIA. I don't understand why you like those places so much.

MOTHER. It was a possibility. Don't deny it.

NATALIA. Morgues ought to be like darkrooms, with one red light bulb and nothing else. Not that hanging neon light. I'd never seen a dead body before. Did you see his eyes? They'd risen out of their sockets and his bottom lip was almost touching his neck. I don't know how I let you drag me here. I must be desperate. There was too much light. Even when I shut my eyes I could still see that face through my eyelids; I can still see it now.

MOTHER. When we get home, I'll bake you a cake and you'll feel better, you'll see. I hope your father's filled up the larder like I asked him to. We left in such a rush.

NATALIA. What did you think when you first saw me? Amongst all those lumps?

MOTHER. Babies, dear. Babies.

NATALIA. Tell me.

MOTHER. Well, that you were a very bonny little girl with big, brown eyes; like mine, when I was young.

NATALIA. Is that why you chose me?

MOTHER. Oh, no. I wanted a little girl so badly. Twice, we came so close, but . . . Your father and I tried everything. Your father . . . Always trying to make me happy. Until we got to that lovely place, full of crying babies. It was paradise. It was you who picked me, Natalia. Here's a taxi . . .

NATALIA. I was about a year old, wasn't I?

MOTHER. . . . . Looks like it's empty. Ooh, he was in a hurry. Sit down, dear; it's dangerous to stand on the kerb. Anyone could come and snatch your bag away. That man keeps looking. Can you see him?

NATALIA. Where?

MOTHER. There, in the middle of the road. What does he want?

NATALIA. He must be looking for someone. I've never walked around this area before; it's dangerous . . . (*Dials her mobile phone. Fails to get through.*)

MOTHER. You were eight months old. Exactly. Barely eight. As soon as you saw me you stretched your little arms up to me. So pretty. You were the only baby that wasn't crying. I picked you up, you smiled at me and . . . It was as if we'd known each other all our lives. You chose your life, Natalia. You're very good at that kind of thing. Not like me.

It starts to rain.

It's late; your father'll be worried.

NATALIA. Here we are. Come on, Mum. Taxi! Over here, please! Stop! (*Opens her umbrella.*) Come on. The idiot's stopped further on. Come on.

MOTHER (*going towards* NATALIA). Did Mario know, then?

NATALIA. Know what?

MOTHER. About the baby.

NATALIA (*stops*). What are you talking about?

MOTHER. Watch out for that puddle. He could have parked a bit nearer! Come on, dear; before he drives away.

NATALIA. What baby?

MOTHER. You can't hide life, Natalia.

They are surprised by a screeching of tyres followed by a thunderous crashing of metal and glass. They instinctively cling to one another underneath the umbrella.

Good Lord!

NATALIA. The man . . .

Juan and Sofía.

In Tijuana. The siblings' house.

JUAN (*on the phone*). Yes. That's all. As soon as we know anything . . . Yes. It'll be in the paper. Absolutely. So, who am I talking to . . . ? Yes, I understand. I'm very grateful . . . Let's hope so. Thank you for calling. No. No bother at all.

He hangs up. Takes a videocassette out of a large envelope.
SOFÍA *enters carrying some bags. The telephone rings.*
JUAN *hesitates in answering.* SOFÍA *stops, and they exchange a glance. On the third ring, the phone stops.*

SOFÍA. I brought apple-and-honey yoghurt.

JUAN. Someone asking after Mario.

SOFÍA. I've just been walking back along the avenue and I smelled the smell of freshly baked bread. I couldn't resist. Look: those little banana buns you like so much. Have a smell; they're still warm. I'm dying for one.

JUAN. Did you hear what I said, Sofía?

SOFÍA. Perfectly. How many people call here every day to ask questions? Hmm? Five? Ten? A hundred? The car's out of petrol, by the way. Where did they all spring from, all these people worried about Mario? They're a bunch of idiots, that's what they are. You can hear the brake lining going as well.

JUAN. I've been waiting for you all afternoon and you've been in San Diego, shopping?

SOFÍA. It was a miracle: there was no queue; I only had to wait half an hour. I needed some clothes. (*Takes out a dress from a designer carrier bag.*) Pretty, isn't it? I couldn't decide between this one or a green one but I think this one goes better with those shoes, the ones I haven't had a chance to wear yet. Look: it's a size four and it fits me perfectly. It's been years since I've fitted into a size four. Not bad, eh? I really fancied a colourful dress. Something vivacious. Meche's coming to pick me up at nine, so excuse me, but I want to start getting ready early. You go ahead and watch your film. What is it? A horror film?

JUAN. Where're you going?

SOFÍA. Don't know. Bullet Square, probably. Barhopping. It's Ladies' Night so we'll make the most of that. With a bit of luck we'll meet some guys and they'll pay for all our drinks.

JUAN. You've got a short memory.

SOFÍA. Put the yoghurt in the fridge if you're not going to eat it now. If Meche calls, tell her –

JUAN. I suppose I'll have to come and drag you out of the toilets of some dive, then.

SOFÍA. They must be missing me. They'll probably think I've gone and become a nun. I haven't been there for three whole months.

JUAN. How can you be so cheerful?

SOFÍA. It's too much.

JUAN. That'll look great: the sister of –

SOFÍA. Don't worry, 'Mummy', the 'little girl' won't be naughty.

JUAN. You switched your mobile off. I called you over ten times.

SOFÍA. He's gone! OK? He left us. Drop it now. Why should I care about Mario when he doesn't give a fuck about us? He wanted to get out of here and he did it. He was dying to see Europe, wasn't he? Any day now we'll get a postcard.

JUAN. You don't know what you're saying.

SOFÍA. And you do? I'm fed up. I've had it up to here! Look at me. Look at the pair of us, the state we're in. Do you think I don't notice you jumping every time the phone rings? Look: I've got no nails left, or fingers, or hands, or arms; I've chewed them all off. I'm trembling. Have you noticed that, at least? I keep trembling and I can't stop; it's stupid. But enough now! There's been no sign of him; it's not normal. Maybe he's dead, maybe he's merrily waltzing around Venice on a gondola, maybe he's hiding somewhere and laughing at us like when he was little. I don't know; the only thing I do know is that I can't do anything more. I need to go out, get some air, get wasted or crash my car into a lamp post.

JUAN. It's my responsibility.

SOFÍA. If that's what you want to believe, go ahead. We're a family of magicians. Poof! We disappear when least you expect it. Maybe I'll be next, or you; who knows? I'm having a bath.

JUAN. The police –

SOFÍA. The police couldn't care less about yet another missing person. They haven't done anything and they aren't going to. People get shot when they step out from their front door, or chopped into pieces and scattered around the desert. People get stabbed for a measly fifteen pesos. (*Pause*.) In the baker's, there was a photo of Mario, in the middle of four others, all of missing people. What the hell are the fucking police going to do? Hmm? Nothing.

JUAN. Have you finished? Mario had a bank account. In dollars. A big account.

SOFÍA. What?

JUAN. A cheque was cashed a few days ago.

SOFÍA. What are you talking about? Mario went to the bank? So he's –

JUAN. They're not sure it was him.

SOFÍA. I don't get it.

JUAN. This is the video from the day and the time when the cheque was cashed. It's the only thing that they – the police – have found. We have to ID the person who cashed it. But I believe you're in a hurry.

JUAN *puts the tape into the video recorder. He takes the remote control. He sits in front of the television. In disbelief,* SOFÍA *approaches and sits next to* JUAN.

Weren't you going to have a bath?

SOFÍA. He's alive – I knew it. Have you already watched this?

JUAN. I wanted us to see it together. (*Starts the video*.)

SOFÍA. Turn the sound up.

JUAN. There is no sound.

They watch.

SOFÍA. Where is he?

JUAN (*taking a piece of paper from the same envelope*). According to the bank's report, 'the man in the blue cap corresponds with the time the withdrawal took place'.

SOFÍA. Blue cap? Press 'pause'! There! It doesn't look like Mario.

JUAN. No . . . It doesn't.

SOFÍA. When did he sign the cheque?

JUAN. It could have been any day. It was made out to the bearer.

SOFÍA. Why would Mario be using cheques? What did I miss? We lived together; we were a family. It was all we had.

Takes the paper that JUAN *took from the envelope. Reads.*

Where did he get so much money?

JUAN. Pay attention, Sofía. We must be missing something.

SOFÍA (*reading*). Who's this Natalia Pollack that he left as the only beneficiary?

JUAN. I don't know.

SOFÍA. Don't mess with me, Juan. Don't treat me like an idiot. Trust me. What was Mario mixed up in?

JUAN. I don't know.

SOFÍA. Who's Natalia Pollack?

JUAN. I don't know.

SOFÍA. Was he trafficking? That's it, isn't it? Was he dealing drugs? Was he selling coke or what? Was he smuggling it, or . . . I won't be frightened; I just want to know.

JUAN. Don't talk rubbish.

SOFÍA. Why did you two argue that night? Tell me. You were the last one to see him. Where did he go? Tell me. I'll find out somehow. Did he get into trouble with money? What is it you don't want to tell me? Was he . . . kidnapped?

JUAN. Let's watch the video again.

> SOFÍA *grabs the remote control.*

Give me that.

SOFÍA. No. Why did you argue?

> JUAN *offers* SOFÍA *a red folder.*

JUAN. I'll swap you.

> SOFÍA *accepts the swap. She opens the folder and examines the papers inside it. Little by little, she begins to understand as* JUAN *rewinds the tape.*

SOFÍA. This looks like . . .

JUAN. Not 'looks like'. Is.

SOFÍA. Your signature's on it. And mine. How did he . . . ? Where did you get this?

JUAN. Will you pay attention to the video now?

SOFÍA. It really is a horror film.

JUAN. I can't see the guy's face, his cap's covering it. Why do they put the cameras up so high?

SOFÍA. He took it from us . . . But, why? What for?

JUAN. Pull yourself together.

SOFÍA. Bastard. Bastard. Bastard! Bastard!!

JUAN. Don't get hysterical; you wanted to know, didn't you?

SOFÍA. What did he say to you? Why did he do this to us?

JUAN. He didn't give me any explanations.

SOFÍA. What did he say to you?!

JUAN (*pause*). That he didn't want to end up like . . . us.

Silence.

Sofía.

At the bar.

SOFÍA. I envy him. I'd disappear like that, if I could. I think I understand him, that's the funny thing. He could never get used to the idea of living like dead people, like Juan, like me. Mario was all light. I think I always envied him. Bastard. I'd like to see him just one more time to punch his lights out or . . . to ask him to take me with him. Why didn't he say anything to me? He's alive; I know it. He's not the dying kind. (*Pause.*) We used to stay up watching TV. Until dawn. We bought a set of knives, the ones they show on infomercials, with Juan's credit card. Hey, they looked pretty good. All right? (*Laughs.*) It's been hell going outside, you know? I can't concentrate, even when I'm driving. I nearly crashed last week. I drive along looking at people, at everyone, at their faces; I think I'm going to spot him at any moment and I'm going to shout out and he'll hold out his hand and wave at me with that harlequin smile of his and we'll hug each other. Oh, I think I'm going to end up in the madhouse. The . . . the other day I went and sat on the beach to see if he'd come out of the sea. He loved water. I stayed sitting there till dawn and . . . and nothing. Sometimes I think I could have prevented it from the start. If I'd started crying that night, crying my eyes out, at least Mum wouldn't have gone out and she'd have stayed with us. At least her. Everything would have been different. I'd like so much to be a different person. Different. It's hellish being here; it's really hellish staying here, searching, living. It's a living hell, Meche.

Natalia and Olga.

Mexico City. The waiting room of a private medical clinic.

OLGA. Apparently this girl's problem was that one of her teeth had come out twisted or in the middle of her palate or something like that. She looked like a sweet little thing in the paper, by the way. But what it was, was that the witch doctor or the priest in the little Hindu village she lived in said that the crooked tooth was an unmistakable sign that she was possessed by a demon. D'you know what I mean?

NATALIA. And what does that have to do with the dog?

OLGA. The only way to cure her was to get her married straight away. D'you know what I mean?

NATALIA. I need some water. Are you sure I had to come here with an empty stomach?

OLGA. Yes. You can't imagine the number of people that come here, honestly. If I gave you names, you wouldn't believe me. People you'd least expect have already been through here and walk around now as if nothing had happened. I know you hear stories about people's insides ending up in a mess, but none of that happens here.

NATALIA. What time is it?

OLGA. We got here early.

NATALIA. How long will it take?

OLGA. Don't worry; I won't get bored; I brought some magazines. I'll be here when you come out. Here, have a look at one.

NATALIA *shakes her head.* OLGA *flicks through a magazine. She finds something and shows it to her.*

Look: those photos you took of the Polanco ladies at their charity ball. You find the best angle for everything, don't you? You really should start taking pictures again.

NATALIA. Do you think I'll see him again one day?

OLGA. The most important thing right now is to get Mario out of your head – and out of your whole body. And believe me: this is the best place to do it. Don't give me that face. Listen: you can't back out now; you're almost out of time. I had to bust a gut to get an appointment here! Just look at the place; it's lovely, isn't it? (*Pause.*) Oh, Natalia, stop pulling that face! Here: flick through one of these; take it: this one, with your work in. (NATALIA *takes it.*) Who needs men from the provinces with all these gorgeous Argentines in here? Look at those two. (*Shows her the magazine*.) See? Could just gobble them up, couldn't you? Although their hair's far too good. Mmm. No. Forget it; they must be gay.

NATALIA. I feel sick. Just from listening to you, I think. Can't you just tell me that everything's going to be all right and leave it at that? Mario and I have – had – plans. Have. He gave me something important the last time we saw each other – something you only give to people you trust.

OLGA. Gave you something? How many carats?

NATALIA. No! You've no idea, Olga. Not all people are the same. He grew up all by himself. He's worked all his life. He has no family. He wants to have one.

OLGA. And what about you? What do you want?

Silence.

NATALIA. I need some water.

OLGA *takes a bottle of Swiss-brand water out of her bag and offers it to* NATALIA.

OLGA. Here. You shouldn't trust water from any old place. I don't deny it: the furthest north I've ever been is Puerto Vallarta, but things really must be different in Tijuana. Don't you watch the news? Who knows who Mario might really have been, to have come to an end like that?

NATALIA. He hasn't come to an end.

OLGA. Even worse.

NATALIA (*drinks*). I know who Mario is. There was one thing that made us the same. (*Drinks*.) Have you never regretted it?

OLGA. Regretted what? Regretted . . . ? Oh, no, of course not. Can you picture me, now, pushing prams and heating up bottles at midnight? No thanks. What I'd really have liked is to have come here for the first time with a friend to support me and not judge me. Relax. You're with me. We're young. We can do whatever we want with our lives. Unlike that little girl with the crooked tooth and the dog. D'you know what I mean?

NATALIA. What? Oh, the thing you were saying about the girl and the dog.

OLGA. Exactly. You weren't sure what the dog had to do with it, were you? Well, it turns out they married the poor little Hindu girl to a dog. Her father was poor – so poor that he couldn't find anyone willing to marry his little daughter and wipe out the evil curse, so he had to marry her to a dog: a stray scavenger with fleas. It's not a joke; there was a photo in the paper. Girl and dog at the altar. It's the most honest image of marriage I've ever seen: no metaphors, just the naked truth. Didn't anyone ask the little girl if she'd rather walk around with a crooked tooth than live a dog's life, literally? And I ask myself, are there no dentists in India? What kind of culture is that, where your family prefers marrying you to a dog to letting you be yourself? It's a sign; it's a wake-up call for women everywhere. I'm taking action, me; I have to protest against a country that does things like that. I've no intention of going to India even by mistake and I've already cancelled my belly-dancing classes.

NATALIA. What about your yoga classes?

OLGA. That's Chinese. Isn't it?

Silence. They both flick through their magazines somewhat disinterestedly.

NATALIA. My mother knows about this.

OLGA. You told her?!

NATALIA. Of course not. But she knows.

OLGA. Look, your mum's a darling, I love her to bits and she makes a chocolate cake to die for. But, if truth be told, she's always scared me a bit, ever since we were little. She's got eyes in the back of her head.

NATALIA. When I told her I was going to stay at your house in Tepoztlan for a few days –

OLGA. To recuperate. Tepoz did wonders for me when I needed it.

NATALIA. She hardly said a word; she was so sad.

OLGA. Why?

NATALIA. She was mourning another one of her dead.

OLGA. What?!

NATALIA. She claimed a man we saw in the street. A car came past at full speed and crashed into the taxi we were hailing. It overturned and crushed him. He was the only one killed. The rest of us came out unscathed. Unscathed. If only we hadn't stopped that cab. No one knew who he was. My mum claimed him; I couldn't stop her. She pretended he was her nephew; I'm not sure. She felt responsible. She convinced my dad that we should pay for his funeral. It was a long night, very long.

OLGA. Another funeral?

NATALIA. She cried buckets; if only you'd seen her. As if it really were her flesh and blood, someone who belonged to her, even though she never knew him.

OLGA. I am sorry, Natalia.

NATALIA. Are you offering me your condolences?

OLGA. No. Well, it's just that your family's so weird. I don't know why your father lets her do those things.

NATALIA. My mum feels a lot better afterwards, a lot better. Funerals do her good.

OLGA takes back her magazine and tries to concentrate on reading something, but fails. She closes it, uneasy.

OLGA. I'm going to get a coffee. I need a good shot of caffeine. With all these stories. Want one? I won't be long.

NATALIA. No.

OLGA. You'll feel better.

NATALIA. No.

OLGA. All right.

NATALIA. No.

OLGA. I heard you.

NATALIA. No.

NATALIA *gets up. She exits.*

Olga.

Drinking a Martini.

OLGA. I have this paranoia that a person can end up in any old place. That's why I never go out without some kind of photo ID in my bag. Do you remember that film about Mozart? The one where they sing 'Amadeus, Amadeus'. Do you remember that at the end of the film they chuck the body into a mass grave? Mozart's body! Imagine. They didn't know who he was! It shocked me so much. Because if that happened to him, it could happen to anyone. Natalia says Mozart ended up in a mass grave because he was poor, but it wasn't that. How could poor Mozart have been poor? (*Drinks.*) That won't happen to me. Everyone knows me here. I'm a regular. (*Drinks.*) Between you and me, I was the one who pulled that Mario, right here in the bar. Natalia was just moping about, 'working', hiding behind her camera as usual. (*Drinks.*) I introduced her to Mario. Then he asked her out. I feel a bit responsible sometimes, you know? But, no. It's just that Natalia doesn't understand that a good relationship can only last a week, tops. It's stupid to drag it out any longer. (*Drinks.*) Do you know that she hasn't taken a single picture since? I don't know what's wrong with her. She walks around like a zombie. She can't get anything right. I don't know what she'd do without me. (*Drinks.*) Oh, it's been a while since I came into this bar on my own; it's not like it used to be, is it? You used to sit at the bar and in two minutes some gent would appear, asking for a light and buying you a drink. Where do people go these days? I didn't realise; Natalia always used to come with me. (*Drinks.*) *C'est la vie.* Make me another Martini?

Natalia and the Mother.

Mexico City. In an airport waiting room. The MOTHER *waits, with a small suitcase by her side and her hands clasped on her lap.*

An unintelligible voice makes an announcement over the loudspeaker.

NATALIA *enters with a suitcase in her hand. She stops and sees her* MOTHER *there.*

NATALIA. What are you doing here?

MOTHER. I haven't many talents, daughter dear, but the one thing I do well, I do very well: looking after you.

NATALIA. Mum . . .

MOTHER. I know you don't need me, Natalia, but don't deprive me of one of the few things I'm good at . . .

NATALIA. I don't even know what I'm going for. All I've got is an address written on a scrunched-up scrap of paper, nothing else. For all I know, I'll just get there, stand outside the place, wait for I don't know what and then catch the plane back; I don't know. I'm not even thinking. I'm not like you, Mum. You don't need to be told something to be sure about it; you always know, somehow. It's hard talking to you. Very hard. Because people talk to tell other people things, to let them know things, to feel that they have something to say, whether it's important or not, but before I even open my mouth, you always know already. It drives me mad, Mum. Yes. I'm going to give birth, to a little lump, to the child of a ghost. It was to be expected, wasn't it? I'm a child of ghosts myself. And things can't be like that; normal people aren't born from ghosts. People are people, flesh and blood; people live, die and are buried and there's a gravestone that you can visit and leave flowers at. There's at least a photo in a wallet to prove that they existed, that they were real: real parents, a real lover, that they weren't figments of the imagination. Photographs in wallets at least give that little certainty and I don't have that. Not even that. I need to know. I don't know what, but I need to know. Try to understand: my eyes don't look like yours. I'm not your daughter. (*Pause.* NATALIA *pulls herself together.*) I'm sorry.

MOTHER. Don't worry. My daughter.

An unintelligible voice makes an announcement over the loudspeaker. They both listen to the message.

I left plenty of frozen dinners for your father.

NATALIA *smiles. The* MOTHER *reacts happily to the gesture.* NATALIA *decides to go. The* MOTHER *hurries, takes her suitcase and follows her.*

An aeroplane takes off.

PROCESSING

Juan, Natalia, Sofía, the Mother.

Tijuana. NATALIA *and the* MOTHER's *suitcases. Expectant silence. Broken by the laughter of* SOFÍA.

JUAN. Shut up.

SOFÍA. You've got to laugh, otherwise you'd cry.

JUAN. They'll hear you.

SOFÍA. Did you know about this, too?

JUAN. No.

SOFÍA. Do you think we're too old to go to the orphanage?

JUAN. Shut up. I didn't expect this.

SOFÍA. And what's with that other woman? Did you see how –

JUAN. Shh.

The MOTHER *appears.*

MOTHER. There, there we are. I am sorry. There was a bit of turbulence during the flight and what with the surprise at meeting you . . . We didn't know exactly –

SOFÍA. Nor did we.

JUAN. Take a seat, Mrs Pollack. This has been a surprise. For all of us.

NATALIA *appears, somewhat shaken.*

NATALIA. I'm sorry.

JUAN. Are you feeling better, Natalia?

MOTHER. She won't be the first or the last person to feel sick after such a long flight.

JUAN. Sit down, please.

MOTHER. It looks like this boy, Mario, has led us all a merry dance.

NATALIA. Mum, let me be the one who –

JUAN. Are you sure that's what he said to you?

SOFÍA. Didn't you hear? 'A man who grew up by himself, with no family, who worked all his life.' (*Laughs.*) 'Worked.' (*Laughs.*)

MOTHER. It must have been a misunderstanding, that's all. Family is the most beautiful thing of all.

Silence.

JUAN. So how long did you know him for?

MOTHER. It'd be a few months, wouldn't it, dear?

SOFÍA. A few months. Is that *before* he fucked off, or –

JUAN. Stop it.

SOFÍA. – or including all this time since?

NATALIA. A few months.

SOFÍA. Where d'you meet?

MOTHER: Ooh, young people go out so much these days; you see them out in the streets even on a Monday night. There are just so many lovely places with such excellent food.

Silence.

JUAN. I am sorry; we haven't offered you anything. Would you like a coffee, a tea? Have we any Coke?

MOTHER. A tea would be lovely. What with the turbulence. What a thing! We were flying for nearly four hours; I'd never realised just how far Tijuana is from the city. Luckily we found a taxi driver, didn't we, dear? Ever such a nice man: he took us along I don't know which roads but he brought us here in the end. How funny: all those hills covered in little coloured houses; they look like they're going to collapse at any moment. Ever such a pretty town. Very modern. The taxi driver gave us his card in case we needed it later. He said, 'I can take you any place, any time,' didn't he, dear?

NATALIA. Yes. Two teas would be good.

Neither JUAN *nor* SOFÍA *moves.*

JUAN. Sofía, could you . . . ?

SOFÍA. I don't know how to make tea.

JUAN (*pause*). I'll be right back. I'll heat the water up in the microwave. (*Exits.*)

Silence.

MOTHER. It's a lovely house. Very big, very tasteful. You must have a beautiful view of the sea.

SOFÍA. It's our house. Our parents' house.

Silence.

MOTHER. It's been a terrible few days for everyone.

SOFÍA. Knowing him for a few fucking days in Mexico City doesn't give you the right to anything. All right?

MOTHER. Oh, but what with the internet, you youngsters keep in touch better than ever before and –

NATALIA. There's no need for you to take that tone with us. We just want to know what happened to him.

SOFÍA. And you came all this way just for that? Please!

MOTHER. Mario and Natalia were very close.

NATALIA. I didn't even know if anyone would open the door to me.

MOTHER. We'd like to help in some way.

SOFÍA. 'Close.' Who do you think you are? Nobody knew him better than I did. Until now.

NATALIA (*getting up*). Get up, Mum; we'd better leave.

MOTHER. But there's tea coming, dear.

SOFÍA. No. Don't go. It's just my way. Sit down. Please.

Pause. NATALIA *sits down. Silence.*

Have you got brothers and sisters?

NATALIA. No.

MOTHER. She's an only child.

SOFÍA. It must be better that way.

NATALIA. I don't know.

Silence.

SOFÍA. Mario was the life and soul of this house. Always coming up with the right wisecracks; making us laugh; driving Juan up the wall, calling him 'the Chief'. I wasn't the baby in the family once Mario came along. I was still the only girl – their little 'Petal' – but that wasn't enough to compete with his charms. He never left me in peace. He used to hide my Barbies.

MOTHER. Oh, Barbie dolls.

SOFÍA. He was so manipulative. When he felt like giving them back to me, he would give me a kiss on the cheek and leave me covered in spit. He used to like hiding the things that I loved the most. First it was my Barbies, then my earrings, then my make-up and then . . . then himself.

Silence. JUAN *enters with a tea set.*

JUAN. Careful, it's quite hot.

MOTHER. Thank you very much . . . It's Juan, isn't it?

JUAN. That's right. (*Pours the tea.*) So, you arrived here today from Mexico City. You live there. Mario was there for a while. Before . . . So, you . . . you met him there and I gather you became very –

SOFÍA. 'Close.'

JUAN. Yes. And you . . . What do you do, Natalia?

NATALIA. I'm a photographer. Society stuff.

MOTHER. You always say it in that tone, as if you were ashamed of it. Her work is wonderful. Have you not seen it? She's been published in all of the major magazines in Mexico City.

SOFÍA. I'm not interested in society magazines. Especially ones from the bloody capital.

MOTHER. Well, they're more than just society photographs; some people have the wrong idea about it. My Natalia photographs people at the very moment when they want to see themselves and be seen by other people. When people want to remember themselves, what do they do? They look at photos of when they were happy, and that way they can believe they've been happy all their lives. That's what my Natalia takes pictures of. She has the gift of capturing people's souls. (*Looking at the photograph that is somewhere in the house.*) They must be your parents, are they? And what lovely children. Very nice picture: the whole happy family at the beach. You can probably see this same view from here. Yes. And what a distinguished-looking lady. Will they be long?

SOFÍA. All eternity.

JUAN. They passed away.

MOTHER. Oh, Lord, I'm so sorry. I do apologise. I shouldn't have –

JUAN. Don't worry. It was a long time ago.

MOTHER. What a terrible loss. How did it happen?

NATALIA. Mum, leave it.

SOFÍA. A crash. Quick. Instant. Poof!

MOTHER. Heaven protect us! I lost a nephew not long ago in the same circumstances.

NATALIA. Don't start.

JUAN. So, Natalia, you were telling us that you met Mario in . . .

SOFÍA. Mum was thrown into the windscreen; she wasn't wearing a seat belt. They were only going to the chemist's. But she did make Mario wear one; he was in the back seat. He was only little so he bounced back; he just had a scratch on his forehead. He used to say he didn't even remember it; he was fast asleep and when he woke up he was already in hospital. They'd left me with Juan; he was having one of his asthma attacks. He was a very sickly child – all to seek attention, of course. 'His imaginary enemy was squeezing his chest and he couldn't breathe.' That was it, wasn't it? It's never happened since then, funnily enough.

JUAN. We don't need to hear your stories.

SOFÍA. Dad was wearing his.

MOTHER. Quite right, too.

SOFÍA. Fat lot of good it did him. In the forensic report that I read later, much later, and hidden away, like always – because no one can do anything in this house without Juan's permission – it said that my dad didn't die from his injuries; it was his heart.

JUAN. Do you take sugar?

SOFÍA. It was his own decision to die. It didn't bother him, leaving us on our own. The funny thing is: I understand him. He worshipped my mum.

The MOTHER *takes* SOFÍA*'s hand tenderly.*

JUAN. Your tea's ready.

NATALIA. Yes. (*Takes it.*)

MOTHER (*to* SOFÍA). You have mine, Petal.

JUAN. Mario never told us about you either.

They drink.

SOFÍA (*lights a cigarette, smokes*). 'Close.' Did you sleep with him?

JUAN. Sofía!

SOFÍA. What's the matter? It's a perfectly simple question.

JUAN. Don't be a smart-arse.

SOFÍA. I want to understand why he left everything to her that we –

JUAN. Just wait.

MOTHER. There's no problem. Sex isn't a taboo subject these days.

NATALIA. Do you have a photo of Mario?

SOFÍA. For your magazines?

NATALIA. That's all I came for.

The telephone rings. JUAN *tenses. He goes to it, picks up and hangs up immediately.*

SOFÍA. She can sort it out, can't she?

JUAN. Does she know?

NATALIA. I can sort what out?

SOFÍA. Doesn't look like it. Ask her.

JUAN. Natalia . . . I hope you understand that what Mario did . . . He shouldn't have done it. I don't doubt that you are good people and that you'll be willing to work with us. It's only fair. And . . .

MOTHER. Yes, of course. Whatever you need.

NATALIA. I don't understand.

SOFÍA. You're like a dyslexic, Juan. Can you never say anything clearly? (*To* NATALIA.) Mario opened a bank account – in dollars – and you're named as the sole beneficiary.

NATALIA. And?

JUAN. You knew?

NATALIA. No. I didn't know.

SOFÍA. He didn't say anything to you when he left?

NATALIA. Just that he'd be back soon.

JUAN. Mario robbed us. He forged our signatures and mortgaged our house. He put the funds into the bank in the name of a woman we don't know. You. That was wrong. Very wrong.

SOFÍA. If you really want to help us, get that money back for us, Natalia Pollack.

Silence.

MOTHER. An angel. They say that, when there's a pause in a conversation, it means an angel has flown by.

The Mother and Sofía.

In a bedroom.

SOFÍA. You'll be more comfortable in here.

MOTHER. It's very kind of you to offer us your house for the night. You're very sweet, Petal.

SOFÍA. If there's one thing this house has plenty of, it's empty spaces. No one's called me that for a long time.

MOTHER. The bathroom is . . .

SOFÍA. At the end of the corridor. If you need anything, knock on my door; I'm in the room on the left. Have a good rest.

MOTHER. Do you still have your Barbies?

SOFÍA. No. Just one.

MOTHER. I knew it.

SOFÍA. You're funny. Don't get me wrong; it's just . . .

MOTHER. Natalia tells me the same thing. In her own way, of course. She didn't want me to come with her but it's a good thing I did. Do you always wear black, Petal?

SOFÍA. No. Well, lately. Although I did buy myself a gorgeous dress not long ago. I hardly ever wear dresses but I just felt like it; I still haven't worn it.

MOTHER. You're very beautiful. Do you have a boyfriend?

SOFÍA. No.

MOTHER. You'd be fighting them off in Mexico City. Are you still at university?

SOFÍA. Ha! No. That was a long time ago. Anyway, school was never really my thing. I work at a travel agent's.

MOTHER. Oh, how lovely. And have you travelled very much?

SOFÍA. No. I've never been away from round here. But I like convincing other people to leave. With a bit of luck they'll leave the whole city empty. Just for me.

MOTHER. I know very well what it's like to lose loved ones. You've been very brave, Petal.

SOFÍA (*pause*). Want me to help you with your suitcase?

MOTHER. Thank you. I don't have much with me.

SOFÍA. You're wearing a black dress, too.

MOTHER. It's all right for someone my age, though. I hardly travel anywhere; I don't really like leaving the house. Natalia's father gets anxious when I'm not there. You've got your mother's eyes.

SOFÍA. No. Do you think? Mario's the one who looks like her.

MOTHER. Never. You look much more like her. The same bearing.

SOFÍA (*blushes*). Well. I'll leave you to it. Can I get you anything else?

MOTHER. Everything's perfect.

SOFÍA. Well. Goodnight.

MOTHER. Goodnight. Dream with the angels, Petal.

SOFÍA. Thanks. (*Half turns to go. Turns back.*) Do you want to see my new dress?

MOTHER. I'd love to! Come on . . .

Juan and Natalia.

In a bedroom.

JUAN. This was Mario's room. You can both share the guest room if you feel uncomfortable here.

NATALIA. No. It's fine. I'll sleep here.

JUAN. The bank opens at nine. We can go first thing to sort this out; it won't take long to transfer the account over to my name. Then I can take you both to breakfast and then –

NATALIA. And then straight to the airport. Back home. You already said, Juan.

JUAN. The thing is: I can't keep not going to work.

NATALIA. What do you do?

JUAN. I'm a production supervisor. Medical equipment. There are lots of factories here, so, you know. There's a lot of pressure, but the money's good.

NATALIA. Yes.

JUAN. If you'd like to stay until the weekend . . .

NATALIA. There won't be any need.

JUAN. You're being very quiet, Natalia.

NATALIA (*picks up a photograph from somewhere*). I never knew if he could swim.

JUAN. He was never out of the water.

NATALIA. This is him. Always laughing.

JUAN. He was good with jokes.

NATALIA. Yes.

The both seem to remember him; they laugh.

JUAN. You can keep that.

NATALIA. Thank you.

JUAN. Why didn't you have one?

NATALIA. Things.

JUAN. You had a really good time together, didn't you?

NATALIA. That's his suitcase.

JUAN. He was going on his travels again. But I stopped him; I confronted him. I had to; I couldn't just take it lying down. You understand, don't you?

NATALIA. I think so.

JUAN (*pause*). Can I ask you a question?

NATALIA. Sure.

JUAN. What did he do to win you over?

NATALIA *just looks away.*

I'm sorry. I didn't mean to upset you. I'm just surprised that . . . a woman like you could have fallen into his . . . I'm sorry; don't take this the wrong way. I'm sure you were special to him. Natalia Pollack. The name sounded to me like a sophisticated woman, like someone different, I don't know. I hope you won't pay any mind to what Sofía was saying. Now that I've met you, the last thing I would want is for you to get the wrong impression of us. Of me.

NATALIA. Don't worry, Juan. I'm shattered.

JUAN. Of course. Sleep well. My room's just next door if you need anything. (*Moving closer.*) We . . . we found it difficult to get on. Everything was very easy for him; he never understood that I . . . I had too much on my shoulders. But – well – he was my brother. My little brother. We used to play a lot when we were children and . . . and I taught him how to ride a bike. A little bike, one that used to be mine. I was his hero. Until something, snapped. (*Pause*.) I didn't mean it. What I said to him that night, I didn't mean it.

NATALIA. Didn't mean what?

JUAN. That I didn't want to see him again, ever.

NATALIA. Juan . . .

JUAN. I didn't mean it. I was too angry. Too angry. He came out of this room. He said he needed some air and . . . I haven't seen him since. That was the last thing I said to him, Natalia, and it came true, like a curse. But I didn't mean it. (*Coming closer.*) No, I can't cope with this as well, not now. I can't. I've never told anyone this, Natalia, no one. (*Hugs her.*) You make me –

NATALIA. Juan . . . Please.

JUAN. – speak and talk and want . . . It feels so good to be near you; I understand why he chose you . . .

NATALIA *wriggles free*. JUAN *pulls himself together*.

I'm sorry. Don't take it the wrong way . . . We, I've been very tense and . . . You'd better get some rest. Goodnight.

NATALIA. Goodnight. The house belongs to the three of you, is that right?

JUAN. Why? Yes.

NATALIA. No reason. See you tomorrow.

JUAN *exits*. NATALIA *looks at* MARIO's *photo*.

You bastard.

Juan.

On the telephone.

JUAN. She's here. She. She's here. The woman I told you about. Yes. Everything's going to be better now. Yes, don't you understand? I thought Mario had run away with her – I told you – that they were off living the high life, but it's turned out that's not it. She's here, in the room next door. Asleep. Forgive me for calling you so late but I thought it was important and I couldn't wait until Tuesday to . . . Why should it? I told you everything's going to be better. He, he's not here right now. He's just not here, that's all. Something must have gone wrong for him. No. No. Yes. Yes, I am 'experiencing a certain sensation of pleasure' now that something has finally gone wrong for him but . . . No, it's just that I'm a bit worked up; I am breathing normally, I promise you, I've got it under control. Listen to me: everything's going to be all right now; I can get the house back and start repairing the damage that Mario did, too, starting with Natalia, of course. She's called Natalia; you'll have to meet her. She's a wonderful person and she might want to stay here to get to know us better and I could start getting everything straight again, making a home. Dad would be proud of me for being able to sort everything out and . . . That doesn't matter now . . . Mario will turn up any day now; the phone will ring and it'll be him; that's what'll happen, I've told you. When he gets hungry he'll come out of his hiding place and ask us for a sweetie and . . . No! You listen to me! What matters is that I'm going to get everything straight again. This is a sign and . . . No! No! (*Pause. Recovers.*) Yes, Doctor. I'm sorry. Yes, yes. I'm fine now. Yes, I am breathing. Yes. Yes. I'll take it straight away. Yes, I have been taking them. It's been a strange day, you know? Yes. Tuesday at your office. See you then. Goodnight.

Hangs up.

The Mother.

Dawn. The MOTHER, *in an apron, stirs a mixture in a bowl. She looks for a bottle of spirits. She finds one that suits her and pours a dash of it into the mixture.* NATALIA *enters.*

NATALIA. What are you doing?

MOTHER. Making a chocolate cake. Oh, I was in Petal's room for ages chatting to her. Such a sweet girl. My sleep's all over the place what with changing the clocks. I just felt like coming downstairs and before I knew it I was looking for ingredients. They don't have any cognac – that's the secret ingredient – but this brandy'll taste lovely. She'll be so pleased. What about you? What did you come down for?

NATALIA. I was thirsty. (*Pours herself some water. Drinks.*) I've got a photo of Mario. On the beach.

MOTHER. Oh, good. That's what you wanted.

NATALIA. I don't know. (*Puts the photo down on the table.*) I don't know who I was with any more. (*Drinks.*)

MOTHER. The man who was with you. Oh, you really were parched.

NATALIA. Mario used to spend so much time in the water. Do you think those things are hereditary?

MOTHER. Everyone likes the water.

NATALIA. No. I mean tastes, obsessions, personality, vices, things like that.

MOTHER. Pass me the milk; it's just behind you.

NATALIA *does so.*

NATALIA. Do you think?

The MOTHER *tastes her mixture and is pleased. She offers it to* NATALIA, *who also tastes it.*

MOTHER. I think that . . . you are what you are.

NATALIA. Could you drop the words of wisdom for a second?

MOTHER. A mother should always have words of wisdom handy.

NATALIA. I don't want history to repeat itself.

MOTHER. Have any two of my cakes ever tasted the same?

NATALIA. I'm not talking about that.

MOTHER. One thing can never be exactly the same as another.

NATALIA. Stop it! Can't you see what I'm going through?!

MOTHER. Of course I can. You're the one who doesn't want to see: we're in this situation because you provoked it.

NATALIA. I didn't bring you here.

MOTHER. Of course you did. Ever since you stretched your arms out to me, I've gone wherever you've wanted, Natalia. That's how it is. And I'm not the only one. You've a real talent for doing that sort of thing, even though you'd prefer not to notice, even though you'd like to slip away in the night without leaving a trace, according to you, as if you didn't exist.

NATALIA. Not existing would have been better.

MOTHER. You haven't any idea what you're saying! You're full of life right now, more than ever, and that doesn't happen to just anybody. No matter how much a person prays. So you're wasting your time with regrets.

NATALIA. We were going to disappear. Both together. We'd planned everything and I wasn't going to tell you, Mum. I wasn't going to tell you. And there's something else: I –

MOTHER. I have to confess something to you, too, dear: cognac isn't really the secret ingredient in my cakes. No, sir. Nor is unsalted butter, not even sieving the flour twice. I've pulled the wool over all your eyes. But don't think that I always knew it; oh no, not at all. Your father sometimes used to forget the things I told him to get from the supermarket even though I wrote them down clearly for him. But I never scolded him, I never told him off for forgetting; your father would have felt terrible. So I had to reinvent my recipe with what I had. And you see: it always came out delicious. As time went by, I learnt that the real secret is knowing how to combine the things you have. That's the only way to make a perfect chocolate cake. If life were perfect, Natalia, we would always find all the ingredients we needed in the right place at the right time. But that's not how it is. Clinging on to someone who's not in our larder any more, it just stops us from appreciating the flavour and the qualities of the people we have nearby. We all have to find life's pathways, Natalia. You see: this cake will taste wonderful with brandy.

Silence.

NATALIA. I've only got one thing in my larder. Right?

MOTHER. And it'll have your eyes.

NATALIA. I've got to get moving before this all crushes me.

MOTHER. I know. Oh, I'm sorry; you don't like me saying 'I know.' But, well, I do know, Natalia. (*Gives her a taste.*) Delicious, isn't it?

NATALIA. I'll never find a better chocolate cake than yours anywhere.

MOTHER. You'll learn how to bake it yourself.

NATALIA. On my own.

MOTHER. That's right.

NATALIA. You'll be OK.

MOTHER. Yes. They need me here. I'll take care of everything.

NATALIA. I need to do it this way.

MOTHER. I understand. I understand.

NATALIA. Mum –

MOTHER. Oh, I'm sorry I'm not following you, but I need to put this mixture into the oven quickly before it turns.

NATALIA. How come you always know what I'm going to do even before *I* know?

MOTHER. You're my daughter, Natalia Pollack.

NATALIA *stretches her arms out towards her.*

(*Without responding to the gesture.*) It's turning, it's turning. (*Exits.*)

NATALIA *drops her arms.*

NATALIA. Thanks.

She looks at the photo and leaves it face down.

I need some air.

Exits.

The MOTHER *returns without the cake mixture. She looks in the direction in which* NATALIA *has gone. She sits down and clasps her hands in her lap.*

The telephone rings. The MOTHER *reacts immediately, barely letting it ring, and answers in a quiet voice.*

MOTHER. Hello . . . Good evening, morning nearly . . . Yes, that's here . . . No, don't worry; I'm baking a cake . . . Yes, of course you can talk to me, I'm one of the family. Yes . . . Yes . . . That's right, it all matches up . . . No, no, don't worry . . . I understand. When was this . . . ? All right, give me the address, please . . . Yes . . . Yes . . . A taxi will find the address, won't it . . . ? I'll get myself there, then. Thank you.

Hangs up. She takes a card out of her pocket and dials the number written on it. She waits for an answer.

Yes? Mister, erm . . . ? (*Reads.*) 'Speedycabs'? I'm sorry for calling at this hour. It's Mrs Pollack speaking, the one you took in the taxi today to . . . Yes, the very same. How's your back . . . ? I told you, it's a wonderful remedy. Listen: you were so kind and since you said you could take me any place at any time . . . Well, I need your services. How long would it take you to come to the place where you dropped me off? It's an emergency. Good, perfect. I'll wait for you outside the house. See you soon.

She hangs up. Takes off her apron. Lays the palm of her hand on the photo of MARIO *and decides not to look at it.*

They really do need me round here.

Mario.

Morning.

JUAN. Sofía! Sofía! Where are you? (*Sees a note on the counter; reads it.*) 'Take out of the oven and allow to cool for at least fifteen minutes before the first bite.'

SOFÍA *appears with the cake. She is wearing her dress, wrinkled from having been slept in.*

SOFÍA (*sleepy*). Look! How delicious.

JUAN. Neither of them are in their room.

SOFÍA. 'PS: I'll be right back; I had to deal with an emergency.' You didn't finish reading it. Do you really think I have to wait fifteen minutes?

JUAN. They've gone!

SOFÍA *takes a chunk of cake in her hands; she burns herself a little but doesn't mind. She eats.*

SOFÍA. Mmm. Good God! It's delicious. Want some?

JUAN. Are you retarded or something?!

SOFÍA. Drop dead! Nothing you can do will change anything! Eat, come on; eat up before the cake disappears as well.

JUAN. You're crazy! Crazy!

SOFÍA. Don't chuck it away!

JUAN. She can't leave! And if you said or did anything to make her leave, you've no idea what you've got yourself into. Do you hear?!

SOFÍA. What's up with you?!

JUAN. Natalia's come this far already; she can't leave now, not like this. Everything happens for a reason. Every cloud has a silver lining. She can't leave!

SOFÍA. You're out of your mind.

JUAN. It's a sign. Don't you understand?

SOFÍA. Sign of what?! Get off me!

The MOTHER *enters. They compose themselves.*

MOTHER. Good morning. You're very impatient, Petal. You see? If you don't wait fifteen minutes it goes all crumbly.

JUAN. Where were you?

MOTHER. I didn't want to wake you. I brought milk to have with the cake and, well, there'll be coffee in a moment for whoever wants it.

JUAN. Where's Natalia?

SOFÍA. I prefer milk.

MOTHER. And you, Juan?

JUAN. Where's Natalia?

MOTHER. She went out for some air.

JUAN. Why did she go on her own? I'd have gone with her.

MOTHER. Natalia can manage on her own. Shall I pour you some milk, Petal?

JUAN. Where have you been?

MOTHER. I told you, I wanted to help. And the only way I can do that is by doing what I know: baking a chocolate cake and . . .

JUAN. And what?

MOTHER. Somebody phoned this morning; I didn't want to disturb you.

SOFÍA. I thought I dreamt the phone ringing.

JUAN. Who was it?

MOTHER. The police. They found a body on the beach; it looked like it had been at sea for months. The description matched Mario's. They needed someone to identify him. I went straight away.

JUAN. Who the hell do you think you are? How could you take the liberty of –

SOFÍA. Shut up. And? And? Was it my brother?

MOTHER (*pause*). It was him, Petal. It was him. I've arranged everything. We'll be having the wake tonight.

JUAN*'s face collapses. The* MOTHER *holds out her arms towards* SOFÍA; *she responds and they hug.*

Shh, Petal. Shh. We needed a dead body and we've got one. This funeral will do us all the world of good. The world of good.

JUAN *has an asthma attack.*

BLURRED IMAGE

Natalia.

Mexico City. A hotel room. A gift-wrapped box, tied with a red ribbon, is seen sticking out of MARIO's *suitcase. Water can be heard falling on* MARIO *in the shower through the half-opened bathroom door.* NATALIA *looks out of the window and takes a few pictures with a Polaroid camera.*

NATALIA. What does Tijuana look like? Don't you want me to come with you? (*Takes a photo.*) Mario, don't pretend you can't hear me, Mario . . . Can I open it now? (*Reads the label on the gift.*) 'To Natalia.' (*Takes a photo of the gift.*) 'Natalia.' Do you like that name? Sometimes, when I couldn't get to sleep, I used to start wondering if that really was my name, the first name I was given. It probably was; maybe no one would've given me a different name before. Do I look like a Natalia? (*Takes a photo of herself.*) They used to think I was half-deaf at primary school; I sometimes wouldn't answer when they did the register. (*Spells.*) N. A. T. A. L. I. A. I like your idea of starting over again. Somewhere else. With different names. Like Bonnie and Clyde, isn't it? I'd be called . . . Hey, don't laugh. Idiot. (*Smiles.*) I really didn't like you when we first met, you know? I really didn't. You seemed so stand-offish. We seemed so different then. But there's one thing that makes you and me the same, Mario: both of us should have died a long time ago.

MARIO *is heard humming in the shower.*

Come on; let me open it. And I'll take that picture of you like you asked. It's not that I don't want to take it; it's just that . . . if I've got the original, what do I need a copy for? Don't you think?

She opens the gift as if it were an act of mischief. She takes out a red folder, opens it, examines the papers, does not manage to understand fully but smiles enthusiastically. The water and Mario's humming stops. She puts down the folder.

We'll do it. Together. Do you always take so long in the

water, Mr Tenor? Hey, you forgot your towel. Shall I dry you off?

She sneaks into the bathroom. They are both heard laughing.

PRINTS

Tijuana. Different spaces at a funeral parlour. They all stand among many people. The coffin is closed.

Each print comes later than the other.

Coffee and styrofoam cups for those who want to help themselves.

OLGA (*just arrived, taking everything in*). Wow.

MOTHER (*appearing*). Olga, I'm so glad you got here. Thank you so much.

OLGA. Good evening, Mrs Pollack. There's nothing to thank me for, quite the opposite. I took the first available flight I could find as soon as you told me. The taxi driver you sent for me asked me to tell you that he was going to the house to follow your instructions.

MOTHER. Yes, thank you, he's a lovely man; he's been so helpful. Look: let me introduce you to Mario's sister.

OLGA. Hello. Nice to meet you. Olga.

MOTHER. Olga has been a lifelong friend of the family. I thought she should be here to keep us company, seeing as my husband couldn't come.

SOFÍA. There's already too many people 'keeping us company'.

OLGA. I'm very sorry for your loss. Although, well, he had already been lost for a long time, but it's better to know, isn't it? The coffin's closed. Just as well. After all that time in the water. So how did you find out in the end?

MOTHER. The details don't matter right now.

JUAN (*appearing, surprised to see* OLGA). Where's Natalia?

MOTHER. She won't be long.

OLGA. What? Isn't Natalia here?

JUAN. We haven't seen her all day. She doesn't even know we're here. I'm going back to the house.

MOTHER. There's no need, Juan, I've just told you. The taxi driver's there waiting for her, to bring her here as soon as she gets back.

OLGA. Hi, I'm Olga, Natalia's best friend. I introduced her to Mario. And you are . . . ?

MOTHER. This is Juan. Mario's brother. He's normally a very polite boy but you'll appreciate this is a very difficult time.

OLGA. I understand.

JUAN. How can you possibly not be worried that she's wandering about on her own?

OLGA. I don't know what you mean. Why's Natalia missing?

MOTHER. She's not missing.

OLGA. Is she still getting the nausea . . . ?

MOTHER. Olga –

SOFÍA. Nausea?

JUAN. We agreed we'd go to the bank today. I'm going to look for her.

SOFÍA. Run and put her photo up at the baker's!

MOTHER. You should all calm down; this isn't the place for arguments.

SOFÍA *lights a cigarette.*

OLGA. Excuse me, but, talking of arguments, I went on at your husband until I was blue in the face to get him to come with me but he wouldn't be told. He said he wasn't going to go to any more funerals and that anyway you ought to be –

MOTHER. Yes, yes, Olga dear. He told me that, too, over the phone. He's turned very headstrong in his old age; I'll have to ask you to excuse him. It's not that he doesn't like funerals; it's just that he gets ever so anxious when I'm not at home. Juan, are you feeling all right? Your chest's wheezing. That smoking, Petal . . .

SOFÍA. It's not the smoke. His imaginary enemy came back.

JUAN. I'm fine. I'll be fine when Natalia turns up.

SOFÍA. Is that all you care about, Juan? Our brother's over there dead. Dead.

Silence.

OLGA. It was a long flight. Could you show me where the bathroom is?

MOTHER. Of course, Olga dear. Over there, on one side of those big wreaths.

OLGA *gestures and exits.*

Civility costs nothing, even at the worst of times. Things like this ought to bring our two families together.

SOFÍA. I don't have a family any more.

MOTHER. Don't say that.

SOFÍA. Or a house. Speak your mind for once, Juan; I'm thinking the same. Your daughter must have run away to who knows where with all of the cash. That's why she hasn't arrived and never will. I'd have done the same. We'll be out on the street before long.

JUAN. That can't be. She wouldn't be capable of . . . Tell me, Mrs Pollack; tell me the truth.

MOTHER. I told you that –

SOFÍA. Anyhow, it's starting to be a health risk, living in that house. It's like a curse. Haven't you two felt it?

JUAN. Don't be stupid.

SOFÍA. Not as stupid as dreaming about hooking up with your own brother's girlfriend.

JUAN. Shut up!

MOTHER. Juan! Don't raise your voice to your sister. And you, Petal, stop saying those things; you're upsetting your brother. You're both speculating too much.

JUAN. Mrs Pollack, you are taking too many liberties and –

MOTHER. And nothing, Juan. There's a dead man to be mourned tonight and that's all that ought to matter to us. To all of us! I'm going to say my rosary; whoever wants to join me is welcome.

The MOTHER *leaves them. They are silent.*

SOFÍA. It's a long time since I saw anyone put you in your place.

JUAN. Drop it, Sofía.

SOFÍA. You realise there's only you and me left.

JUAN. And our house. And I'm not going to lose it. I'm not going to. We've got to breathe life back into it, start afresh, with new people. With Natalia, I could . . .

SOFÍA. The house is just that: just a house. A thing, that's all. No one's coming back to life there. No one.

JUAN. Where are you going?

SOFÍA. To . . . I don't know.

*

OLGA. I read a really interesting article on the plane. It was talking about how the human body has the natural capacity to recover its vital functions even when one of its organs has been removed. D'you know what I mean? Somehow, the organism knows, it communicates with itself or I don't know, and if the gall bladder or a kidney or an ovary or the tonsils – which is the most common – are missing, then our body's amazing design readjusts itself and tells the other organs to take over its functions. So you can keep on walking around and from the outside no one can tell there's anything wrong. It's wonderful, isn't it! Although, of course, if your heart's been stolen there's no way to replace it. And, what's more, you can tell from a mile off. (*Laughs*.)

SOFÍA. . . .

OLGA (*drinks*). Mmm. It's not bad for coffee from a funeral parlour. Can I bum a cigarette?

SOFÍA. Here.

OLGA *takes it;* SOFÍA *lights it.*

OLGA. Thanks. (*Smokes*.)

SOFÍA. Natalia's 'organism'. Pregnant, isn't it?

OLGA. Erm. Don't know.

SOFÍA. It's all right. Don't tell me. You already did.

OLGA. I didn't tell you anything.

SOFÍA. You didn't deny it.

OLGA. How was I supposed to know it was a secret? I don't know why she decided to have it if she wasn't going to boast about it.

SOFÍA. Now you really have told me.

OLGA. Hold on. I didn't come here to –

SOFÍA. Why did you come? Were you 'close' to Mario, too?

OLGA. It's 'good manners'. You know? Like it or not, you should always go to someone's funeral, especially if you're invited.

SOFÍA. You can't have had anything better to do. What do you do?

OLGA. Lots of things. Listen: is everyone around here like you or is it just your family?

SOFÍA. Go find out.

*

OLGA. Lot of people, aren't there? All very nice.

JUAN. Yes.

OLGA. I didn't know Mario had any family.

JUAN. . . .

OLGA. They're saying over there it was suicide.

JUAN. Who is?

OLGA. Because he had debts and he'd bought loads of stuff lately and you were the last person he saw and you got so furious with him. They're saying you two had terrible problems. That he'd been talking. People are very chatty round here, apart from you. It'd be easy to put two and two together and think that he felt under pressure and . . . Plus what with everything with Natalia – who wouldn't want to run away? D'you know what I mean? My theory was that he'd just run off and that was that. But no one believed me; bunch of fatalists, insisting something had happened to him, but it's not always like that. Men sense commitment looming and suddenly it's like Scotch mist. They don't have to die for that. I should know.

JUAN. What are you saying about Natalia?

OLGA. Nothing. Did Mario have any enemies? Because the other thing I heard was that it was some kind of payback, because money doesn't grow on trees. I'm surprised you're not interested in clearing it all up, especially if –

JUAN. It's Olga, isn't it? Well, we don't need to clear anything up, and we don't need you coming here to do it for us. We know quite well who Mario was. Mario liked the sea. Maybe a wave washed him away. I don't know. I haven't had time to think.

OLGA. Washed away by a wave? Like in a cartoon?

JUAN. What do you mean?

OLGA. You're as attractive as he is, but your moodiness and your wrinkled brow make you more . . . mature, more interesting.

JUAN. I'm going for more coffee. (*Exits*.)

OLGA. Oh. They're the same everywhere.

*

MOTHER. Hail Mary, full of grace. The Lord is with thee. Blessed art thou among women and blessed is the fruit of thy womb, Jesus.

SOFÍA *(appearing)*. Amen.

MOTHER. Come here with me, Petal; give me your hand.

SOFÍA *draws close*.

JUAN *(appearing)*. They're ready to take the body away.

MOTHER. It's time.

OLGA *(appearing)*. Mrs Pollack, that taxi driver's looking for you outside.

MOTHER. In a minute, Olga.

JUAN. Has he brought Natalia?

OLGA. I didn't see her.

SOFÍA. It seems impossible that Mario's in that coffin.

MOTHER. He isn't really. He's in all of our hearts.

SOFÍA. He's not the dying kind.

JUAN. He is, unfortunately.

SOFÍA. Not quite.

The three women exchange complicit looks.

MOTHER. Let's say goodbye to him. All the family together.

The MOTHER *takes* SOFÍA *and* JUAN*'s hands.* OLGA, *despite* JUAN*'s reticence, takes his hand.*

ALL. Our Father, who art in Heaven, hallowed be Thy name. Thy kingdom come, Thy will be done, on Earth as it is in Heaven. Give us this day our daily bread, and forgive us our trespasses, as we forgive those who trespass against us. And lead us not into temptation, but deliver us from evil.

MOTHER. Amen.

SOFÍA. Amen.

JUAN *and* OLGA. Amen.

OLGA. Mrs Pollack, the taxi driver's at the door; he says he needs to give you something.

MOTHER. Do me a favour, Olga: you deal with him, go on; this is an awkward moment.

OLGA. OK. I'll go. (*Exits*.)

Silence.

SOFÍA. Juan . . . are you crying?

JUAN. Leave me alone.

SOFÍA. Hey, everything's going to be all right.

JUAN. No. No, it isn't! She's right. He had plans. Why would he have drowned? Waves don't wash people away like in cartoons. Mario knew perfectly well how to swim. He spent more time in the water than anywhere else. It's absurd that he should have drowned, unless he wanted to. I cursed him. I said I'd prefer him dead. And he'd have done it just to upset me.

SOFÍA. Stop it, Juan.

JUAN. I pushed him into it. I killed him.

SOFÍA. I'm going to give you one of my pills.

JUAN. I don't want anything! Don't you understand what I'm saying to you?

MOTHER. Calm down, son.

JUAN. Don't call me 'son'! I already had a mother and she died, too. Don't try to fill gaps that aren't yours to fill. This isn't your family!

SOFÍA. Don't shout.

JUAN. Why did she come here and then leave? To make me feel worse? That girl just wanted to laugh at us. To hell with everything! They can all get lost, Sofía; you're right: they're a bunch of idiots, that's what they are. Idiots who don't know anything. Do you know what they're saying? Have you heard them? Who has ever cared if we live or die? No one! They can just leave us in peace! They can fuck off!

OLGA *returns. She carries a gift-wrapped box tied with a red ribbon, which no one seems to notice for the moment.*

OLGA. What happened? We were all having such a nice time.

MOTHER. It's the shock.

SOFÍA. Take this.

JUAN. No! I'm not going to be treated like an idiot any more. I'm fed up of fucking tablets.

SOFÍA. Are you on medication? Since when?

JUAN. To hell with all of it. It's me next, Sofía; I'll be the next one to disappear.

SOFÍA. Juanito, I thought you didn't care. I'm sorry. Come on, sit down.

OLGA. People are looking.

MOTHER. We'll all feel much better after the burial.

SOFÍA. Mrs Pollack, we're very grateful to you for identifying Mario; I couldn't . . . I couldn't have done it. But for now –

JUAN. It's all over, it's over.

OLGA. She identified him?

SOFÍA. Calm down, Juan; breathe. Breathe.

OLGA. But Mrs Pollack never knew Mario.

A disturbed pause.

SOFÍA. What?

OLGA. You scare me, Mrs Pollack.

JUAN. She never . . . ? What games are you playing now?

SOFÍA. Is it true what she says? You never knew Mario?

MOTHER. No. Not exactly.

JUAN. What are you doing to us? So who's in that box? For God's sake! Who are we burying?

MOTHER. I can explain.

SOFÍA. Yes, do! Now!

MOTHER. I . . . I did know Mario. Very well. I saw him every day in Natalia's eyes. I saw him when I got to your house, in the two of you; you've turned into nothing more than his reflection and you've forgotten to live your own lives. It's true. Yes. I never did see Mario in the flesh. But I've seen him in the faces of the people I love, the people I've come to love. And I'd recognise him anywhere, even better than you would. I promise you.

SOFÍA *breaks down.* JUAN *seems unmoved.*

OLGA (*dares to speak*). Someone sent this. It's for you two.

She gives the box to JUAN.

SOFÍA. Oh, for Christ's sake, another bloody box of surprises!

After a moment, JUAN *throws himself furiously at the coffin.* OLGA *stops him.*

OLGA. No! No, please, don't open it, Juan. You're frightening people.

JUAN. Get off me!

OLGA. I'm sorry, but someone has to maintain decorum. It doesn't matter who's in the coffin; the fact is that it's a dead person, and out here there's a lot of living people, and we'll all drop down dead if you get hysterical now and take the lid off. Let me . . . let me talk to everyone and get them out of here. It's 'good manners'.

SOFÍA. Let her do it.

JUAN (*containing himself*). All right.

MOTHER. I think that –

JUAN. Get her out first. I want her out of my sight.

MOTHER. I meant it for the best, believe me.

OLGA. Mrs Pollack . . .

MOTHER. I'm not needed around here any more, am I?

SOFÍA *and* JUAN. . . .

OLGA. Come with me. You should go home.

MOTHER. Petal . . .

SOFÍA. Please go.

OLGA. Come on – take my arm.

They exit. SOFÍA *and* JUAN *are left alone with the coffin.*

JUAN. What shall we do now?

SOFÍA. Open the boxes.

JUAN. Which one first?

SOFÍA. They're both for us.

JUAN. Give me your hand.

SOFÍA. Like when we were children.

JUAN. Yes.

SOFÍA. And we would spy from the staircase; all those boxes, wrapped just for us, under the Christmas tree.

JUAN. Our hearts beating so hard.

SOFÍA. We'd go down the stairs, holding each other's hands to stay calm.

JUAN. Together.

SOFÍA. Together. Are you ready?

SOFÍA. Yes.

They squeeze each other's hands. They open the coffin.

They look inside.

An indescribable expression forms on their faces. Blackout.

The aeroplanes take off.

THE PHOTO IN THE WALLET

An empty space.

Six lights illuminate six places.

NATALIA, *the* MOTHER, OLGA, SOFÍA *and* JUAN *move independently amongst them.*

There is one light too many. They adjust.

Five lights illuminate five places.

They each find their place, their time.

NATALIA. Good morning. I'd like to make a withdrawal from this account.

JUAN (*on the telephone*). I'd like to place an ad in your paper.

SOFÍA. I'm looking for a flight to . . . I don't know. Where would you recommend?

NATALIA. Give me one third of the total, exactly one third. In cash.

JUAN (*on the telephone*). Yes, the 'houses for sale' section.

NATALIA. I'd like to leave the rest in two other people's names.

SOFÍA. Let's make it long-haul. No, I didn't win the lottery. It's, erm . . . I inherited some money.

NATALIA. Could you tell me where I can hire a car? I need to . . . we need to move on.

OLGA (*on the telephone*). Juan. It's Olga. Remember me? We met at a difficult time but a lot of time's gone by and I woke up today and thought of you. D'you know what I mean?

JUAN (*on the telephone*). How could I forget you . . . ? No, of course you're not interrupting anything. I'm on my own. (*Laughs.*) Yes, I know what you mean. (*Laughs.*)

MOTHER. Come here; put that paper down and come here; bring your glasses. At last, some news. (*Opens an envelope.*)

It's just a photograph. (*Reads the back.*) 'Something to put in your wallet.' (*Looks at the photo. Smiles.*) Got her eyes; I knew it.

A final flash.

Blackout.

SEVEN-ELEVEN

IVÁN OLIVARES
translated by
WILLIAM GREGORY

Characters

CABRÓN, *thirty-two*

JESÚS, *twenty-two*

BOY (MARTÍN), *ten*

PAULINA, *thirty-nine*

SHOP ASSISTANT

SECURITY GUARD

OLD WOMAN

POLICEMAN

MAN (*off*)

A forward slash (/) indicates a point of interruption by the next speaker.

Seven-Eleven was first performed in English as a rehearsed reading as part of the *Arena Mexico* season in the Jerwood Theatre Upstairs, Royal Court Theatre, London, on 12 January 2006 with the following cast:

CABRÓN	Justin Salinger
JESÚS	Tom McKay
SHOP ASSISTANT/OLD WOMAN	Rosalind March
BOY	Harry Treadaway
PAULINA	Lolita Chakrabarti
FELIPE/POLICEMAN	Daniel Crowther

Director Indhu Rubasingham

Scene One

Seven-Eleven store. Fast-food section, tables and chairs. JESÚS *and* CABRÓN *sit eating hot dogs. The* SHOP ASSISTANT *at the counter and a* SECURITY GUARD *in the background. There are no other clients.*

CABRÓN. Whatever happens.

JESÚS. Yeah.

CABRÓN. You'll do everything you have to do.

JESÚS. Is she thin? So I know how much rope to buy . . .

CABRÓN. We're not gonna tie her up.

JESÚS. She could escape.

CABRÓN. No one escapes from me.

JESÚS. What if she doesn't accept?

CABRÓN. She'll do it.

JESÚS. And don't we have to cover our faces? She could recognise us.

CABRÓN. She'll do it of her own free will.

JESÚS. Shouldn't I take just a little bit of rope?

CABRÓN. Is it showing?

JESÚS. What?

CABRÓN. My cock.

JESÚS. What?

CABRÓN. It's not showing, then.

JESÚS. Why?

CABRÓN. Wipe your hand.

JESÚS. I'm eating.

CABRÓN. Touch it, stupid; you didn't even notice it.

JESÚS. I'm not grabbing your cock while I'm eating.

CABRÓN. It's sticking right up and you didn't see it?

JESÚS touches CABRÓN's crotch.

CABRÓN. All right, let go. Giz a kiss.

JESÚS kisses him. CABRÓN grabs him by the hair and pulls him away from his mouth.

You're so stupid!

JESÚS. You could hurt me . . .

CABRÓN. Be more discerning.

JESÚS. What's that?

CABRÓN. You're useless; you're a pushover.

CABRÓN sits looking at JESÚS. The SHOP ASSISTANT approaches.

SHOP ASSISTANT. You can't kiss each other here.

CABRÓN laughs. JESÚS continues eating.

JESÚS. You know you can count on me, but you help me out, too.

CABRÓN. Are you bargaining with me?

SHOP ASSISTANT. What bad manners.

CABRÓN. Why d'you always do as you're told?

JESÚS. I need you.

SHOP ASSISTANT. Doing that in a public place.

JESÚS. She's not taking away what's mine.

CABRÓN. She's an old woman.

JESÚS. You don't know her.

SHOP ASSISTANT (*to the* SECURITY GUARD). Leave them; don't touch them.

SECURITY GUARD. But they were kissing.

CABRÓN (*referring to the* SECURITY GUARD). Does he fancy some?

SECURITY GUARD. What did you say?

CABRÓN. Forget it.

The SECURITY GUARD *withdraws.*

JESÚS. I'm not gonna give her my money. My dad left it to her.

CABRÓN *picks up a newspaper to read.*

CABRÓN. You'll get enough just by scaring her.

JESÚS. I have to finish it.

CABRÓN. It's gonna snow.

JESÚS. Snow?

CABRÓN. It's gonna snow here for the first time in eighty years.

JESÚS. No way. How come?

CABRÓN. 'Cause of global climate change. You ever seen snow?

JESÚS. On telly.

CABRÓN. People could go skiing in the streets.

JESÚS. That's dangerous.

CABRÓN. I went skiing in the States once.

JESÚS. Really?

CABRÓN. There was a whole city full of millionaires. That's where I first saw reindeer.

JESÚS. What are reindeer?

CABRÓN. Reindeer are . . . There's no point explaining to you.

JESÚS. I don't know what reindeer are.

CABRÓN. Just imagine: we can come to the Seven-Eleven and the snow outside'll make us feel like we're in the States. (*Sighs.*) We're already starting to be more like them. (*Pause.*) Get me another hot dog.

JESÚS. Look: decaff coffee.

CABRÓN. I don't like it with hot dogs. I'd rather have a Diet Coke and an instant soup. Shit! There's no sauces! (*Shouts at the* SHOP ASSISTANT.) Oy, Fatso, there's no sauces.

SHOP ASSISTANT. Give me your hot dog. I have to put it through the scanner. I can't give you any sauce otherwise.

SECURITY GUARD. You have to behave.

CABRÓN. Fuck you, man. Don't be like that. I've known you since your days dealing speed on street corners.

SECURITY GUARD. Behave yourself, Cabrón, please, or they'll sack us.

CABRÓN. 'Behave yourself, *Sir*.'

JESÚS (*showing him a soup*). This one all right?

CABRÓN. Yeah. (*Eats his hot dog in one mouthful.*)

SHOP ASSISTANT. That's not allowed: eating it like that. I have to put the barcode through the scanner.

SECURITY GUARD. We need the barcode.

SHOP ASSISTANT (*to* JESÚS). Give it to me. Everything has to go through the scanner.

She passes the products through the scanner.

CABRÓN. Everything'll be different when I'm in the States.

SHOP ASSISTANT. It says so in the Seven-Eleven manual. That's eighty pesos and twenty cents.

CABRÓN. Cough up, Jesús.

JESÚS. All of it?

CABRÓN. You're gonna be rich, aren't you?

JESÚS. But I haven't got enough just now.

CABRÓN. Ask the drug dealer.

SECURITY GUARD. Cabrón, please.

CABRÓN. I've got some top-notch acid at home.

SECURITY GUARD. I don't do that any more.

JESÚS. Shall we rape her?

CABRÓN. She could infect me with fuck knows what; plus which, she's dog-ugly. You rape her if you like.

His mobile rings.

(*On the phone.*) Hello, gorgeous. How have you been, beautiful? I have to see you tomorrow . . . The usual place: the Seven-Eleven.

JESÚS (*to the* SHOP ASSISTANT *and the* SECURITY GUARD). I wouldn't argue with him if I were you.

CABRÓN (*on the phone*). It'll be worth both our whiles; I'm not telling you now . . . At . . . Hang on. (*To* JESÚS.) What time's the thing with your old mum?

JESÚS. Four o'clock.

CABRÓN (*on the phone*). At five – no – better make it six. (*To* JESÚS.) We'll finish her off quick. (*To the phone.*) Don't go having sex tonight, darling. Wait for me, tomorrow . . . OK. *Hasta la vista*, baby.

JESÚS *and* CABRÓN *go to the food area.*

JESÚS. Six o'clock?

CABRÓN. What?

JESÚS. Will you have time?

CABRÓN. Will *we* have time? Depends on you.

JESÚS. Does she still not know anything?

[CABRÓN. *What do you think?*

JESÚS. What?

CABRÓN. Idiot, you'll never get anywhere if you don't speak English.

JESÚS. It's very difficult.

CABRÓN. If you want to be someone these days you have to speak English.

JESÚS. What do I want to think about the future for?

CABRÓN. Didn't you say you wanted to be free? '*What do you think?*' is 'What do you think?' '*Of course not.*' 'Of course not.']*

JESÚS. You ought to tell her.

CABRÓN. Fool. Are you gonna touch it or not? I won't help you if you don't.

JESÚS. I can't touch it in here.

CABRÓN: You daren't. So I can't count on you, then.

JESÚS. If you want.

CABRÓN. This is gonna cost you big-time. Touch it.

JESÚS touches CABRÓN's crotch.

Now get me a coffee. Here. (*Gives him some coins.*) Pay with this.

JESÚS gets the coffee and then goes to the counter to pay. CABRÓN takes in the scene.

It must look gorgeous with snow all over!

JESÚS. D'you really think so?

CABRÓN. Course. I wish I was there already.

---

* *The italicised words in this bracketed section are in English in the original. Given that this is unlikely to work in an English-language version, the following replacement is suggested:*

[CABRÓN. What d'you think?

JESÚS. What?

CABRÓN. Idiot. You'll never get anywhere being this stupid.]

JESÚS. When they gonna give you the visa?

CABRÓN. When I've got all Paulina's money in my bank account.

JESÚS. I'm giving you half the old lady's money.

CABRÓN. I'm buying my plane ticket with that.

JESÚS. And d'you think they'll come?

CABRÓN. Who?

JESÚS. The reindeer.

CABRÓN. I reckon they'll take a few days.

JESÚS. Sweet. (*Pause*). How long does a person take to die?

CABRÓN. Depends how old they are.

JESÚS. She's pretty old.

CABRÓN. Not too long, I shouldn't think. It's quicker if she's boring.

JESÚS. I don't think she is.

CABRÓN (*laughs*). You wanna gimme a kiss, don't you?

JESÚS. No.

CABRÓN. Sure you do.

JESÚS. Where'd you get that from?

CABRÓN. What do you want, then?

JESÚS. To get rid of her.

CABRÓN. So you *are* a poof.

CABRÓN *kisses him*.

SHOP ASSISTANT. He's kissing him to annoy me, isn't he!

SECURITY GUARD. Leave them.

SHOP ASSISTANT. But I . . .

SECURITY GUARD. No one's noticing and I don't want any trouble. If it bothers you that much, tell him you fancy him.

Scene Two

The OLD WOMAN's *room. An old radio is heard but the interference is more audible than the music. The* OLD WOMAN *wears a dressing gown. The* BOY *sits on a high chair with a lollipop in his mouth.*

OLD WOMAN. Where did we leave off?

The BOY *points to his thigh.*

BOY. Here.

OLD WOMAN. Your mother's very happy to bring you here.

BOY. She was crying all night last night.

OLD WOMAN. Children shouldn't listen when grown-ups are crying.

BOY. She wasn't crying loudly.

OLD WOMAN. Were you spying on her?

BOY. I knew she was crying.

OLD WOMAN. It's naughty to spy.

BOY. I wasn't spying. I can just tell when she's crying.

OLD WOMAN. Poppycock.

BOY. Can I go and play?

OLD WOMAN. After we've finished.

BOY. I don't want to today.

OLD WOMAN. You have to study.

BOY. I prefer maths.

OLD WOMAN. This will be more use to you.

BOY. She's going to leave me with you, isn't she?

OLD WOMAN. Do you remember the last part?

BOY. That's why she left me with a suitcase. I don't want to stay here.

OLD WOMAN. When they crucify Him. At that moment, the heavens opened and the sun shone brightly through the clouds.

BOY. I know.

OLD WOMAN. You'll like the next part. The destruction of all things.

BOY. That bit's boring, too.

OLD WOMAN. No, and it starts just here, on my leg. (*Points to her thigh.*)

The OLD WOMAN *opens her robe and lets it fall gently. She stands naked in front of the* BOY. *Her body, apart from her breasts, is completely covered with tattooed phrases.*

Point to the place where we left off. Come closer.

The BOY *approaches and puts his finger halfway down the* OLD WOMAN*'s thigh.*

BOY. Here.

OLD WOMAN. Then begin.

The OLD WOMAN *lies back on a sofa with her legs open. The* BOY *begins to read the* OLD WOMAN*'s leg.*

BOY. A-po-ca . . . ! What's 'Apo-ca-lypse'?

OLD WOMAN. That's what you're going to learn today. (*Pause.*) Don't let go; touch me with your finger as you read.

The BOY *reads the body of the* OLD WOMAN, *who writhes with pleasure.*

Scene Three

The Seven-Eleven. CABRÓN *pays for some sweets at the till.*

CABRÓN. Those bastards.

SHOP ASSISTANT. Who?

CABRÓN. Outside the embassy.

SHOP ASSISTANT. Where?

CABRÓN. Should be arrested.

SHOP ASSISTANT. I thought it was some sort of street concert.

CABRÓN. City looks so ugly.

SHOP ASSISTANT. Can't tell if they're complaining or celebrating.

CABRÓN. They ought to come and take them all away.

SHOP ASSISTANT. They should leave them for a while.

CABRÓN. But not at this hour. They ought to give them a timetable.

SHOP ASSISTANT. Are you taking anything else . . . ? Are there many of them?

CABRÓN. Have you not looked out? Come on.

The SHOP ASSISTANT *and* CABRÓN *go to the window.*

SHOP ASSISTANT. There's more than five hundred of them.

CABRÓN. Much more than that, I reckon.

SHOP ASSISTANT. They're very aggressive, aren't they?

CABRÓN. No respect for private property.

SHOP ASSISTANT. An embassy isn't private property. Is it?

CABRÓN. They're saying they're against them, against globalisation.

SHOP ASSISTANT. They're right.

CABRÓN. If they were right, you wouldn't have this job.

SHOP ASSISTANT. I could have a different job.

CABRÓN. Dream on.

SHOP ASSISTANT. Do you like kissing that friend of yours?

CABRÓN. Why?

SHOP ASSISTANT. Just curious.

CABRÓN. You fancy a bit, do you?

SHOP ASSISTANT. It's not that. It's just . . .

CABRÓN. If you want my services, here's my card. Gimme another pack of chewing gum; my mouth tastes foul.

JESÚS enters the Seven-Eleven.

You took your time.

JESÚS. I went to make sure she was there.

CABRÓN. Come on, then. We have to be quick; I've got things to do later.

Scene Four

The OLD WOMAN'*s room. The* OLD WOMAN, *naked, with the* BOY *pointing to various parts of her body.* JESÚS *opens the door, accompanied by* CABRÓN. *They are both masked. The* OLD WOMAN *gets up and looks for her robe.*

OLD WOMAN. What are you doing? Get out of here!

JESÚS (*to* CABRÓN). That's her.

OLD WOMAN. 'Her' who?

CABRÓN. Button it, Grandma, and say your prayers; I don't want / you wasting my time.

OLD WOMAN. Who are you?

CABRÓN. Are you gonna pray or not? / For fuck's sake.

OLD WOMAN. This is my house.

CABRÓN. Say your prayers, you stupid cow.

He takes some gloves from his bag and puts them on.

OLD WOMAN. What do you want?

CABRÓN. Jesús, where are you going? You're not leaving me alone; this is your business; I just came to help you.

JESÚS. I just think that . . . I'd better . . . I don't think . . .

OLD WOMAN. Jesús?

CABRÓN. Oh, no, shit-for-brains, / you're not bottling out now!

JESÚS. She's recognised me.

CABRÓN. I told you I don't want any trouble. / You're such a poof.

OLD WOMAN. It's Jesús, isn't it?

JESÚS. Shut up. I'm not Jesús.

OLD WOMAN. I'm calling the police.

JESÚS hits her in the face.

CABRÓN (*to* JESÚS). Now the pipe. You first.

JESÚS. I can't. You hit her.

CABRÓN. This is gonna cost you, poofter.

The OLD WOMAN *tries to get out of the room.* CABRÓN *grabs hold of her.*

Take the kid.

JESÚS. What?

OLD WOMAN. Unhand me.

CABRÓN. Grab his arm, stupid. Don't let him see.

JESÚS. Come on, short-arse.

BOY. But . . .

OLD WOMAN. Don't hurt me, please.

JESÚS. Be quiet.

He covers the BOY's *mouth with his hand.*

CABRÓN. Keep still.

JESÚS (*to the* BOY). We're going to keep quiet.

BOY. Let me go.

JESÚS. Hang on, Cabrón; we'd better not do this; the kid's here.

CABRÓN. You made me come all this way; I'm not wasting my time. Wasting time fucks me right off.

OLD WOMAN. Take whatever you like.

JESÚS. But the kid's here.

CABRÓN. Take him away. Do something with him.

JESÚS covers the BOY's *ears and turns him with his back to the scene.* CABRÓN *beats the* OLD WOMAN *about the head with a pipe; she falls face-down on the ground. She keeps moving and* CABRÓN *hesitates, not sure whether to hit her again.*

What shall we do, Jesús?

JESÚS. I dunno, Cabrón; you're the clever bastard here.

CABRÓN. She's still moving.

CABRÓN *does not dare hit her again and opts instead to kick her in the head.*

That'll do it.

JESÚS. You sure?

CABRÓN. She won't be able to move.

JESÚS. They say it's best to finish them off.

CABRÓN. She'll die by herself.

JESÚS. She recognised me, didn't she?

CABRÓN. She's ancient.

JESÚS. Finish her off; you never know.

CABRÓN. She's bound to have a heart attack. Christ, your old lady was a clever cow. Did she fit the whole Bible on?

JESÚS. Just one part.

CABRÓN. Look: she did it in zig-zags.

JESÚS. It used to be in a cross but it went cock-eyed.

CABRÓN. We should sell her.

JESÚS. Fuck off! What?

CABRÓN. We'll say she's a saint. Imagine: your old lady in a glass case in some church. Keep his ears covered, stupid; we don't want him having traumas.

JESÚS. I'm nervous.

CABRÓN. Don't be a poof.

JESÚS. What shall we do?

CABRÓN. You deal with the rest. I'm out of here.

JESÚS. Aren't you gonna do anything else?

CABRÓN. She'll die all by herself. You work out what to with her.

JESÚS. You can't leave me on my own. What about the kid?

CABRÓN. That's your problem.

JESÚS. Take him with you.

CABRÓN. You're being an idiot. You get rid of him.

JESÚS. Look: he's trying to speak.

CABRÓN. So? Are you scared of him?

JESÚS. No, but . . .

CABRÓN. Just put an end to your problems once and for all; it's almost over . . . Think about your freedom, stupid. You've got no bollocks.

BOY. I want to go.

CABRÓN. Shut it, idiot, or you'll end up traumatised like my friend here.

JESÚS. Don't talk to him like that; he's a kid.

BOY. Please.

CABRÓN. Your mum must be even worse than this old bag, to send you over to a madwoman's house, eh?

JESÚS. Where are you going?

CABRÓN. It's very late.

JESÚS. You said you'd help me if I helped you.

CABRÓN. You finish off here; this is your life and I don't want you fucking up mine.

He gives the pipe to JESÚS.

And put your gloves on.

CABRÓN *exits, leaving* JESÚS *and the* BOY *together with the* OLD WOMAN *still alive on the floor.*

BOY. Let me go.

The BOY *struggles with* JESÚS, *who covers his mouth and prevents him from seeing the* OLD WOMAN.

JESÚS. It's all right; I'm not gonna hurt you, but promise you'll stay calm.

BOY. OK.

JESÚS. What's your name?

BOY. Martín.

JESÚS. I'm Jesús. (*Takes off his mask.*) Where's your mum?

BOY. Dunno.

JESÚS. She coming after your class?

BOY. You're her son, aren't you? (*Points to the* OLD WOMAN.)

JESÚS. No. Get that straight.

BOY. I know you, don't I?

JESÚS. We're gonna make a deal: I'll wait till your mum gets here and you'll forget that you ever saw us, unless you want something bad to happen to you.

BOY. You're not gonna hurt me, are you?

JESÚS. Are you deaf?

BOY. I just . . . (*Sees* JESÚS's *piercing*.) Did it hurt when you had that done?

JESÚS. No.

BOY. I want one, but my mum says 'No'. I like them. You got one you could give me?

JESÚS. Later; you can put it in when you grow up, when your mum can't tell you not to.

The BOY *turns round and sees the* OLD WOMAN.

BOY. Why did the lady do that to herself?

JESÚS. What?

BOY. The tattoos.

JESÚS. Grown-ups' things. Don't turn round; we made a deal.

Scene Five

The Seven-Eleven. PAULINA *arrives. She stops in the doorway and looks around. She walks around in silence, looking around the shelves to see if there is anyone behind them. She arrives at the frozen-food section, looks at it, turns around and notices* CABRÓN.

PAULINA. Why here? Couldn't you think of anywhere else?

CABRÓN. I wondered what you were like in the outside world.

PAULINA. Let's have a drink.

CABRÓN. Gatorade? There's gallons in the fridge . . .

PAULINA. What's the matter?

CABRÓN. You wanted to see me, didn't you?

PAULINA. Do you want more money?

CABRÓN. Don't you want a hot dog? They're well tasty here.

CABRÓN *serves himself a hot dog and makes one up for* PAULINA.

PAULINA. I really wanted to see you.

CABRÓN. And now you don't? (*Gives her a hot dog.*) All the sauces and things are over there.

PAULINA. You're acting funny.

CABRÓN. *You're* acting funny.

PAULINA. Don't mess about.

CABRÓN *sits down to eat his hot dog.*

CABRÓN. I just beat someone up with a bit of pipe.

PAULINA. Have you been in a fight?

CABRÓN. The hot dog's well tasty, innit? I like these shops; they're so modern. Plus which, they help the needy.

PAULINA. Cabrón, who did you beat up?

CABRÓN. We need your PIN number.

PAULINA. So you do want money? Joshua's been checking through my bank accounts.

CABRÓN. He's gonna kill you, gorgeous.

PAULINA. Who is?

CABRÓN. Your husband.

PAULINA. Cabrón, stop playing around. What do you want? I can give you some money, if that's what you want, and we can sort everything out, but I can't . . .

CABRÓN. Your husband's gonna kill you.

PAULINA. You're insane.

CABRÓN. I called him and told him everything. I'm getting another one; I love them. What about yours? You haven't touched it.

PAULINA. Are you joking? I love it when you make jokes, but this time . . .

CABRÓN. I'm being serious. (*Kisses her.*) You forgot about me, didn't you. He said he'd rather miss the plane.

PAULINA. The plane?

CABRÓN. You two are sure in for a rough ride.

PAULINA. OK, time out. You didn't call him, did you?

CABRÓN. Shall I start again? D'you wanna drink? A beer would be good for the shock; I'll get you one. He'll be here in no time.

PAULINA. What on earth made you think that . . . ?

CABRÓN. He's on his way now.

PAULINA. On his way where?

CABRÓN. Here.

PAULINA. Here? You called Joshua so he'd come here? He's on a plane now.

CABRÓN. I described your wedding ring to him.

PAULINA. What?

CABRÓN. I described the initials on your ring; I said I thought it was in poor taste not to bother putting your whole name on.

PAULINA. You called him and told him that?

CABRÓN. Oh, yeah, and that being spanked when you come really turns you on.

She slaps him in the face. It begins to snow outside.

Sorry, gorgeous. You know I'm not like that with you; I like being sweet; but I had to tell him something big to convince him.

PAULINA. How did you find out his number?

CABRÓN. If you didn't take so long in the bathroom . . .

She goes to slap him again but CABRÓN *blocks her.*

PAULINA. You son of a bitch, I'm going to have you wiped out.

CABRÓN. Are you horny? I love it when you're angry.

PAULINA. Drop dead.

CABRÓN. Would it turn you on to fuck my corpse?

PAULINA. Get me a drink.

CABRÓN. Gatorade?

PAULINA. What did you tell him?

CABRÓN. That you're a fantastic fuck. (*Offers her a Gatorade*.)

PAULINA. I'm so stupid; how could I stay mixed up with you for so long?

CABRÓN. Don't you wanna do it one last time?

PAULINA. I'll have to come up with something quickly.

CABRÓN. I told him I'd kidnapped you.

PAULINA is lost for words. She takes a swig of Gatorade.

That I'd been stalking you for months; that when I first met you, at the entrance to a museum, something exploded inside me; that you were the most beautiful woman on the planet and that I'd found out what you do every day so I could kidnap you today and have you to myself; that I've never wanted anything more in my whole life . . . That if he wants his wedding ring back I'll send it to him with your finger still inside. (*Takes her hand*.) It's the perfect plan, isn't it?

SHOP ASSISTANT. You can't take what isn't yours. You have to pay for the merchandise before you consume it.

PAULINA (*to the* SHOP ASSISTANT). This is life or death. (*To* CABRÓN). Did he believe you?

SHOP ASSISTANT. You have to pay for it.

CABRÓN (*to the* SHOP ASSISTANT). Keep your hair on. (*To* PAULINA.) He sounded convinced; I think I know you so well I described you exactly as you are, babe.

PAULINA. What am I going to do?

CABRÓN. Choose.

PAULINA. Choose what? I'm married.

CABRÓN. I need money.

PAULINA. You should have asked me.

CABRÓN. More money than you've got. I need your husband's cooperation.

PAULINA. Why didn't you ask me first?

CABRÓN. I can't wait. Seventy for me, thirty for you; what d'you say?

PAULINA. What have you done, Cabrón? Who do you owe so much money to? How much did you ask Joshua for?

CABRÓN. One and 'alf million. And I owe it to myself. I wanna retire.

PAULINA. From what?

CABRÓN. From fucking for money.

PAULINA. That's what this is about. You should have said before.

CABRÓN. You're married and that doesn't fit my plans.

PAULINA. And you arranged to meet him here?

CABRÓN (*takes her hands*). Beautiful, will you consent to be my kidnapped woman? (*Pause.*) Your hands'd look horrible with a finger missing, wouldn't they!

PAULINA. Cabrón . . . I accept.

CABRÓN. You're the perfect woman, more wonderful but, more importantly, more intelligent than any other woman on the planet!

His mobile rings.

This must be him.

PAULINA (*grabs the phone*). Let me see the number.

CABRÓN (*smiles*). Keep your knickers on; it's not him. I was hardly gonna call him from this phone. I nicked one to call him from. (*Answers the phone.*) Well? . . . Why the fuck are you calling me from your house? . . . I don't wanna know; it's your problem. (*Turns to look outside the shop.*) You're right . . . It's snow! Are you in the street?

He gets up and signals to PAULINA *to look outside to see the snow.*

What does it look like where you are? Everything's turning white . . . I never wanna see you again. Forget that I exist.

Hangs up. Meanwhile, the SHOP ASSISTANT *and the* SECURITY GUARD *have gone up to the window overlooking the street, and stare out motionlessly. They are all watching the snow.* PAULINA *fidgets nervously with her hands.*

SHOP ASSISTANT. What's this?

Pause.

CABRÓN. Isn't it gorgeous?!

PAULINA. I can't believe it.

SHOP ASSISTANT. I'm going to shut the shop.

CABRÓN. You can't. It's twenty-four hours.

PAULINA. It's never snowed here before.

SHOP ASSISTANT. Is it dangerous? (*To* PAULINA.) Could you lend me your phone, please?

PAULINA. Sure. (*Takes a mobile phone out from her bag.*)

The SHOP ASSISTANT *dials a number.*

CABRÓN. It's like in the States; I'm getting some coffee.

PAULINA. No, wait.

SHOP ASSISTANT (*on the phone*). Have you seen?

PAULINA. What if I say 'No'?

CABRÓN. Then he finds out everything.

SHOP ASSISTANT (*on the phone*). Are you all all right?

PAULINA. I don't want you messing me about.

CABRÓN. We'll have some fun with him.

SHOP ASSISTANT (*on the phone*). Don't even think of going outside until I get there. It might be dangerous.

CABRÓN (*to the* SECURITY GUARD). It's like an acid trip, isn't it?

SECURITY GUARD. Cabrón, please . . .

SHOP ASSISTANT (*on the phone*). Bring those clothes in that I've left out to dry.

SECURITY GUARD. It's better than that.

CABRÓN. Now we're part of the Developed World.

SHOP ASSISTANT (*on the phone*). Put my son on.

PAULINA. I can't believe it.

CABRÓN. That you're finally mine?

PAULINA. The snow; but, yes, that too . . .

SHOP ASSISTANT (*on the phone*). Calm down, dear; I've never seen anything like it either.

PAULINA. So where are you keeping me hostage?

CABRÓN. At my place, sweetheart, if you accept.

PAULINA. I do. (*They kiss.*)

SHOP ASSISTANT (*on the phone*). Don't let the dog out.

Scene Six

Dusk. Street outside the OLD WOMAN's *apartment block.* JESÚS *and the* BOY *look with amazement at the first snowflakes falling over the city. Neither of them speaks for some time.*

JESÚS. I thought snow was different.

BOY. We'll get wet.

JESÚS. No. It's like foam.

BOY. It's white.

JESÚS. Everyone's come outside to look.

BOY. I'm frightened.

JESÚS. It's all right.

BOY. My mum's not coming.

JESÚS. Sure she is. She won't be long.

Silence.

She must be held up watching the snow like us.

BOY. I heard when she told your mum.

JESÚS. That wasn't my mum.

BOY. She told her she wasn't coming back.

JESÚS. Who?

BOY. My mum. I heard her say she was leaving me with her.

JESÚS. No way.

BOY. She couldn't cope with the burden.

JESÚS. You can't say that.

BOY. Have you met her?

JESÚS. You should never give up hope.

BOY. She said she was going far away to look for a job.

JESÚS. Maybe she meant 'one day'.

BOY. She's going to the border.

JESÚS. I don't reckon she'd leave you on your own.

BOY. I heard her. She said she loves me a lot.

JESÚS. Are you sure you heard her say that?

BOY. Yeah.

JESÚS. You imagined it.

BOY. I never.

Silence.

Why did you live with her?

JESÚS. 'Cause I got in the way.

BOY. In her way?

JESÚS. In my dad's way.

BOY. How?

JESÚS. He wanted to live his life and one day he left.

BOY. What about your mum?

JESÚS. I don't think I ever met her.

BOY. What if she never comes back?

JESÚS. Your mum?

BOY. Yeah; yours isn't gonna.

JESÚS (*smiles*). It's no big deal. See: I was worse off.

BOY. But she really was my mum.

Scene Seven

Night. A large basement where CABRÓN *lives. The bed in the background, a screen and small windows.* CABRÓN *and* PAULINA *sit on the sofa.* CABRÓN *dials a number on the mobile.*

CABRÓN. Now I need you to groan.

PAULINA. What?

CABRÓN. Groan, as if I'd smacked you one. What's your number at home?

PAULINA. 56 88 88 73.

CABRÓN. Engaged.

PAULINA. Are you going to talk to him?

CABRÓN. Course I am. Can you cook?

PAULINA. It's dangerous.

CABRÓN. Not if you learn. (*Dials again.*)

PAULINA. I mean it's dangerous calling him.

CABRÓN. Groan.

PAULINA groans.

CABRÓN. You'd better just pant; we don't want it sounding fake. (*On the phone.*) Mr Joskowicz, I have your wife here in front of me. Tied by her hands and feet to a chair. If you want to see her again it'll cost you one and a half million pesos . . . I want the money the day after tomorrow, the seventh, *comprende*? . . . I'll call you again to tell you where and when. Oh, and don't trace the call; it's a stolen phone . . . Wanna hear her?

He puts the phone to PAULINA's mouth.

PAULINA. I'm all right.

CABRÓN. There you are! . . . If you don't get the money to me sharpish, I'll send you the lady's wedding ring with her finger still inside it. I'll be in touch again later. (*Hangs up.*)

PAULINA. You hadn't called him before, had you?

CABRÓN. Shall I fix you something to eat, sweetness?

PAULINA. Answer me.

CABRÓN. Are you really interested in me answering that question?

PAULINA. Do you want the truth?

CABRÓN. Tell me.

PAULINA. No. Besides, you've just confirmed to him that I've been kidnapped right in front of me.

CABRÓN. You having second thoughts?

PAULINA. Shall we cook together?

They hug and kiss, then go into the small kitchen and begin to cook something.

CABRÓN. I went to the Seven-Eleven this morning and bought everything for tonight. (*Pause.*) D'you think I should call the police?

PAULINA. He prefers avoiding that kind of trouble and sorting things out for himself. He thinks he's some sort of hero.

CABRÓN. Good for you!

PAULINA. Are you laughing at me?

CABRÓN. Must be amazing to live with a hero.

PAULINA. The excitement lasted five years at most.

CABRÓN. Houses, cars, travel, jewellery; what more could you want? Don't tell me 'love' or 'passion'; no one believes that these days. A few more days and you'll be free again.

PAULINA. Free for a few days and then . . .

There is an insistent knock on the door. They both jump.

Shall I hide?

CABRÓN. Don't move.

He looks for something to defend himself with. Finds a pipe.

Fucking hell! Just what we need!

PAULINA. Could it be the police?

CABRÓN. The police don't knock. (*Goes to the door.*) Who is it?

JESÚS. It's me.

CABRÓN. Who?

JESÚS. Jesús.

CABRÓN *opens the door.*

CABRÓN. What are you doing here?

JESÚS. It's really cold.

CABRÓN. So what?

JESÚS. It's freezing. Haven't you seen the snow?

CABRÓN. What's it to me?

JESÚS. I couldn't stay there.

CABRÓN. What about the old bird?

JESÚS (*noticing* PAULINA*'s presence*). Is that her?

CABRÓN. Mind your own business.

JESÚS (*to* PAULINA). Evening. Are you my friend's hostage?

PAULINA. Good evening.

JESÚS. Paulina?

PAULINA. And you are . . . ?

JESÚS. Jesús.

PAULINA. Pleased to meet you, Jesús. So, Cabrón, it wasn't just a secret between the two of us.

CABRÓN. Sweetness, please, I'll explain later.

JESÚS. Can we talk in private?

The BOY *appears in the doorway.*

PAULINA. Is there anything wrong?

CABRÓN. Nothing, babe. What's he doing here?

BOY. Hello.

CABRÓN. What d'you bring him here for?

JESÚS. We were waiting.

CABRÓN. Why didn't you leave him?

JESÚS. I couldn't abandon him.

CABRÓN. What d'you mean, you 'couldn't abandon him'? You decided to bring him here?

JESÚS. His mum never turned up.

CABRÓN. You should have left him there.

JESÚS. It could traumatise him.

CABRÓN. In the street, then.

PAULINA. Can I help you?

JESÚS. No thanks, Miss.

PAULINA. Cabrón, you have to explain this to me.

CABRÓN. Course I do, beautiful.

JESÚS. We'd better not talk about this in front of him.

CABRÓN flings himself at JESÚS, grabs him by his clothes and pulls him into the flat.

CABRÓN. Look, you little fool: you're no use for anything. I don't know what you've got in your head. Pure shit! Why the fuck are you turning up at my house with little short-arse here in tow? He'll have worked everything out by now. Do you realise, stupid? Answer me . . . (*Hits him.*) You are capable of thought, aren't you? (*Hits him.*) Even just a little bit?

PAULINA. Calm down, Cabrón.

CABRÓN (*to* JESÚS). Cat got your tongue, you piece of shit? (*Hits him.*)

BOY. Leave him alone.

CABRÓN. Fuck off, stupid, and take short-arse with you.

BOY. Let's go, Jesús.

JESÚS. I just wanted . . .

CABRÓN. Have you any idea what a fuck-up you could cause?

PAULINA. Stop it, Cabrón; you'll kill him.

CABRÓN. Do you realise the shit you're getting me into?

The BOY *runs out.*

Where are you going?

CABRÓN *runs after him.*

You're not going anywhere.

JESÚS. Let the kid go.

CABRÓN. No, I won't let him go. Do you realise how dangerous this is? He works the whole thing out and then you bring him here.

PAULINA. What's going on? Worked what out? What have you done?

CABRÓN. Nothing, sugar.

BOY. I didn't see nothing, I swear.

CABRÓN. Zip it.

BOY. Don't hurt me, please.

PAULINA. Enough! Leave it; calm down, please, all of you. I don't understand what's going on here.

JESÚS. What did you expect me to do?

PAULINA. Are you related to him?

JESÚS. No.

PAULINA (*to the* BOY). What about you?

BOY. I don't know him, honest.

CABRÓN. Paulina, stop asking questions, please.

PAULINA. Don't tell me what to do.

CABRÓN. You're my hostage!

BOY. Are you his mum?

PAULINA. A friend.

CABRÓN. I'm sorry, darling, I didn't mean to shout at you.

PAULINA. Forget it; you've a lot of explaining to do.

CABRÓN (*to* JESÚS). I'm going to crack your skull open and try and pour some brains in through the hole; see if you can learn to think a bit . . .

JESÚS. Can we stay here tonight?

CABRÓN. What about the old woman?

JESÚS. Don't say anything. The kid's here.

BOY. I never saw nothing, I swear.

PAULINA. What old woman?

BOY. His mum.

JESÚS. She's not my mum.

CABRÓN. See? Does he know everything?

PAULINA. This child should be taken home.

CABRÓN (*to* PAULINA). You can't leave. (*To the* BOY.) And you: sit there, quick.

PAULINA. You're very worked up.

CABRÓN. What do you expect?

PAULINA. Don't you speak to me like that.

CABRÓN. Sorry, baby.

PAULINA. Are you abducting this child?

BOY. No, please. Let me go if you like and I'll leave on my own.

JESÚS. Quiet, Martín.

CABRÓN. You even know his name.

PAULINA. We're all very tense; let's take some deep breaths.

The BOY *begins to cry a little.*

What if we adopt him?

Silence as the others look at her.

Was that a stupid thing to say?

CABRÓN. Yes.

PAULINA (*to* CABRÓN). I just thought that you and I . . .

JESÚS. The kid's not feeling well.

CABRÓN. Thanks to you.

PAULINA. How do you expect him not to cry when you take that attitude?

JESÚS. What shall we do, Cabrón?

PAULINA. We have to get things under control.

CABRÓN. You had to finish your thing off.

JESÚS. And you didn't wait for me to help you kidnap her.

PAULINA. You weren't supposed to tell anyone.

JESÚS. You didn't wait for me; I've got a bit of rope back there.

CABRÓN. You're gonna drive me mad.

JESÚS (*to* PAULINA). And you must love Cabrón – to be kidnapped and not tied up.

PAULINA. That's between him and me.

CABRÓN (*to* JESÚS). You've no reason to get mixed up in this.

PAULINA. Who did you beat up with a pipe? Was it to kidnap this child?

JESÚS. She knows about the pipe? (*To* PAULINA.) We haven't kidnapped him.

BOY. My mum left me with his mum. Don't kidnap me, please.

CABRÓN. You shouldn't be coming here talking about this. Know what? You'd better just go.

BOY. Can I go?

CABRÓN. Jesús, sling your hook and take him with you.

PAULINA. You can't leave.

CABRÓN. Why not?

JESÚS. Now the hostage is calling the shots.

BOY. Thank you, Miss.

PAULINA. We can't take the risk. Think about it, Cabrón: I don't know what you've got going with these two, but I can't take the risk. At least until Joshua pays the ransom.

CABRÓN. Baby, we can't do this.

PAULINA. Of course we can. And you – sit yourselves down; it's going to be a long night.

BOY. I don't wanna stay here. Don't kidnap me, please.

PAULINA. And where's your mother?

JESÚS. She never came to pick him up.

PAULINA. We're not going to kidnap you, all right?

BOY. All right.

PAULINA. Do you know where she lives?

BOY. She won't be there.

PAULINA. We're not going to get far with that attitude, sonny. Why do you say that?

BOY. She went to the States and left me with Jesús's mum – well, no – with his dad's wife.

CABRÓN *(to* JESÚS*)*. You idiot.

PAULINA. Don't speak to him like that. We have to calm this child down.

BOY. I'm all right.

CABRÓN. We'll be done for abducting a minor.

PAULINA. Have you got aunts and uncles or cousins?

BOY. In the village. I've got an aunt who lives near the old lady's house.

PAULINA. So for now everything's fine.

BOY. Are you going to hurt me?

PAULINA. We're not going to do anything to you. Do you want something to eat?

BOY. I'm not hungry.

JESÚS. I left a note for his mum.

CABRÓN. How thoughtful!

PAULINA (*to the* BOY). Come on, let's go to the kitchen, find you something to eat.

CABRÓN (*to* PAULINA). But you don't know how to cook.

PAULINA. At times like this a person can learn anything.

They exit.

CABRÓN. A note?

JESÚS. I said if she gets there and doesn't find us to call me on the mobile.

CABRÓN. To say 'hello'?

JESÚS. I said I had to go out and I couldn't leave the kid on his own in the flat.

CABRÓN. And you think she's gonna call to pick him up?

JESÚS. We're not sure.

CABRÓN. That means they've got your phone number.

JESÚS. Yeah.

CABRÓN. You have to call the police.

JESÚS. What if she's not dead?

CABRÓN. Have you got shit for brains? Stick your head between her tits – if she's not dead yet, whack her again with the pipe.

JESÚS. It's snowing. Can you lend me something for the cold?

CABRÓN *hands him a jacket from the sofa.*

I'm scared of sleeping on my own.

CABRÓN *bursts out laughing.*

CABRÓN. Poof!

JESÚS. What about the kid?

CABRÓN. He's staying here.

Scene Eight

JESÚS *walks cautiously into the* OLD WOMAN's *flat. There is no light except for the light coming from the corridor outside.*

The body of the OLD WOMAN *can be seen lying a few metres away from where she originally fell.* JESÚS *comes into the room without closing the door and switches on a lamp. He looks for some time at the body and stifles his reflex to vomit. He decides to close the door of the flat.*

He sits and watches the body, trying to spot any kind of movement. He gets up, approaches her fearfully and feels her wrist to check for a pulse. There is nothing. He places his head against her chest and stands in this position for a few seconds.

He makes a phone call.

JESÚS. I don't know what to do . . . I did what you told me and . . . She's still warm . . . I daren't; if I don't do it right and then make it worse and she wakes up and sees me and does something to me . . . Don't hang up, please; just . . . What shall I do? Can I leave her here and come back to yours? All right, with the pipe, right? And . . . Where? Because she's on the floor; how can I do it so it looks like it was part of the same thing? What if, tomorrow . . . No, not tomorrow; I didn't mean that, but . . . The blood that's all over the place, it's dry and they have machines that can tell when you hit her and so if I hit her again, well, they'll know that it wasn't at the same time . . . No, please don't hang up . . . I'll finish her off now and . . . Oh, Cabrón, what if she heard me just now; I'm so stupid, aren't I . . . ? Cabrón? Hello, Cabrón? Don't . . .

Hangs up. Starts to untidy things.

Where would a burglar look? Just throw some of these around, make a bit of a mess . . . Where d'you keep it . . . ? They have to believe it's a crime scene. Anyway, I'm gonna need that money. (*To the* OLD WOMAN.) You've no right selling this flat.

Goes to the phone.

Police? Good evening, Miss; some people have broken into my house and burgled me; they've taken a few things and some money, but they've beaten up my dad's wife, they wanted to . . . Her head's all smashed open; I think they must have hit her with something very heavy and . . . She doesn't seem to be breathing; I don't know what to do; please, send a squad car and an ambulance or something . . . Yes. Flat 2, 375 Valley Street. Yes, thank you.

Hangs up. Silence. He takes out some gloves and picks up the pipe that is lying there. He gives her a sharp whack.

Blackout.

Scene Nine

CABRÓN's *basement. Dawn. A very intense light filters through the solitude of the room.* PAULINA *is seated on a sofa. She smokes a cigarette. After a few minutes there is an insistent knock on the door.*

MAN'S VOICE (*off*). Cabrón, open the door. I know you're there.

Pause. PAULINA *stands up, not knowing what to do. She goes to the door and hesitates. She does not know whether to open it or not. She decides to stay still so as not to give herself away.*

Open this door. (*Knocking.*) I know you're there, or somebody's there. Show your face, Cabrón; open the door. (*Pause. Knocking.*) Cabrón . . . Cabrón . . . ! I'm talking to you ... Open the damn door or I'll knock it down! You've been hiding for days. I know you're there. All right, you asked for it; you'll be sorry.

PAULINA, *disconcerted, tries to remain static. After checking that the MAN has gone, she heads for the sofa; she smokes again. After a while, CABRÓN and the BOY enter. CABRÓN locks the door. They carry bags from the Seven-Eleven.*

CABRÓN. We're back, babe.

PAULINA. You took your time.

CABRÓN. We went for a walk.

BOY. Even the cars are covered in snow.

PAULINA. Is it still snowing?

CABRÓN. Not any more.

BOY. People couldn't get into them.

CABRÓN. Nearly everything was shut.

BOY. And all the roofs on the houses were white.

CABRÓN. Apart from the Seven-Eleven. We had coffee and doughnuts, didn't we?

BOY. All the people were wearing long coats and carrying umbrellas.

PAULINA. You look very pleased with yourselves.

CABRÓN. You should have come with us.

PAULINA. The pain hasn't gone off yet.

CABRÓN. I brought the tablets.

BOY. The city looked amazing.

CABRÓN. D'you wanna glass of water?

PAULINA. Someone came looking for you.

BOY. People were building snowmen.

CABRÓN. Who?

PAULINA. I didn't open the door. They were shouting.

BOY. It's not as cold as it was yesterday.

CABRÓN. What did they say?

PAULINA. That you'd be sorry.

CABRÓN. Is that all? Was it a woman?

PAULINA. Yes.

CABRÓN. Some mad cow.

PAULINA. I thought you'd cancelled your clients.

CABRÓN. Jealous? (*Pause.*) D'you want breakfast?

BOY. Yeah.

PAULINA. No, thanks.

BOY. The city's empty.

CABRÓN *prepares breakfast as* PAULINA *smokes on the sofa. The* BOY *walks from side to side and takes something from the sofa.*

CABRÓN. As if no one lived here. I'll make you something. And you, Martín, remember our deal: don't budge from there.

PAULINA. I was in Moscow one winter. Darkness nearly all day and snow that came up to here; absolutely freezing.

BOY. Where's that? In the States?

PAULINA. In Russia.

CABRÓN. They used to be bad but they turned good.

PAULINA. Life isn't that simple. Do you not know which woman would come and shout at you like that?

CABRÓN. There's so many of them; I dunno who it was.

BOY. I wanna go to the bathroom.

CABRÓN. I'm not stopping you.

PAULINA. Why did you take him out?

CABRÓN. To explain a few things to him.

PAULINA. You've done something serious, Cabrón. Why won't you tell me?

CABRÓN. 'Cause I don't wanna get you involved. Besides, my hands are clean.

PAULINA. Do you like me?

CABRÓN. I'm mad about you.

PAULINA. If I asked to stay with you . . .

CABRÓN. It'd be a bit more expensive.

PAULINA. Do you like my hands? Don't they look very old?

CABRÓN. Like a piano player. Tomorrow's the day.

There is a loud knock at the door. The same MAN*'s voice as a while ago.*

MAN'S VOICE (*off*). Cabrón, open up. (*Knocking.*) You haven't shown your face in weeks. I don't deserve this from you. You're breaking the deal.

CABRÓN *signals to* PAULINA *to keep quiet. The* BOY *opens the bathroom door and* CABRÓN *tells him to be quiet too.*

You're not fooling me. I know you're there. If you don't want to open the door, fine; next time I'll bring the police with me.

After a moment, silence.

CABRÓN. It was him, wasn't it? It wasn't a woman.

PAULINA. I got mixed up. Perhaps it was another client shouting like he does.

CABRÓN. None of them know where I live.

PAULINA. You don't have to tell me.

CABRÓN. You were my first.

The BOY *shuts himself in the bathroom.*

PAULINA. You're wonderful. I want to have a lie down.

CABRÓN. I'll tell you when breakfast's ready.

> PAULINA *goes out to lie down.* CABRÓN *continues preparing breakfast. He knocks at the bathroom door.*

Don't fall asleep in there.

There is a knock at the door. A moment of tension.

JESÚS (*off*). Cabrón, it's me.

> CABRÓN *opens the door.*

CABRÓN. Why didn't you call?

JESÚS. You didn't wanna hear from me.

CABRÓN. Where've you been all night?

JESÚS. I'm hungry.

CABRÓN. Did the police turn up?

JESÚS. I've had nothing to eat.

CABRÓN. You should've phoned.

JESÚS. I had to pay.

CABRÓN. A bribe?

JESÚS. The wake. My head's killing me.

CABRÓN. Have a tablet. They've had the wake?

JESÚS. Tonight, when they give the body back. Where's the kid?

CABRÓN. In the bathroom. They didn't suspect anything?

JESÚS. Don't ask me now. I need to sleep.

CABRÓN. Tell me.

JESÚS. They opened her skull right up.

CABRÓN. Not that.

JESÚS. They wanted to know what size the pipe was; where's your girlfriend?

CABRÓN. She's my hostage.

JESÚS. She's not listening?

CABRÓN. She's not here.

JESÚS. You haven't hurt the kid, have you?

CABRÓN. Where've you been?

JESÚS. I've been talking non-stop all night. Word after word. I've never talked as much as I did last night, and the worst thing is that none of what I said was true, Cabrón. All lies. It took them an hour to turn up, another hour to get the body out, half an hour to take her to the forensic, a fifteen-minute walk to the Public Ministry . . .

CABRÓN. I'm not interested. Just tell me what they asked you and what you said.

JESÚS. Three hours waiting at the Public Ministry till they finally sent me through to an office and I had to repeat the same thing I'd said to the doctor at the house, to the policeman who took me to the Ministry and to the secretaries.

CABRÓN. D'you realise what you're saying?

JESÚS. Why didn't you hit her harder?

CABRÓN. She was so old she'd have died all by herself.

JESÚS. Where's the kid?

CABRÓN. I told you: in the bathroom.

JESÚS. You're sure you haven't taken him anywhere?

CABRÓN. What about the money? Did you find all the money?

JESÚS. You didn't finish your job.

CABRÓN. You've gotta pay me my money.

JESÚS. There was hardly any left over.

CABRÓN. What do you mean 'left over'?

JESÚS. Hardly anything. I had to pay.

CABRÓN. Pay what?

JESÚS. For the wake.

CABRÓN. What the hell made you spend it on a wake? What about the note?

JESÚS. It wasn't there. His mum must've come back.

CABRÓN. No way.

JESÚS. I've still got this funny feeling in my mouth. You should've seen her; she was bleeding again. I wanna throw up.

CABRÓN. Not in the living room you don't. (*Gets up. Goes to the bathroom. Knocks on the door.*) Out, short-arse; come out of there. (*To* JESÚS.) Hold it in or go to the kitchen. Come on out!

The BOY *opens the door and comes out.* JESÚS *goes into the bathroom and vomits.*

What were you doing in there for so long?

BOY. I felt poorly.

CABRÓN. That's all I need. Come on. I'll give you some medicine.

BOY (*sits at the table*). Please let me go.

CABRÓN. You're not going anywhere.

BOY. I don't wanna be here.

CABRÓN. Don't you shout at me.

BOY. I never did nothing to you and now you're kidnapping me.

CABRÓN. Stop fucking me off and shut up!

JESÚS *comes out of the bathroom.*

JESÚS. A bucket.

CABRÓN. What for?

JESÚS. The bog's on fire.

CABRÓN *fetches a bucket.*

CABRÓN (*to the* BOY). Idiot. What were you trying to do?

JESÚS. Come and help me.

CABRÓN. Think you're really clever, do you? Wanna burn the house down?

Picks him up from the chair, pushes him, pulls him towards him and hits him.

BOY. You two killed that lady.

CABRÓN. Fuck your bitch mother, man.

JESÚS. Leave him alone.

CABRÓN. Butt out. Put that bog out and you, little piece of shit, don't ever say that again.

BOY. I don't want to be here.

CABRÓN. You're in just as much shit as we are.

JESÚS brings the fire under control. He throws himself at CABRÓN.

JESÚS. Get off him, Cabrón.

CABRÓN pushes JESÚS away. PAULINA enters.

PAULINA. What's going on?

CABRÓN. Get off me, wanker.

JESÚS. Didn't you say she wasn't here?

He rises and throws himself at CABRÓN.

Leave him alone. It's not his fault.

CABRÓN. Get off.

PAULINA. Cabrón, he's a child.

JESÚS. Let him go.

CABRÓN. Pair of idiots!

JESÚS. And she's worked everything out, has she?

PAULINA. I don't know what you're mixed up in, but . . .

BOY. I won't say anything.

CABRÓN. Too right you won't.

JESÚS. What did you hear, Miss?

CABRÓN. Say that again: 'I won't say anything, I won't say anything.'

BOY. I – won't – say . . .

JESÚS. I should never have listened to you, Cabrón.

CABRÓN. Get lost, then.

JESÚS. You're not the clever bastard you say you are.

CABRÓN *hits the* BOY *again.*

PAULINA. Cabrón, don't do that.

JESÚS. Yeah.

CABRÓN. You're making me angry. Of course you're not gonna say anything; don't go getting ideas.

PAULINA. We're all very tense.

JESÚS *vomits in the living room.*

CABRÓN. You pig! Shit. Listen to me, you useless pair. And you, too, Paulina. The world's gone arse over tit and we're gonna set it straight. Give me the rope, Jesús; we're gonna tie him up; and wipe your mouth.

JESÚS *hands the rope to* CABRÓN; *they tie the* BOY *to a chair.*

Hold his legs.

JESÚS. I might hurt him.

PAULINA. I can't stand to watch this. (*She sits on the sofa.*) Finish that and then we need to talk.

CABRÓN. Cover his mouth.

BOY. I'm not shouting.

They cover his mouth.

CABRÓN. Gotta be cruel to be kind.

JESÚS *sits at the other end of the sofa.*

Paulina, darling, don't look at me like that.

PAULINA. How do you expect me not to look at you like this when you've got that boy tied up? I at least hoped you would have made love to me last night.

CABRÓN. He could escape.

PAULINA. You could have invited me to sleep with you on the sofa.

CABRÓN. You were sleeping like an angel; I didn't wanna wake you.

PAULINA. I spent a night away from home.

CABRÓN. You're not telling me you're not happy?

PAULINA. The first time since I married Joshua.

CABRÓN. And didn't you like it?

PAULINA. I slept with that boy; he could have got up and strangled me to escape from this place.

CABRÓN (*to* JESÚS). Put the headphones on him so he doesn't hear anything.

JESÚS *places the headphones on the* BOY.

PAULINA. I didn't go to work today.

CABRÓN. It's your day off.

PAULINA. I have to phone and tell them.

CABRÓN. Do you think your kidnapper would give you permission to make a phone call? The world's turned upside down, my angel; it won't be that easy to put right. The price has gone up too much and we have to pay it. Don't be scared, beautiful; if he loves you he'll give us the money. (*Pause.*) Fancy a fuck?

PAULINA. There's a child here.

CABRÓN. I can blindfold him.

PAULINA. Kiss me.

PAULINA *rises, goes up to* CABRÓN *and gives him a kiss.*
JESÚS *closes his eyes and sleeps.*

CABRÓN. Do you wanna hit me, torture me, bite me, spit on me? I'm your slave, angel.

PAULINA. I need some air.

CABRÓN. Air to fly through?

PAULINA *smiles. Her eyes fill with tears.*

PAULINA. Air to breathe; I'm suffocating. I'll be right back.

CABRÓN *accompanies her as far as the door; he opens it and* PAULINA *exits.* CABRÓN *closes the door again and sits on the sofa beside* JESÚS.

CABRÓN. Go to sleep.

JESÚS. Do you love her?

CABRÓN. She's not ugly.

JESÚS. What you gonna do to her?

CABRÓN. *I* don't do anything. Other people do. Jealous?

JESÚS. What of?

CABRÓN (*smiles*). So your rope was some use. (*Referring to the* BOY.) Get up, Jesús. (*Hugs him.*) This is a very special and very painful moment. It's normal for you to feel this way, because you lost her and at the same time you wanted it to happen. Even killing someone you don't know hurts, so I can imagine how you feel. *Hakuna matata!*

JESÚS. I need to sleep.

CABRÓN. Not yet – gimme a hand. You got any cigarettes?

JESÚS *takes out a packet of cigarettes.* CABRÓN *lights one. He gives one to* JESÚS. *He goes to the* BOY, *takes the gag from his mouth and the headphones, and offers him a cigarette.*

Think you're all grown up? Smoke one of these.

BOY. Don't want to.

CABRÓN. I started smoking at your age.

JESÚS. He's very young.

CABRÓN. Let him learn.

He gives the BOY *a cigarette.*

BOY (*smokes*). Like this?

CABRÓN. Breathe in and hold. That's it. Hold it and then blow it out. In, hold and out. Learn to hold it in for longer.

BOY. I can't.

CABRÓN. Don't be a poof. You want a piercing and you don't know how to smoke? If you can hold on, you'll survive. (*Pause.*) Now, get this straight, you little bastard: you saw what you saw, but you realise it's best for you to keep quiet? It's not your fault you're here and it's not ours neither, so we're just gonna make the best of it: you keep your gob shut and you cooperate. Another lungful? It's good for the nerves. We're one big family and we have to work together.

BOY. I'm scared.

CABRÓN. And you think we're not? We have to believe in what we've started until the last moment; right now is when we can't let ourselves be beaten. You either stand up to it or you don't. We decided to play, everything's shot to hell and I'm a very bad loser. All I want is to make it to the end. (*To* JESÚS.) Gag him and put the headphones on.

BOY. Please, no – I got the message.

CABRÓN. Leave him. Jesús, please, get some sleep; you have to be fresh for that wake. Tomorrow's the big day and you have to help me collect that money.

Smoke comes from the kitchen.

Of course, the water for the coffee's boiled away.

CABRÓN'*s mobile rings; he answers.*

Paulina, why the hell are you calling me from the street? . . . You're right, angel; is it very cold? . . . (*To* JESÚS *and the* BOY.) Do you want anything from the Seven-Eleven?

Scene Ten

Dusk. It is still snowing extremely heavily. Close by CABRÓN's *basement,* PAULINA *walks with some Seven-Eleven bags to a phone box, takes out a card and dials a number.*

PAULINA. Joshua? It's me . . . Your wife . . . I managed to sneak out to call you; they're in the other room . . . A reduction? I'm not on special offer . . . Forget I exist if you don't care . . . You could at least ask if I'm OK . . . I have to hang up; one of them's coming . . . Don't even think of calling the police; they're very dangerous . . . Your ring? Yes, I've still got it . . . Do you care more about your bloody ring than my hands? . . . Forget it. Goodbye, Joshua.

She hangs up. Stops to think. Dials another number.

Cabrón? I have to tell you . . . It's nothing bad. No one knows where I am or anything . . . Yes, but the city looks so beautiful. Cabrón, I'm going to the Seven-Eleven; do you want anything? . . . Nothing else? Ask the boy if he wants a hot dog . . . I won't be long, Cabrón; big kiss; bye.

She hangs up. Takes a deep breath. Sits down on the kerb, makes a snowball and then starts taking it apart with her hands.

Scene Eleven

Evening. The Seven-Eleven, empty. CABRÓN *sits in the dining area drinking a hot coffee. The* SHOP ASSISTANT, *seated behind the counter, tired and bored, looks from time to time at* CABRÓN *and also drinks a hot coffee. The* SECURITY GUARD *paces to and fro, sits, picks up a magazine, reads a little and makes himself a hot coffee.*

SHOP ASSISTANT (*to the* SECURITY GUARD). He spends hours here. Sometimes in the morning or before dawn. He does like coming here.

Long pause.

CABRÓN. Isn't it cold? Let me buy you some doughnuts.

SHOP ASSISTANT. Thank you.

SECURITY GUARD. Cheers, Cabrón.

The SHOP ASSISTANT comes out from behind the counter with a cloth, cleans the café area, goes to the doughnuts and takes three. She gives one to the SECURITY GUARD and takes the other to CABRÓN.

CABRÓN. The embassy was closed, wasn't it?

SHOP ASSISTANT. It was dangerous with the snow.

CABRÓN. So weird!

SHOP ASSISTANT. What?

CABRÓN. That they closed it. The snow makes us more like them.

SHOP ASSISTANT. It was the anti-globalisation people. There were police everywhere all night.

CABRÓN. That's why they don't give us visas. 'Cause of people like that.

Scene Twelve

Evening in CABRÓN's basement. He is sleeping on the sofa. The BOY is still tied up, but has managed to untie his feet and advances with the whole chair to CABRÓN. He wakes him.

BOY. Can you let me go?

CABRÓN. I'm asleep.

BOY. I want to go.

CABRÓN. Again.

BOY. What?

CABRÓN. Say it again.

BOY. Can you let me go?

CABRÓN. You want to leave?

BOY. Yeah.

CABRÓN. Where will you go?

BOY. To my house.

CABRÓN. Again.

BOY. To my house. (CABRÓN *smiles mockingly*.)

CABRÓN. To your mummy?

BOY. Yeah.

CABRÓN. She didn't come for you.

BOY. I'm not sure.

CABRÓN. Are you a poof?

BOY. No.

CABRÓN. You look like a poof.

BOY. I don't.

CABRÓN. What if your mum's not home any more?

BOY. Dunno.

CABRÓN. Think.

BOY. I don't wanna be in the way.

CABRÓN. You won't be.

BOY. Please.

CABRÓN. You got a dad?

BOY. No.

CABRÓN. You're gonna be a poof.

BOY. I'm not. (*Pause*.) Can your mum sometimes not love you?

CABRÓN. Yeah. Did you like the tattoos Jesús's stepmum had?

BOY. They were ugly.

CABRÓN. I've got one, but it's not ugly.

BOY. Jesús is gonna give me a piercing like his. (*Pause*.) Why didn't you sleep with Paulina?

CABRÓN. Grown-ups' things.

BOY. You're mad at each other, aren't you?

CABRÓN. Doesn't sir ask a lot of questions!

BOY. She must have a lot of money; she's not very pretty.

CABRÓN *smiles*.

It's good that you didn't leave me with the old woman; I didn't want to stay with her!

CABRÓN. You should be thanking us. Why leave? You're better off here.

BOY. Dunno.

CABRÓN. Again.

BOY. I'll stay.

CABRÓN's *mobile rings*.

CABRÓN (*on the phone*). How are you? . . . Everything go all right? . . . I'm very pleased for you . . . Jesús, do a good job of that wake so no one suspects; I'll be waiting for you here first thing . . . That's normal . . . We're resting up for tomorrow. I spoke to the husband and I've rendezvoused with him tomorrow to pick up the money. What time d'you think? . . . Eleven-oh-seven a.m. Tomorrow's the big day . . . We'll be here; we'll go out for some dinner tonight . . . The Seven-Eleven, where else? (*Hangs up*.) Mates?

BOY. OK. Was Jesús all right?

CABRÓN. Crying.

BOY. He's worse off than I am, isn't he?

CABRÓN. Yeah.

PAULINA (*off*). Can you two not sleep?

CABRÓN. Yeah, that's what we're doing.

PAULINA (*off*). Are you having a chat?

CABRÓN. Man talk. (*To the* BOY.) Now, go to sleep and let me do the same.

BOY. OK.

PAULINA approaches as far as the sofa where CABRÓN is sleeping; she climbs onto him, kisses him and removes her clothes.

PAULINA. Fuck me, Cabrón.

CABRÓN. The kid's here.

The BOY watches the action. PAULINA stops, goes for the handkerchief and blindfolds the BOY.

PAULINA. Grown-ups' things.

CABRÓN. He'll hear.

PAULINA. That's what the headphones are for.

CABRÓN. Hang on.

He stops and pulls away from where PAULINA is. He goes to the BOY. He loosens the blindfold.

If you wanna watch and learn, the choice is yours.

He returns to PAULINA and kisses her.

Scene Thirteen

Seven-Eleven. Night. CABRÓN, PAULINA *and the* BOY, *eating hot dogs.*

CABRÓN. It's very late. We have to go.

BOY. Please, a bit longer.

PAULINA. So I surface tomorrow?

CABRÓN. You surface tomorrow, angel.

PAULINA. Won't I see you again?

CABRÓN. I can send postcards to your work.

PAULINA. I would have liked to be happy.

CABRÓN. You've lots of money.

BOY. There's no sauces.

CABRÓN. There never is. Go and ask Fatso. Then go sit at the other table; we're talking about grown-ups' things.

The BOY *goes to the counter.*

PAULINA. He was the biggest deal of my life. He has money in his blood.

CABRÓN. Do you love him?

PAULINA. I decided to invest my whole self. It was a high price, but he was the best candidate to father my children.

CABRÓN. And you're still waiting for them?

PAULINA. I'm talking crap. I love being a hostage, Cabrón.

CABRÓN. This is my best investment. (*Pause.*) The snow's very romantic, isn't it?

PAULINA. Are you going to make love to me?

CABRÓN. Have you ever done it in the snow?

PAULINA. It was the most expensive fuck of my life.

CABRÓN. Gimme your hand.

   PAULINA *offers him her hand. He removes the ring.*

   I don't want you scratching me.

   PAULINA *smiles.* CABRÓN *puts the ring in his pocket.*

   You shouldn't fall in love with a salary.

PAULINA. Kiss me.

CABRÓN. Yes, ma'am!

   JESÚS *enters with a birthday cake.*

JESÚS. Happy birthday to you, happy birthday to you . . .

CABRÓN. What's that in aid of?

JESÚS. Happy birthday, Cabrón.

PAULINA. A cake?

JESÚS. For you.

PAULINA. Is it your birthday?

CABRÓN. Not today.

JESÚS. It nearly is; it's twenty-five to twelve.

PAULINA. Why didn't you tell us?

SHOP ASSISTANT. What's going on here?

PAULINA (*to the* SHOP ASSISTANT). It's going to be his birthday in twenty-five minutes.

CABRÓN. What about the wake?

JESÚS. I got bored; I left someone else in charge.

CABRÓN. Get rid of it.

JESÚS. It's yours.

SHOP ASSISTANT. You can't bring food in here, young man.

PAULINA. Take it, Cabrón.

JESÚS. You can't say that.

SHOP ASSISTANT. Is it his birthday?

CABRÓN. I don't like cake.

SHOP ASSISTANT. All right, we'll make an exception today.

JESÚS. Where's the kid?

PAULINA. Picking out sweets.

CABRÓN. Get rid of it.

JESÚS. Buy some disposable plates.

    PAULINA *goes to the* SHOP ASSISTANT *to ask for a knife.*

I just fancied a party.

PAULINA. How old will you be?

CABRÓN. None of your business.

SHOP ASSISTANT. Yes, tell us; how old will you be?

JESÚS. Thirty-two.

PAULINA. I thought it was more.

CABRÓN. I don't wanna cake.

JESÚS. I know you do.

The BOY *has come over to them.*

I brought you this.

Takes a package out from his trouser pocket.

BOY. For me?

JESÚS. A piercing.

PAULINA. You're barely a child . . .

BOY. None of your business.

CABRÓN. A kid after my own heart.

PAULINA. You should have been brought up better.

JESÚS. I remembered this afternoon; I wanted to surprise you.

BOY. Look, Cabrón: I got a present, too.

JESÚS. We needed a party to cheer us all up.

PAULINA. Tomorrow's the big day, Cabrón.

JESÚS. What shall we do until midnight?

PAULINA. We could sing a song.

BOY. How boring!

CABRÓN. And how Jewish.

PAULINA. Funny.

BOY. Can you put it here on my eyebrow?

PAULINA. Why don't you make a wish?

CABRÓN. They never come true.

BOY. Course they do.

PAULINA. What flavour cake is it?

JESÚS. Strawberry.

BOY. My mum never made me a cake.

JESÚS. I'll start lighting the candles.

PAULINA. Let's party.

CABRÓN. What the hell made you come here and start a party, Jesús?

PAULINA. Cabrón, what did you want most when you were a child?

BOY. Where's your mum?

CABRÓN. Far away, like yours.

PAULINA. You haven't answered.

JESÚS. What did you used to want?

CABRÓN. Nothing.

JESÚS. We all dreamt of something when we were kids.

CABRÓN. I didn't.

BOY. Me neither.

CABRÓN. No one asked you.

BOY. I'd like to be lots of things when I grow up, but real things.

PAULINA. You haven't answered; what did you want most when you were small?

JESÚS. Come on – think.

CABRÓN. I never dreamed.

PAULINA. Don't say that.

JESÚS. Not even I say that and things have been worse for me.

CABRÓN. I barely dream at all these days.

BOY. I don't believe you.

JESÚS. Nor do I.

CABRÓN. I dunno.

BOY. Something.

CABRÓN. Nothing.

JESÚS. Nothing?

CABRÓN: I wanted money.

JESÚS. Something else.

CABRÓN. I always wanted to have money.

PAULINA. What for?

JESÚS. We all dreamt of that.

PAULINA. I understand you want money.

BOY. Something else.

PAULINA. But since you were a boy?

CABRÓN. I wanted to have money.

BOY. Something real.

JESÚS. You have to surprise us.

SHOP ASSISTANT. Sorry for interrupting, but I used to dream of that, too.

CABRÓN. A kite.

JESÚS. A kite?

PAULINA. A kite?

SHOP ASSISTANT. What?

BOY. One that flies.

PAULINA. You were very poor.

JESÚS. I don't believe you.

CABRÓN. A kite.

JESÚS. Something else.

CABRÓN. I always really liked them . . .

BOY. My mum showed me how to make them . . .

CABRÓN. Yeah, but my mum never abandoned me.

Pause.

JESÚS. Let's light the candles!

PAULINA *and* JESÚS *sing, joined later by the* BOY. *The* SHOP ASSISTANT *joins in:*

[(*In Spanish.*) 'Happy birthday to you . . .'

CABRÓN. It's better in English.

ALL (*except* CABRÓN, *singing in English*).]*
  'Happy birthday to you,
  Happy birthday to you,
  Happy birthday, dear Cabrón,
  Happy birthday to you!'

JESÚS. Blow them out; blow them out.

PAULINA. Blow out the candles.

CABRÓN *blows out the candles. Applause.*

JESÚS. Now cut it.

CABRÓN. This is ridiculous.

PAULINA. We want cake.

JESÚS. Cut it.

CABRÓN. I've never had a birthday party before.

SHOP ASSISTANT. There's always a first time.

---

* *As in Scene One, this section is included for completeness, but is probably best cut for an English-language performance as its meaning is lost.*

BOY. Will you put my piercing in?

JESÚS. Not yet. In a bit.

> CABRÓN *cuts the cake*. PAULINA *puts the slices onto plates and hands them out. Long silence.*

SHOP ASSISTANT. I'll get the coffees. Courtesy of Seven-Eleven.

JESÚS. I brought wine.

He uncorks a bottle and serves glasses.

SHOP ASSISTANT. You can't consume food or drink from outside.

PAULINA. Don't be like that.

SHOP ASSISTANT. All right, anything goes today.

JESÚS (*to the* BOY). Don't eat it yet; not till we've had a toast.

CABRÓN. This is stupid.

PAULINA. What's wrong with it?

BOY. Can you put my piercing in?

JESÚS. Not just now.

PAULINA. My condolences, Jesús; I am sorry.

JESÚS. Did you tell her?

CABRÓN. No.

JESÚS. So how . . . ?

PAULINA. We're like a family.

BOY. I don't want to – well, yes – it was his mum.

JESÚS. She wasn't my mum.

CABRÓN. Can you not keep quiet?

JESÚS. Let's have a toast and then talk, all right?

CABRÓN. A toast, Paulina.

SHOP ASSISTANT. Who died?

CABRÓN. No one; they're joking.

He raises his glass and waits for the others to join him. They toast. A silence that no one dares break. They each eat their cake until they have none left.

JESÚS. Cheers for tomorrow.

PAULINA. Cheers.

CABRÓN (*to the* BOY). You not saying 'cheers'?

BOY. Yes.

SHOP ASSISTANT. Isn't it cold?

CABRÓN. You should close up for the party.

SHOP ASSISTANT. No, I shouldn't. It's twenty-four hours.

Scene Fourteen

Seven-Eleven, morning. CABRÓN *outside, on the phone.*

CABRÓN (*on the phone*). You'll receive instructions by telephone; we'll have the whole area watched, so no funny business . . . Eleven-oh-seven a.m.; don't forget. A black briefcase and a tracksuit. (*Hangs up.*)

The BOY *passes hot dogs through the scanner while* CABRÓN *approaches the* SHOP ASSISTANT.

How do you expect the customers to find them when you don't stack them properly?

SHOP ASSISTANT. They let us give the place our own personal touch.

BOY. What else shall we take?

PAULINA. This is plenty.

CABRÓN (*to the* SHOP ASSISTANT). You ought to keep everything in order.

BOY. We'll get hungry later on.

PAULINA. Why do you want so much?

BOY. I want more hot dogs. (*Goes over to make up some more.*)

CABRÓN (*to the* SHOP ASSISTANT). Give me one strawberry flavour and one grapefruit.

BOY. We need lots of energy.

SHOP ASSISTANT. These ones are new. They come out better.

PAULINA. Why are you taking so many?

BOY. And some popcorn?

PAULINA. Cabrón hasn't got a microwave.

BOY. Course he has.

PAULINA. Where did you see it?

BOY. I don't believe Cabrón doesn't have a microwave. Anyway I want to put them through the scanner and when we get back you won't be there.

PAULINA. No one's ever given you a good slap.

CABRÓN *comes over to* PAULINA *and the* BOY *at the checkout.*

CABRÓN. And these too. (*Puts the juices on the table.*)

SHOP ASSISTANT. Is that everything?

CABRÓN. Yes.

SHOP ASSISTANT. Four-two-five.

CABRÓN (*to* PAULINA). You pay. I left my money in the house.

SHOP ASSISTANT. Don't you want any chocolates?

BOY. Yeah. (*Takes some.*)

SHOP ASSISTANT. For the cold.

BOY. Have you not got a microwave?

CABRÓN. No.

PAULINA. Told you.

BOY. Butt out.

SHOP ASSISTANT. Four-fifty.

PAULINA (*paying*). There you are.

BOY. What shall we do now?

CABRÓN. We're gonna wait for him.

SHOP ASSISTANT. It was a nice party last night.

PAULINA. It tired me out. I couldn't sleep.

SHOP ASSISTANT. And what are you going to do today to celebrate your birthday?

CABRÓN. Buy a plane ticket.

SHOP ASSISTANT. How exciting!

They go to the fast-food section and sit down.

CABRÓN. Are you clear on everything?

BOY. I'm not stupid.

CABRÓN. One slip-up and we're dead meat. He's late.

BOY. He said he'd put my piercing in.

PAULINA. I'm nervous.

CABRÓN. You don't have to do anything.

BOY. Can I eat a hot dog?

CABRÓN. Go ahead. It's yours. (*To* PAULINA.) Do you think he'll have all the money?

PAULINA. Of course he will.

CABRÓN. There's an hour to go and he's not here.

BOY. She told me it was a shame she wasn't staying with you.

PAULINA. I'm not going to argue with you.

BOY. Me neither.

CABRÓN. Don't you wanna hot dog?

PAULINA (*wringing her hands*). Doing things like this at my age.

CABRÓN (*referring to the hot dogs*). I love them. He's been ages.

BOY. This is exciting!

Silence. CABRÓN *and the* BOY *finish their hot dogs. The* BOY *looks through the window.*

A kite!

CABRÓN. One of the ugly kind.

BOY. It's a good flyer.

CABRÓN. The first thing in my life I ever stole was a kite.

BOY. Why? They're dead easy to make.

CABRÓN. I never learnt; it was easier to steal one.

BOY. I'll teach you.

CABRÓN. I liked feeling as though I was flying; now I think life's like that: if you don't put up a fight the wind can tear you to pieces. What can have happened to him? He should be here by now.

PAULINA. It's late.

CABRÓN (*to the* BOY). Let's go.

PAULINA. Are you going on your own with the boy?

CABRÓN. What are you so scared of?

PAULINA. Please, do be careful.

BOY. We'll be all right.

PAULINA. It's dangerous.

CABRÓN. Don't worry; it'll be fine.

PAULINA. What time do I have to surface?

CABRÓN. After two. Say that we treated you well. So they say we were good kidnappers.

PAULINA. I'll wait for your postcards, Cabrón.

CABRÓN. One day I'll kidnap you for real and take you to the States.

PAULINA. You're mad, really. It was the best fuck. (*In* CABRÓN*'s ear.*) Give me my ring?

CABRÓN. Let him get you a new one.

PAULINA. Seriously?

CABRÓN. I didn't keep your finger.

PAULINA. You stole something else from me. Good luck, Cabrón.

CABRÓN. Don't say goodbye yet. Wait till I've got the money and I'll give you your cut.

PAULINA. Keep it; you earned it.

CABRÓN. Really? (*Kisses her.*) Angel, thanks for everything.

PAULINA. Good luck, Cabrón.

CABRÓN. I don't wanna be Cabrón any more.

PAULINA. Have you ever flown before?

CABRÓN. You taught me.

PAULINA. Goodbye.

BOY. There's Jesús.

He watches JESÚS. CABRÓN *and the* BOY *leave.* PAULINA *sits deep in thought. She calls the* SHOP ASSISTANT *over.*

PAULINA. Do you sell hand-cream?

SHOP ASSISTANT. I can lend you some.

PAULINA. Thanks.

SHOP ASSISTANT. Is he your boyfriend?

PAULINA. My nephew. Don't I have ugly hands?

SHOP ASSISTANT. I don't think so.

PAULINA. They show my age. And with this cold . . .

SHOP ASSISTANT. He's very attractive.

PAULINA. Do you think?

SHOP ASSISTANT. But I'm a mother.

> PAULINA *is silent*.

> It wouldn't be right to . . . Are you feeling all right?

PAULINA. You should hire him one day.

SHOP ASSISTANT. Is he very expensive?

PAULINA. He's worth it.

Scene Fifteen

By the ticket office and gates of a metro station. Coming up the stairs.

JESÚS. I'm sure they saw you. I saw the guy's face when he realised you were picking up the briefcase.

CABRÓN. You're imagining things. Walk.

BOY. You're going very fast.

CABRÓN. We'll get caught. Walk.

JESÚS. I wanna throw up.

CABRÓN. So throw up.

BOY. Have you got tickets?

CABRÓN. Careful, there's a guard. Jesús, get the tickets out.

JESÚS. I've none left.

CABRÓN. Idiot!

> *He punches* JESÚS *in the stomach.* JESÚS *doubles up in pain.*

POLICEMAN. Is there a problem?

CABRÓN. No, Officer.

POLICEMAN *(to* JESÚS*)*. Are you feeling all right?

BOY. He's got a really bad stomach ache.

POLICEMAN. Are you sure?

JESÚS. Yes, Officer; it's going off though.

The POLICEMAN *moves away.*

Do you think we're being watched?

CABRÓN. Course we are. They'll stay cool until Paulina surfaces, but then . . .

JESÚS. I've gotta go to the funeral.

BOY. Shall I come with you?

CABRÓN. You're coming with me.

JESÚS. I bought the coffin last night.

CABRÓN *(to the* BOY*)*. Go and buy three tickets.

The BOY *obeys.*

JESÚS. Wood was the cheapest.

CABRÓN. I don't wanna hear it.

JESÚS. So that's the one I bought.

CABRÓN. Sorry. It's the nerves.

JESÚS. He's gotta be taken to his aunt's.

CABRÓN. Tomorrow.

JESÚS. Today. Did you get it all?

CABRÓN. At least a million.

BOY. Lend me for some crisps?

CABRÓN *(to* JESÚS*)*. Lend him ten pesos.

JESÚS. Here.

BOY. I'm gonna buy some crisps. What about my piercing?

JESÚS. Later.

The BOY goes to buy some crisps from a machine.

What now?

CABRÓN. I'm going to the house to remove any traces.

BOY. The machine doesn't work. It ate my money.

CABRÓN. Wait till the Seven-Eleven.

BOY. I want some crisps.

JESÚS. I'll go with him.

JESÚS and the BOY go to the machine. The BOY begins to yell.

BOY. Police!

CABRÓN (*to himself*). Idiot.

BOY. Police!

CABRÓN moves away to avoid being recognised.

JESÚS (*shouts*). Cabrón, get over here!

CABRÓN covers the BOY's mouth and whacks him on the head.

CABRÓN. Shut up, you little fucker!

BOY. It ate my money.

A POLICEMAN appears.

POLICEMAN. What are you doing to him?

CABRÓN. Nothing. The machine ate his money.

POLICEMAN. Why did you hit him?

CABRÓN. People shouldn't shout in stations.

POLICEMAN (*to the* BOY). Are you all right?

BOY. No.

POLICEMAN (*to the* BOY). What's the matter?

BOY. It ate my money.

POLICEMAN (*to the* BOY). Are they mistreating you?

BOY (*hesitating*). No.

POLICEMAN (*to the* BOY). Do you know them?

BOY. They're my uncles.

POLICEMAN. Are you sure? What have you got in that briefcase?

CABRÓN. Exercise clothes. We've been to the park.

POLICEMAN. Can I see?

CABRÓN. Yes, of course.

He opens the briefcase so the POLICEMAN *can check; he finds nothing suspicious.*

POLICEMAN (*gives him a coin*). OK, take this. I'll go and report the machine.

JESÚS, *terrified throughout the scene so far, finally reacts. The* POLICEMAN *leaves.* CABRÓN *laughs.*

JESÚS. I'm gonna smash your face in.

BOY. Want me to start shouting?

JESÚS. We could've been caught thanks to you. I'm not gonna let you put me in danger.

CABRÓN. Stop talking.

JESÚS (*to the* BOY). You never saw anything.

BOY. She was your mum.

CABRÓN. You have to go, Jesús; you can't arrive late.

JESÚS. Get it straight: she was not my mum.

Scene Sixteen

A phone booth in a snow-covered street. PAULINA *comes up to the phone. She dials a number.*

PAULINA. I don't know where I am; they just came here and left me here; I can take a taxi; you can pay for it at that end . . . They let me go as soon as they had the money; I'm fine . . . They just took my ring. I won't be long. I'm on my way.

She hangs up.

Scene Seventeen

A distant landscape: a field covered in snow. A delicate blizzard falls and a few rays of sun break through the dusk. The scene is dominated by the silhouette of a tree with a thick trunk.

JESÚS *and the* BOY *are wrapped up in a somewhat improvised way for such an unexpected winter.* JESÚS *has a kite in his hand.*

JESÚS. I always wanted to learn how to make one.

BOY. It's not hard.

JESÚS. You were up to the Apocalypse, right?

BOY. What?

JESÚS. When me and Cabrón got there.

BOY. Yeah, something like that. Ap-oc-a . . .

JESÚS. That piercing looks good on you.

BOY. Thanks. Weren't you scared of her?

JESÚS. The old woman? Yeah. But the best bit came after.

> JESÚS *stuffs a handkerchief into the* BOY*'s mouth as he holds him down to tie his hands and feet, takes out another*

piece of rope, ties one end around the BOY*'s neck and tightens it. The blizzard ends.*

JESÚS *takes the other end of the rope and ties it to the tree trunk, leaving the* BOY *like a dog tied to a post. He leaves. He comes back moments later with the kite and puts it in the* BOY*'s hands. He pulls the other end of the rope that the* BOY *has around his neck. The* BOY *begins to hit him before gradually falling motionless.*

Scene Eighteen

The Seven-Eleven. Night. JESÚS *throws a bottle of beer against the refrigerator.*

SHOP ASSISTANT. You can't do that.

CABRÓN. You're on camera.

SHOP ASSISTANT. You're disturbing public order.

JESÚS (*throws something else*). This is my public order.

CABRÓN. Sit down.

JESÚS *goes to the fridges, takes out more beers and starts throwing them.*

SHOP ASSISTANT. I shall call the police.

JESÚS. Call them if you want.

CABRÓN. No, wait, I'll pay for the damage. (*To* JESÚS.) Idiot.

SHOP ASSISTANT. He's destroying everything.

JESÚS. You're a fucking cowardly piece of shit!

CABRÓN *hits* JESÚS *in the face.*

CABRÓN. Are you gonna calm down or what?

JESÚS *is stunned by the blow, but carries on.*

JESÚS (*shouting at* CABRÓN). You never stopped me. And that's not the worst of it; the worst is that you didn't even do it yourself. The worst of it is that you did nothing.

CABRÓN. It was your job. Not mine.

JESÚS. You're a piece of shit; you've never had the guts to do anything.

CABRÓN *stops. He looks at* JESÚS *and hurls himself at him to punch him in the face, the chest and the abdomen.* JESÚS *falls doubled up to the floor.* CABRÓN *grabs him by the hair, lifts his head and hits* JESÚS *several times in the face.*

CABRÓN. Freedom is a prize. (*Punch.*) And you had to win it with your own hands. (*Punch.*) And being free hurts.

CABRÓN *leaves* JESÚS *lying on the floor.*

You're not getting a cent out of me.

The SHOP ASSISTANT *approaches.*

SHOP ASSISTANT. You hit him too hard. It wasn't worth that.

CABRÓN. I'll help you tidy up.

SHOP ASSISTANT. Don't trouble yourself.

CABRÓN. As a favour. You didn't call anyone?

SHOP ASSISTANT. No.

CABRÓN. Let's close up, so no one can come in.

SHOP ASSISTANT. What's wrong with you? It's twenty-four hours.

CABRÓN. I'll pay for the damage.

SHOP ASSISTANT. The supervisor might come.

CABRÓN. No one's gonna come at this time of night.

SHOP ASSISTANT. You broke lots of things.

CABRÓN. Close up. We'll do an inventory.

SHOP ASSISTANT. All right, I'll close up, but I'll still need to stay until the end of the day.

CABRÓN. When I own a Seven-Eleven I'll give you a job.

JESÚS *cries with rage on the floor, doubled up in pain from the beatings to his face. He dares say nothing. The* SHOP ASSISTANT *closes the door of the Seven-Eleven.*

SHOP ASSISTANT. We have to count quickly, before anyone notices. (*Pause.*) You see: it's snowing again.

CABRÓN. I can't believe it. I didn't think it'd snow any more.

SHOP ASSISTANT. It looks thicker than last time.

CABRÓN. Yeah, looks like it.

SHOP ASSISTANT. Let's go outside. It isn't wet.

CABRÓN. Please, don't open the door.

SHOP ASSISTANT. Let's go out into the snow.

CABRÓN. Don't. I'm gonna count the rum bottles.

SHOP ASSISTANT. I'll buy us some coffees.

CABRÓN. Decaff for me, please.

The SHOP ASSISTANT *serves coffees.*

(*To* JESÚS.) Want something?

SHOP ASSISTANT. We sell painkillers. Do you want one?

JESÚS *does not respond.*

CABRÓN. Don't give him anything.

SHOP ASSISTANT. Here's your coffee.

CABRÓN. I'll buy us some biscuits; put them on the list of damages.

The SHOP ASSISTANT *joins* CABRÓN *by the window. Pause.*

SHOP ASSISTANT. It doesn't scare me as much as before. When it snows, people get . . .

CABRÓN. Nervous?

SHOP ASSISTANT. No. Warm. I like that.

CABRÓN. Do you reckon?

SHOP ASSISTANT. What I don't like is the colours dying away.

CABRÓN. I don't like them cancelling flights.

SHOP ASSISTANT. Pardon?

CABRÓN. No one can go out or come in.

SHOP ASSISTANT. Security.

CABRÓN. We're not prepared. They closed the airport.

JESÚS (*recovering and joining them*). Kites don't fly when it snows.

CABRÓN. The airport's covered in snow.

JESÚS. So's the kid.

SHOP ASSISTANT. Could you lend me your phone? I need to call home.

CABRÓN *gives her his phone. The* SHOP ASSISTANT *goes to the counter to make the call.*

JESÚS. He tricked us; he didn't know how to fly a kite.

CABRÓN. What d'you say about the kid?

JESÚS. That he's covered in snow.

CABRÓN. Where is he?

JESÚS. I hope it snows more.

CABRÓN. Fucking lunatic. (*Paces.*)

SHOP ASSISTANT (*referring to the phone*). What a lovely screensaver!

CABRÓN. Gimme the phone.

SHOP ASSISTANT. It has a camera, doesn't it? Shall I take your picture?

CABRÓN *snatches back the phone.*

JESÚS. Tell me I did the right thing.

SHOP ASSISTANT. I'm going to count the broken bottles.

JESÚS. Tell me it was for the best.

CABRÓN. Idiot. You killed a child, don't you realise?

JESÚS. You taught me how.

CABRÓN. Goodbye.

JESÚS. What am I gonna do?

CABRÓN. Live.

JESÚS. They found the note I left on the door the first day.

CABRÓN. Throw another beer; I'll pay for it.

JESÚS. Fuck off! (*He throws some beer bottles at the refrigerator*). Go to hell.

CABRÓN (*to the* SHOP ASSISTANT). Open the door.

SHOP ASSISTANT. Your friend's a lunatic.

CABRÓN. Not really. Close the door, please.

The SHOP ASSISTANT *closes the door.*

SHOP ASSISTANT. Just for you.

CABRÓN *sits down to finish his hot dog. He picks up a newspaper and reads. He begins to laugh.*

CABRÓN. 'Boy rescued unconscious from the snow . . . with strangulation marks from a kite-string . . . He is expected to recover in hospital . . . ' (*Laughs.*)

SHOP ASSISTANT. Is that the boy who was with you? Are you a relative?

CABRÓN. The woman I was with was.

SHOP ASSISTANT. Wasn't he her son? (*Pause.*) Nothing's safe in this city.

CABRÓN. We're not responsible for the things we leave unfinished.

SHOP ASSISTANT. What did you say?

CABRÓN. I said I'm going to count the broken bottles.

They count up the damages.

SHOP ASSISTANT. Do you charge very much?

CABRÓN. Are you asking for yourself?

SHOP ASSISTANT. For a friend.

CABRÓN. A fortune.

SHOP ASSISTANT. I'm just curious.

CABRÓN. Tell her it's a hundred dollars minimum.

SHOP ASSISTANT. That much?

CABRÓN. How much did you expect?

SHOP ASSISTANT. I've no idea. I have two children.

CABRÓN. What's that got to with it?

SHOP ASSISTANT. Do you think that I . . . ?

CABRÓN. Why not?

SHOP ASSISTANT. The lady who was with you sent me some flowers and a cheque. Have you some time this week?

CABRÓN. I'm doing nothing till they open the airport.

SHOP ASSISTANT. I don't want to put you out, but the card from the lady said she'd buy me a night with you, and there'd even be money to spare.

CABRÓN. Let's see the cheque.

SHOP ASSISTANT. Are you that expensive?

CABRÓN (*laughs*). You got the wrong person.

SHOP ASSISTANT. You gave me your card.

CABRÓN. You misunderstood. You got the wrong person. You'd best keep the money.

The SHOP ASSISTANT *smiles.*

End.

**THE SÁNCHEZ HUERTA GIRL
KILLED HERSELF**

CLAUDIA RÍOS
translated by
ROXANA SILBERT

Characters

FLORA HUERTA, *the Sánchez Huerta girl's mother*
JUAN SÁNCHEZ, *the Sánchez Huerta girl's father*
BEATRÍZ HUERTA, *the Sánchez Huerta girl's mother's sister*
BERTHA, *the nun*
MOTHER SUPERIOR
GIRL

The Sánchez Huerta Girl Killed Herself (*Sánchez Huerta, se mató la niña*) was first performed in English as a rehearsed reading as part of the *Arena Mexico* season in the Jerwood Theatre Upstairs, Royal Court Theatre, London, on 11 January 2006 with the following cast:

BEATRÍZ HUERTA	Jo McInnes
JUAN SÁNCHEZ	Aaron Neil
FLORA HUERTA	Sandy McDade
HEADMISTRESS	Helen Ryan
BERTHA THE NUN	Linda Bassett

Director Orla O'Loughlin

One

A boarding-school classroom, at dawn: desks, a dais, a blackboard, a teacher's desk and, beside this, a large cupboard. The walls are green and dirty, there's only a thin row of windows running along the top.

Half-light. It is raining heavily. At one of the desks sits a woman in her forties, FLORA, *dressed in outdoor clothes. Visibly upset, she is crying, with her arms wrapped around the desk.*

She gets up, leans against the wall, howls, approaches the blackboard, takes a piece of chalk and writes: EVA ALICIA SÁNCHEZ HUERTA. *She steps away from the blackboard, looks at the name and crosses it out, sits on the edge of the dais and cries. Returns to the board, attempts to erase it with the board rubber, but the name remains there, still visible. She tries unsuccessfully to clean it off with her spit. She walks round and round the classroom, without stopping, getting faster and faster, repeating all the while:*

FLORA. E.V.A. A.L.I.C.I.A. S.Á.N.C.H.E.Z. H.U.E.R.T.A.

Silence.

She hurries back to the desk, stares at the name and repeats it slowly.

Two

In the morning.

The room is lit by artificial lights. A school bell rings loudly to signal the start of classes. Students are shouting in the distance. The classroom door opens slowly, and a woman dressed in black enters. It is FLORA's *younger sister,* BEATRÍZ. *She stands in the doorway.*

She goes and sits at the teacher's desk. She looks around. She stands in front of the blackboard, looks at the name: the writing is still visible.

Pause. BEATRÍZ *cries. She looks through the desks, inspecting them. Finds Eva Alicia's.*

BEATRÍZ. This is horrible. This is horrible.

She takes out a lipstick from her bag, touches up her make-up and puts it back.

There.

She sits at a desk, takes out a comb and tidies her hair.

There is a knock at the door. BEATRÍZ *starts. The door opens. A man enters:* JUAN, *almost in his fifties, nearly bald, formally dressed, wearing a black necktie and carrying a small suitcase. He is soaking wet.*

Ah!

JUAN (*surprised; after a pause*). You look just like your mother.

BEATRÍZ. My mother?

JUAN. Yes, you look just like your mother.

BEATRÍZ. How odd –

She goes up to JUAN *and greets him coldly. Silence.*

So, when – ?

JUAN. It's late – late. Your sister?

BEATRÍZ. Flora?

JUAN. I should have already left.

BEATRÍZ. Oh – Didn't you want to come?

JUAN (*laughs*). This is horrible. No. I got scared – on the plane. I don't know, I don't even know what she was like? (*Pause.*) What was she like?

BEATRÍZ. Very pretty.

JUAN. Yes, she was gorgeous, wasn't she?

BEATRÍZ. Why do you say that?! That's a strange way to put it.

JUAN. Hey! Don't get me wrong!

Silence.

BEATRÍZ. Eva Alicia. Like all girls. Tall and gangly . . . I never knew you cared.

JUAN. I called whenever I could.

Pause.

BEATRÍZ. Yes.

JUAN. She didn't like me, that was always clear. She didn't laugh with me. Strange.

BEATRÍZ. When was the last time?

JUAN. I don't know, she was like so high. (*Demonstrates a certain height with his hand.*)

BEATRÍZ. Oh. So it was a while ago then.

JUAN. Yes. (*Pause.*) Your mother died, didn't she?

BEATRÍZ. A while ago. Her too; she died too.

JUAN. I haven't been able to cry. I can't. Maybe now, seeing the other girls.

BEATRÍZ. I've cried a lot.

JUAN. It's exhausting.

BEATRÍZ. Are you tired?

JUAN. No.

BEATRÍZ. Oh.

JUAN. And your sister?

BEATRÍZ. Flora? In the Mother Superior's office, I think.

JUAN. Do they know anything?

BEATRÍZ. I don't think so. I don't know.

JUAN. I should have already left . . . Sorry, but no, I need to cry, I don't know, that's all right, isn't it? It's how things should be. (*Pause.*) Guilty. Sort of lost. But mostly guilty.

BEATRÍZ. It doesn't help.

JUAN. I hadn't seen her for ages, not since she was so high. (*Illustrates*.) She never loved me. I got annoyed. I didn't know what to talk to her about. I would call her and I didn't know what to talk about.

Silence.

BEATRÍZ. She got straight 'A's.

JUAN. Did she?

BEATRÍZ. Yes.

JUAN. Did she have friends?

BEATRÍZ. Seems so, but I haven't seen any of them crying.

JUAN. Did they find anything? And your sister? It's strange. They sent me here. The nuns are strange. I sound like an idiot. And Flora? Did they find anything?

BEATRÍZ. Nothing.

JUAN. Look.

BEATRÍZ. What?

JUAN. Nothing, nothing. A silly thing, an image.

BEATRÍZ. What?

JUAN. Flora, I don't know, a photo of Flora, of your sister Flora, when she was Eva Alicia's age. She looked, sort of . . .

BEATRÍZ. Dead?

JUAN (*pause*). You look a lot like your mother. How are you? Are you single? Are you still single?

BEATRÍZ (*pause*). None of your business . . . you feel guilty?

JUAN. Walking out's no fun, it was hard for me too.

BEATRÍZ. Oh. (*Pause.*) I thought that . . .

JUAN. What?

BEATRÍZ. Nothing. Got my wires crossed again.

Pause. JUAN *walks around the classroom and reads Eva Alicia's name on the blackboard.*

JUAN. Who wrote that?

BEATRÍZ. It was there when I got here.

JUAN. It's horrible in here. (*Pause.*) I've never liked classrooms.

BEATRÍZ. Yes, that's obvious. (*Laughs.*)

JUAN. Which one was her desk?

BEATRÍZ *points to one.*

This one?

JUAN *approaches and opens it.*

Exercise books, textbooks . . . (*Smells it.*) It doesn't smell.

BEATRÍZ (*looks at him*). As if she'd never been here. As if.

JUAN. None of this is my fault. Only leaving.

BEATRÍZ. Only . . . So just go, go then.

JUAN. I'm her father.

BEATRÍZ *laughs. Silence.*

BEATRÍZ. These days kids are doing it with Drain-o.

JUAN. What?

BEATRÍZ. These days. Kids. They're doing it with Drain-o.

JUAN. Doing what?

BEATRÍZ. Nothing.

JUAN. What's Drain-o?

BEATRÍZ. Nothing.

JUAN. You've lost me.

A nun, BERTHA, *opens the door, sees them and closes it again. They both turn round.*

BEATRÍZ. Have you seen Flora yet?

JUAN. No. I only just heard. I arrived, and they sent me here.

BEATRÍZ. Ah.

JUAN. What's Drain-o?

BEATRÍZ (*barely audible*). It unblocks pipes.

JUAN. None of it makes sense. Have any of her little friends said anything? I can't fucking cry.

BEATRÍZ. They probably don't know anything.

JUAN (*pause*). Drain-o – ? What are they doing with stuff for unblocking pipes?

Silence.

BEATRÍZ. Who called you?

JUAN. Your sister, Rebecca. She called me and said, 'See – ? I told you.' I didn't understand, I didn't know if she wanted to tell me or upset me –

BEATRÍZ. 'I told you.' Why did she say that?

JUAN. I don't know; you're all mad, the lot of you. (*Pause.*) Why do you wear the same make-up as your mother? You wear the same make-up as your mother, don't you?

BEATRÍZ *keeps her eyes on him while opening the door. She turns to look at him resentfully.*

Your sister never . . . never. Depressions. Shouting. She was always accusing me of I never knew what –

BEATRÍZ. And you? What did you do?

JUAN. Nothing. It just ended, that's all.

BEATRÍZ (*pause*). All parents should protect their children.

JUAN. Yes, but . . . you're all mad, all of you.

BEATRÍZ. Yes. And just look what happened. Nothing to do with you, right?

JUAN. What happened?

BEATRÍZ. Let my sister tell you when she comes.

The nun, BERTHA, *opens the door again.*

BERTHA (*to* BEATRÍZ). Are you Flora?

JUAN. Do we have to come now?

BERTHA. No. (*To* BEATRÍZ.) Are you Eva Alicia's mother?

BEATRÍZ. No, Sister, I think she's with the Mother Superior.

BERTHA *closes the door.*

JUAN. They didn't even let me see her. Eva Alicia, or your sister. I'm shaking. That's what you're all like . . . Do you know . . . something?

BEATRÍZ. I'm not allowed to say. (*Pause.*) Even if we are all mad . . . (*Pause.*) God bless you. Poor you.

JUAN. What?

A school bell rings, very loudly. There's a lot of hustle and bustle outside. GIRLS *are heard shouting and running about.*

BEATRÍZ. They didn't have schools like this there.

JUAN. Where?

BEATRÍZ. In Veracruz. There weren't any schools like this.

JUAN. Your sister told me that once. I don't really know, I don't know, she never talked about those times.

BEATRÍZ (*pause*). She'd have done the same thing, wouldn't she?

JUAN. What?

BEATRÍZ. Nothing, let Flora tell you . . . Sorry.

JUAN (*pause*). Did you really never talk about it?

BEATRÍZ. She just . . . The only thing she remembers is that you walked out. Leaving her with the load . . . Sorry. (*Looks at the blackboard.*) Sorry, Eva Alicia.

JUAN. Who are you talking to? Did she really never . . . ?

A tense silence falls.

BEATRÍZ. Children have the right idea, killing themselves –

JUAN. What?

BEATRÍZ. Nothing.

Silence.

JUAN. When I arrived at the airport, at dawn, on my way down through the car park I saw a boy lying in a corner, a street kid, with his trousers pulled down and his chewing-gum strewn all over the floor. He was howling like a –

Suddenly BEATRÍZ starts to punch and kick JUAN uncontrollably. He stops her by hugging her tightly. She calms down. The nun, BERTHA, opens the door, sees them and closes it again. BEATRÍZ composes herself and sits at a desk.

BEATRÍZ. I'm sorry, I'm sorry, I'm sorry . . .

JUAN. It's OK, relax.

BEATRÍZ. I'm sorry. I hurt you . . .

JUAN. Don't worry.

BEATRÍZ. It's all so horrible, I'm sorry. Eva Alicia, Veracruz, Flora, this place – all of it.

Pause. She looks at JUAN intensely; he goes to the door, opens it, stands looking out into the corridors.

JUAN (*to* BEATRÍZ). Wasn't there a better place to send Eva? It's not as if your family were ever very religious.

BEATRÍZ. I don't know, ask Flora – Sorry . . . I think it was because there's a canteen here or something. But I don't know, I think that might be why, because we never were really like that, maybe that's why it occurred to her –

JUAN. Just look at it – I didn't think schools like this existed any more . . . Maybe it was because –

BEATRÍZ. Maybe . . . (*Leaving.*) I'm sorry, all this must be, maybe –

JUAN. Go and calm yourself down –

BEATRÍZ. No, I'm fine now. It's fine. It's over.

The nun, BERTHA, opens the door.

BERTHA. Are you Mr Huerta? (JUAN *nods*.) Come with me, please.

JUAN. It's now, is it, Sister? Where's Flora?

BERTHA. The Police want to see you.

JUAN *goes out.* BEATRÍZ *slides down the door and slumps onto the floor. Leaning back on the door, she bites her nails as if she were seven years old. A* WOMAN *is heard over a loudspeaker ordering the* GIRLS *to line up. Shortly afterwards, the same* WOMAN *is heard over the loudspeaker leading a Rosary. Soon after this begins,* BEATRÍZ *repeats the 'Hail Mary' as if hypnotised; she is about to start an 'Our Father' when there is a knock at the door.*

FLORA. Let me in.

BEATRÍZ *stands up and opens the door. She tries to hug* FLORA *but is gently pushed away.*

BEATRÍZ. I'm sorry. (*After a pause*.) What happened? (*Pause*.) I brought you some clothes – so you can – change. (*Pause*.) I love you very much.

FLORA. She looked very pretty, didn't she – ? And straight 'A's, straight 'A's . . . they told me we should . . . wait here.

BEATRÍZ. What about Eva Alicia?

FLORA. The body?

Silence.

BEATRÍZ. Juan's here, have you seen him?

FLORA *shakes her head.*

He just went out . . . he's bald . . .

FLORA *laughs.*

Do you want a coffee? Do you want me to get you a coffee?

FLORA *shakes her head again.*

FLORA. I was thinking . . . nothing . . . Afterwards . . . No, I don't want a coffee. So you've already seen Juan – ? I haven't seen him . . . I haven't seen him for a long time.

BEATRÍZ. What time did you get here?

Silence.

FLORA (*barely audible*). About . . . I don't know . . . about . . . about three or four hours ago.

BEATRÍZ. I've only just arrived. Didn't you see Juan . . . ? A nun came in and called him to go and see . . . the police.

FLORA. The police . . . They must have some more questions.

BEATRÍZ. They must . . . It's horrible here. Doesn't it remind you . . . ?

FLORA. Did you bring the papers I asked for?

BEATRÍZ *nods, goes to the teacher's desk where she has left her bag and takes out a folder. She gives it to* FLORA.

It's a bad photo, isn't it? (*Pause.*) Sorry, I'm . . . Are the girls coming, then? Have you seen them? Are they crying much?

BEATRÍZ. I didn't see . . . anyone crying . . . Perhaps they don't even know – but no one, no one is crying. Well, I just walked through, I was with the nun, sorry, I didn't mean that no one . . . I just walked through, that's all, to the Mother Superior's office.

FLORA. Her neck is all . . . Poor little thing . . .

BEATRÍZ *hugs her tightly.* FLORA *gently pushes her away.*

BEATRÍZ. Do you know why?

FLORA. No . . . and now her father . . .

BEATRÍZ. Her classmates are in the laboratory, maybe one of them will want to . . . They won't be long, they told me, but we will have to wait, well, I'll wait here with you. (*Pause.*) Hasn't he already gone? He'd even said goodbye to me. I hadn't seen him for years. He's put on weight. Lost his hair. It's funny. He used to be handsome. I remember the two of you. No one thought.

FLORA. No. No one. (*Pause.*) I collected her things, Eva Alicia's. I went through all her things at dawn. She was tidy. I didn't know. Very tidy. All 'A's. Just one 'B'. Straight 'A's. Her pencils had hardly any lead left. She used them up. She didn't lose them. She used them up. Lots of colour in her exercise books . . . Juan's coming, did I tell you?

BEATRÍZ. Flora – Juan's already here –

FLORA. Who told him?

BEATRÍZ. How are you?

FLORA. Destroyed . . . I just . . . I don't understand.

BEATRÍZ. Eva Alicia –

FLORA. This school is perfect . . . The idea was that nothing would happen to her here . . . !

BEATRÍZ. Why?

FLORA. What?

BEATRÍZ. What could have happened to her?

Silence.

Let's see –

FLORA. What?

BEATRÍZ. Her exercise books.

FLORA. No . . . ! Don't get anything out. There's no point.

BEATRÍZ *goes to Eva Alicia's desk and as she looks though its contents:*

BEATRÍZ. What are you going to do with all of this? With it all?

FLORA. She got straight 'A's and . . . it's not fair . . .

BEATRÍZ. Don't say those things. I don't understand . . . She was . . . perfect . . .

FLORA. Do you think I'll need a lawyer?

BEATRÍZ. No – I don't think so . . . What for . . . ?

FLORA (*pause*). Isn't this room horrible . . . ? She didn't leave me anything . . .

BEATRÍZ. What?

FLORA. A short message – nothing.

BEATRÍZ. They asked me – out there – why you hardly ever . . .

FLORA. Visited? I did visit! And we went out for lunch and everyone loved her and she was pretty and . . . She had no problems! (*Pause.*) I can't breathe in this room . . .

BEATRÍZ (*pause*). The tiles in the kitchen –

FLORA *looks at her.*

– they were sort of tarnished. I used to look at them in the evenings. I counted every single tile. I used to stay in there for hours. (*Pause.*) They used to lock me in . . .

FLORA. What are you talking about?

BEATRÍZ. They left me locked inside, like dogs people lock up in their bathrooms. Mother. Mother, before going out, she'd lock me up. After you two had already left. She put a padlock on the kitchen door. Remember?

FLORA. I'd already left by then . . . No, I don't remember anything, Beatríz.

BEATRÍZ. Funny. No one remembers . . .

FLORA (*after a pause*). No message, not even a few words. Nothing. She didn't leave anything.

BEATRÍZ. Have you been through everything?

FLORA. Straight 'A's.

BEATRÍZ (*pause*). Why do you never remember anything?

FLORA. What do you want me to remember?

BEATRÍZ. Everything. The things I don't know about. (*Pause.*) Why did Mother lock you up? And Rebecca, her too. (*Pause.*) Have you heard from her? Did she call you?

FLORA. Rebecca? What on earth would she call for?!

BEATRÍZ. I told her, I swear. I spoke to her. I don't know. Well, she asked me what had happened, I didn't want to tell her. It's not my place to. (*Pause.*) She's got problems.

FLORA. She's always got problems.

BEATRÍZ. No, she didn't complain about anything. She didn't say anything. I could just hear . . . in her voice.

FLORA. I never liked her either . . . (*Cries.*)

BEATRÍZ. Did you never like me either?

FLORA. This isn't the time.

BEATRÍZ. Why have you never loved me?

FLORA. What?

BEATRÍZ. Why do you always act as though you don't love anyone?

FLORA. This boarding school is perfect! It has gardens, a canteen and even a –

BEATRÍZ. Why do you always act as though you don't love anyone?

FLORA. – projection room and a . . . with . . . with . . . (*Looks with profound sadness at* BEATRÍZ.) Don't I love you?

BEATRÍZ. Sorry. Do you want to talk about something else? Hmm? Shall we talk about something else? What do you want to talk about?

Silence.

It's just . . . If Rebecca – she was the eldest – she should have protected us . . . That was her job.

FLORA. She can go to hell and burn . . . I don't want to talk about this. Honestly, another day would be better. Another day. (*Long pause.*) It hasn't stopped raining since May – it's like the world's melting.

BEATRÍZ: Yes.

Silence.

For a while now, I've taken to watching the news all the time. Reading the papers . . . staying informed.

FLORA. What for?

BEATRÍZ. I don't know. I don't know. (*Pause*.) Because there's such a lot, I suppose.

FLORA. A lot of what?

BEATRÍZ. News, newspapers, scandals – and all over the world, not just here.

Silence.

Do you like it where you live?

FLORA. I don't know.

BEATRÍZ. It's pretty where you live.

FLORA. A long way away, though.

BEATRÍZ. Yes, it is a long way.

Long silence. BEATRÍZ *wanders around the room. She pokes around the other* GIRLS' *things. She opens some exercise books.*

FLORA. Put that down.

BEATRÍZ. It's fun.

FLORA. You're not a little girl any more.

BEATRÍZ. I never was.

She continues rummaging around. She finds a little note. She reads it to FLORA.

Look: 'I glow with love and tenderness for you. And when you wear your white trousers, phwoar!'

The two sisters laugh.

FLORA. And the rest, eh?

BEATRÍZ (*pause*). They should already have . . . Why are they taking so long?

FLORA. I don't know.

BEATRÍZ. I didn't see anyone . . . Have the Forensic Team been?

FLORA. Beatríz, the police are –

BEATRÍZ. I see, sorry, sorry.

FLORA. I don't know if they're still here –

BEATRÍZ (*pause*). Some girls asked me, just now when I went past, 'Are you her aunt?' I said I was and they ran away. They were scared.

FLORA (*pause*). I haven't seen Rebecca since –

BEATRÍZ. Since then. I thought she'd come.

FLORA. Do I look terrible? (*Silence.*) I do, I look terrible. Can I borrow some lipstick? I look horrible. It hasn't stopped raining. I got drenched. In case Juan comes –

BEATRÍZ. Flora, he's already here – I already told you, didn't I? Besides, what are you worried about, he's bald.

FLORA. Well, yes –

BEATRÍZ. OK . . .

She goes to her bag and takes out a bright red lipstick.

Here.

FLORA. Oh, no! It's like Mother's. How awful! You wear this? It's horrible!

BEATRÍZ (*pause*). Sometimes I used to sit next to her, in front of the mirror, really close, right up next to her, and she used to do my make-up, slowly, a bit at a time, first my lips . . . I barely remember. And Dad used to watch us and crease up laughing, standing behind us, watching, and then he'd give me a big bear hug . . . Dad. He'd give me five pesos and a smack on the bum, and I'd go out onto the patio. And I'd stay there, with my bright red lips and five pesos.

FLORA. Why do you still wear the same make-up? Why? You shouldn't keep wearing same make-up!

BEATRÍZ. And they used to look at me lovingly. Do you remember the patio?

FLORA. I don't remember anything, Beatríz, anything.

BEATRÍZ. Yes, you remember! The eldest was the eldest but you were a bit older than me . . . I don't blame you for

anything. I'm here after all. But you were older than me,
I could blame you, too . . . (*Pause.*) Sorry, I'm sorry . . . It's
better for you not to remember anything. Not only that, I'm
going to throw this red lipstick away. Look, I'm throwing it
in the bin.

She goes to a bin and throws the lipstick in.

See? Done. Finished.

Silence.

FLORA. What am I going to do with her things? Her clothes.
All her things.

BEATRÍZ. Well, you can't throw anything away yet. You have
to wait.

FLORA. I used to like the rain. I really did like it. Now it just
irritates me. I've lost the pleasure in watching the rain.

BEATRÍZ. Me too.

FLORA (*pause*). I didn't know. Straight 'A's. Straight 'A's
across the board. 'Just look at that!' I thought, as I looked
over her stuff. It's all such a mess, isn't it? Everything's a
bloody mess.

BEATRÍZ. Uh-huh.

FLORA. This room is ghastly.

BEATRÍZ. Like the kitchen. It's ugly. One day I talked about
everything, with Rebecca, about the kitchen, Mother. Why
didn't Mother do anything?

FLORA. Do what? What should she have done?

Silence.

BEATRÍZ. I go out at night. Walking. I think about how mixed
up it all is. I'm sort of thinking and sort of . . . I don't know.
Something hurts me, and I drink gallons and gallons of coffee.
All on my own. And I try, I really do try to understand. I can't.

FLORA. I thought you wanted to help me through this. If you
want to leave, then leave.

BEATRÍZ. No, sorry . . .

She goes up to FLORA *and strokes her back.*

FLORA. Don't . . . touch me . . .

BEATRÍZ. I'm sorry. (*After a pause.*) Can I say something? I was very cruel, wasn't I? I'm sorry . . . I don't want you to remember now . . . But Mother . . . I was sort of scared of her, can you believe that? And then I think about your daughter, about Eva Alicia . . . I don't know, it's like she's sort of blaming me for something . . . something I couldn't do for her . . .

FLORA. That girl never wanted for anything! She was a happy child, she never wanted for anything and nothing bad ever happened to her! She never wanted for anything!

BEATRÍZ. I'm sorry. I don't understand. I just don't understand, that's all.

FLORA. Don't you have any shame? Evil cow!

She collapses onto the floor.

You evil cow . . .

The MOTHER SUPERIOR, *a woman in her sixties, opens the classroom door. She sees* FLORA *and kneels down beside her.*

MOTHER SUPERIOR. Are you all right? (*To* BEATRÍZ.) Help your sister up . . .

FLORA. Get off me!

MOTHER SUPERIOR. Where's your husband?

BEATRÍZ. He's not her husband any more, Mother.

MOTHER SUPERIOR. Where is Mr Sánchez?

FLORA. I don't want anything any more! Not any more!

BEATRÍZ (*trying to stand her up*). Come on, stand up, the Mother Superior is here –

She kneels down beside FLORA.

FLORA. 'Remember!' You want to know? Everyone wants to know! (*To the* MOTHER SUPERIOR.) You too?

BEATRÍZ. Quiet now!

FLORA. No!

MOTHER SUPERIOR. Where is Mr Sánchez?

BEATRÍZ. Get up!

FLORA. Let's see your mouth . . . My hands used to shake and my stomach would hurt . . .

BEATRÍZ. Be quiet, Flora! (*Takes her hands and looks into her eyes.*) Quiet . . . (*To the* MOTHER SUPERIOR.) You sent for him . . . He went to see you, didn't he? Do you want me to go and look for him?

BEATRÍZ *goes out.*

MOTHER SUPERIOR (*to* FLORA). Madam . . . do you need anything?

FLORA *shakes her head.*

I need . . . to . . . Calm down, calm down, please . . . This . . . it's not only embarrassing, it's . . .

FLORA. You have no right – !

MOTHER SUPERIOR. You have to sign some papers . . . They're ready in my office . . .

FLORA. I don't want to leave here . . . I don't want people to see me . . . Anyway, her things . . .

MOTHER SUPERIOR. I understand.

FLORA. I don't understand, I don't understand, I don't understand . . .

MOTHER SUPERIOR. This has been shocking and painful for all of us. Believe me, I . . .

FLORA. What?

MOTHER SUPERIOR. That a girl like Eva Alicia . . .

FLORA. Took us all by surprise, didn't she?

MOTHER SUPERIOR. Yes . . . a girl you could describe as . . . perfect.

FLORA. Perhaps that was why . . .

MOTHER SUPERIOR. You have to sign some papers. They've already prepared the body. You and the girl's father have to inform us officially if you want the wake to happen here . . .

FLORA. I don't know . . .

MOTHER SUPERIOR (*pause*). Why did you hardly ever visit?

FLORA. Who?

MOTHER SUPERIOR (*after a pause*). Forgive me . . . You've seen her exercise books?

FLORA. Mine used to be the same . . .

MOTHER SUPERIOR. Would you let me have one?

FLORA. I wouldn't know what to do with them . . . Keep them all.

MOTHER SUPERIOR. Have you spoken to Bertha?

FLORA. Who's Bertha?

MOTHER SUPERIOR. Your daughter never mentioned Bertha to you?

FLORA. My daughter is . . . was perfect . . . but she had her own world . . . No . . . she never talked about Bertha.

MOTHER SUPERIOR. Speak to her.

FLORA. What about the girl who found her?

MOTHER SUPERIOR. She's already receiving help. She's . . . in shock.

FLORA. Poor thing . . .

MOTHER SUPERIOR. Her parents came at once.

FLORA. Do you need me to speak to them?

MOTHER SUPERIOR. Why did you never visit?

FLORA. Who?

MOTHER SUPERIOR. Nothing, it's nothing. (*Pause.*) Do you know what happened to your . . . Mr Sánchez?

FLORA. I haven't seen him. He's with the police.

MOTHER SUPERIOR. Right. (*Pause*.) What were you talking about with your sister when I came in?

FLORA. Things that don't concern you . . .

MOTHER SUPERIOR. Very well. I hope you'll leave immediately this is over.

The MOTHER SUPERIOR *exits and slams the door.* FLORA *follows her as far as the door and closes it. She goes to her daughter's desk. She sits down, and as she bangs the desk with her fists:*

FLORA. Go to hell! Go to hell, you evil cow! It's not fair! It's not fair –

She collapses onto the desk. After a moment she gets up. She picks up one of her daughter's exercise books, looks at it lingeringly, kisses it, flicks through it, looks around, tears out a page and places it on a desk as she says:

For you, who never wanted to go to lunch with my daughter –

Throughout the following, she tears page after page out of the book and places one on each desk.

For you, who stood us up on her birthday . . . For you, the leech; for you the millionairess; for you, the swot; for you, whose parents never got divorced; for you, the neat one; for you, the perfect one; for you, the pretty one, for you, with the clean knees; for you, who spent the evenings with your mummy; for you, whose homework got checked over; for you, the slim one; for you, who was properly prepared for her first communion; for you, who never had warts on your little hands; for you, whose parents were normal; for you, who never overheard any arguments; for you, who was never scared in bed at night; for you, who never wondered where your father was; for you, who were never threatened; for you, who never thought, 'Why not me?'; for you, who was never made fun of; for you. For you. For you, evil little bitch. For you, who hasn't cried for my daughter. For you. For you, so that you don't forget her. For you, let's see if you can feel the pain. For you, because you're still alive –

FLORA *sits at Eva Alicia's desk, cries.*

At this moment the nun, BERTHA, *opens the door. She has a letter in her hand. She looks at* FLORA. *She stands in the doorway.*

BERTHA. Mrs Sánchez Huerta?

FLORA. Just 'Huerta', Sister . . .

BERTHA. I'm . . . Bertha . . .

She comes too close to FLORA.

Are you crying? Were you crying?

FLORA. I've good reason to, haven't I?

BERTHA. Yes . . .

FLORA. Anything wrong?

BERTHA. No . . .

FLORA. Who are you?

BERTHA. A nun . . .

FLORA. What do you want?

BERTHA. I wanted to meet you . . .

FLORA. You wanted to meet me?

BERTHA. Yes . . .

FLORA. Why did you want to meet me?

BERTHA. I just . . .

FLORA. Who are you?

BERTHA. What were you thinking?

FLORA. That my daughter's dead . . .

Long silence. BERTHA *continues looking at her.*

What do you want?

BERTHA *does not answer.*

Why are you looking at me like that? Do you want to say something to me?

Silence.

What do you want?

Silence.

What do you want from me? What did she have you for?

BERTHA. What?

FLORA. What subject, stupid?

BERTHA. What does that matter?!

FLORA. What subject did you teach her?

Silence.

Aren't you going to answer me?

BERTHA (*through gritted teeth*). Spanish . . .

FLORA. I didn't hear you.

BERTHA. Spanish.

She takes out the letter and reads it.

'I didn't write this letter, Mum, I never even thought of writing you anything. I don't want to say goodbye to you, I don't care about not saying goodbye to you.

FLORA *goes to* BERTHA *and tries to snatch the letter.*

FLORA. It's from her! Give me that!

BERTHA *does not let her and goes to the other side of the room, where she continues to read.*

BERTHA. 'No one did anything to me. I got tired. There's nothing here. In the evenings. On Sundays – '

FLORA. Give me that!

BERTHA. 'I don't want anyone to cry. I don't want anyone to care. I don't want anything to happen, because I didn't write this, Mummy.'

BERTHA *goes up to* FLORA *and gives her the letter.*

I wrote it.

FLORA (*looks at the letter*). This isn't her handwriting.

BERTHA. I wrote it.

FLORA (*crying*). Why . . . ? Are you out of your mind . . . ? What's wrong with you?

BERTHA. I don't know. I don't know why. Maybe because I did love her, maybe because she was important to me. Maybe because I kind of took it personally. But that's not it, is it? But it can't be helped, can it? The girl just went and killed herself . . .

FLORA *looks at her furiously.*

And I don't even feel like forgiving myself, or asking her forgiveness, or even understanding her.

FLORA. I'm going to report you . . .

BERTHA. Nobody'll believe you . . . Report me.

FLORA (*approaches the nun*). Do you know? (*Silence.*) Tell me . . .

BERTHA. No. I don't know anything. Just that I kind of took it personally . . .

FLORA (*after a pause*). Do you think that I'm . . .

BERTHA. Eva Alicia was like all of our pain, wasn't she – ? Your pain, my pain . . .

FLORA. And what do you know about us?! You don't know a thing. You just go ahead and judge us, from whatever little superficial thing you see. You don't know a thing. I'm going to report you . . .

BERTHA. I loved her very much. (*Pause.*) And now she's not here. Nobody could stop her. She was . . . didn't you realise?

FLORA *is silent, then:*

FLORA. Be quiet!

BERTHA. The last few days . . . she was happy; she touched things and saw things and felt things so intensely . . . She looked us in the eyes as if nothing could surprise her . . . Nothing bothered her, she blended in. She shone . . .

FLORA. I never realised. I never realised.

BERTHA. Thank you. I needed to hear that.

She walks towards the door.

FLORA. Are you leaving already?

BERTHA. Yes. I have a class to teach. And your husband?

FLORA. I don't have a husband any more.

BERTHA. Has he already left? (*Pause*.) Could I steal a cigarette?

FLORA (*goes to her bag and gives her a whole packet*). Keep them . . . I'll buy some more later.

BERTHA. Thanks.

She opens the packet and puts the cigarettes into her jumper.

Maybe now you'll start noticing what's happening more . . .

FLORA. Why do you say that?

BERTHA. No reason. I've got a class to teach.

FLORA. What did you come here for?

BERTHA. I wanted to see you. I wanted to see your face – the look of surprise.

FLORA. Are you out of your mind?

BERTHA (*after a long pause*). She used to cut herself.

FLORA. Are you out of your mind?

BERTHA. If you don't want to know . . .

FLORA. Eva Alicia was a girl . . .

BERTHA *tries to leave.* FLORA *stops her.*

BERTHA. You want to rummage around . . . but you don't want to know anything . . . What do you want to know? (*Pause*.) Nothing. There's nothing to know. Or did you want to know something? Now that someone's offering? Do you . . . ? Well, you had the honour of being the mother of a girl who was . . . perfect, intelligent, sensitive – (*Looks in* FLORA*'s eyes*.) and abandoned . . .

FLORA *goes up to the nun and slaps her hard in the face.*
BERTHA *is stunned. Then she tries once more to leave.*

FLORA. Stay where you are!

BERTHA. You've already hit me, haven't you? I can go now.

FLORA. What did she write? Did she write anything? What did she tell you? Did she tell you anything?

BERTHA. You've already hit me, haven't you? (*Pause.*) The truth . . . I don't even want to look at you . . . The truth . . . I came here to hit you . . .

FLORA. She cut herself?

BERTHA (*goes to a desk, takes a pencil*). Like this –

She illustrates, with movements like peeling a potato.

She harmed herself more each day . . . She harmed herself where we wouldn't see . . . like this. I . . . loved her very much . . .

FLORA. Not Eva Alicia. Not Eva Alicia.

BERTHA. A body cut to ribbons under a school uniform . . . Can I go now?

FLORA. She never told me.

BERTHA *looks at her and laughs.*

BERTHA. You're a failure. Look: all around you there are things and people . . . it's not just you, you, you . . .

FLORA. She never talked about anything!

BERTHA. Eva Alicia talked in other ways . . . Did you never stroke her shoulder . . . her arm?

FLORA. I . . . can't . . . I . . . worked for her . . . and this school . . .

BERTHA. I noticed a sort of scratch showing through her blouse . . . another day a little bloodstain on her shoulder . . . Did you really never, never realise?

FLORA. No.

BERTHA. It was like a secret hobby . . . you know? I asked her . . . She'd say 'No'. We went to the infirmary . . . You are stupid . . . I sent messages . . . We needed authorization to – (*Pause.*) There's no point now . . . I hate you.

Pause. FLORA *opens the door. She looks out along the corridor.*

FLORA. The Mother Superior said I had to sign some papers. Do you know where her father is?

Pause.

BERTHA. Why did you never visit, you cruel old witch?!

FLORA. Sister, could you go to the Mother Superior's office and get the papers I need to sign?

BERTHA. Didn't you hear me? Aren't you listening . . . ? For the love of God!

FLORA. You're not Eva Alicia's mother.

BERTHA. There is no Eva Alicia now, Mrs Huerta.

BERTHA *leaves, slamming the door loudly.* FLORA *stands immobile for a long time. In the distance, recorders can be heard playing the Roberto Carlos song.* FLORA *goes to the door, opens it and shouts:*

FLORA. You are not her mother!

FLORA *goes to Eva Alicia's desk, looks though her things, finds nothing. Pause. She gets up, looks in her bag, finds nothing.*

Fuck's sake!

At this moment, JUAN *enters. He sees* FLORA *and is stunned. They look at each other for a long time.* JUAN *approaches* FLORA *intending to hug her, but she withdraws. Long pause.*

JUAN. I didn't know that . . .

FLORA. I'm shaking . . . Got a cigarette?

JUAN. In here?

FLORA. I shouldn't, should I?

JUAN. No.

FLORA. But you've got some?

JUAN. Do you smoke?

FLORA. Yes.

JUAN. You used to hate it.

FLORA. Used to.

JUAN. They told me . . .

FLORA. Have you seen her?

JUAN. Yes.

FLORA. Is she . . . ?

JUAN. It wasn't an accident.

FLORA. No.

Silence.

JUAN. It's horrible.

FLORA. It is.

JUAN. The . . . forensics people have already left . . .

FLORA. We've got to sign some papers.

JUAN. They told me . . .

Long silence.

FLORA (*looking at* JUAN). Do you remember our Sundays? (*Pause.*) Nothing ever happened. We just sat there. I used to like it when nothing happened.

JUAN. Yes.

FLORA. I used to like watching you fix things . . .

JUAN. What?

FLORA. What little time we had together. (*Silence.*) I was . . . it's nothing. (*Pause.*) And now . . . (*Pause.*) Thank you for coming.

JUAN. Yes. That time. I'd forgotten about it . . . the feeling. Now it's all over.

FLORA. Is it? I don't think so.

JUAN. What?

FLORA. Nothing.

JUAN. This is very painful for you. All of this. I can't ask your forgiveness, it wouldn't be genuine.

FLORA. Don't worry.

JUAN. I'm already going bald.

FLORA (*laughs*). Yes, I noticed. You've put on weight. I look horrible, don't I?

JUAN tries to approach her. FLORA *doesn't let him.*

No, don't come near me, thanks. (*Moves a little further away.*) Leave me. (*Pause.*) Did you notice the indifference of all the girls?

JUAN. I didn't. I just came straight in. And your sister, wasn't she here?

FLORA. I don't know . . . stupid woman. She only came here to dig up the past and then . . .

JUAN. She attacked me a while ago.

FLORA. Why?

JUAN. No reason . . . I told her about this awful thing I saw yesterday . . . and that was it, she just flew at me. (*Pause.*) So we have to sign something?

FLORA. It's still raining . . .

JUAN. This place . . . why can't we be out there?

FLORA. I always loved you very much.

Silence.

JUAN. I'm going to be sick.

FLORA. Anything. Aren't you going to say anything?

JUAN. Do you want me to say, 'Me too'? Why? Out of pity?

FLORA. Go away. Go away, please.

JUAN. I'm going.

   JUAN *tries to leave, but* FLORA *stops him.*

FLORA. I'd like . . . You left too . . . I have to talk about this.

JUAN. You tire me. You shock me. You want it your way. I left . . . That was what you wanted, wasn't it? (*Pause.*) I'm sorry. What's the point of talking now? This is fucking painful for me too.

FLORA. It all slipped through my fingers. I couldn't . . .

JUAN. I'm suffocating!

FLORA. A moment ago they were playing that awful Roberto Carlos song. Did you hear it?

JUAN. Yes. What about it?

FLORA. It's ridiculous, isn't it?

JUAN. You and Roberto Carlos, me and my stupid face, this sodding, nightmare school, it's all ridiculous. I'm sorry, I feel like I'm going to be sick, I can't stand any more of this.

   He opens the door and looks lingeringly at FLORA. *Pause.*

   Our Sundays . . . how funny you should remember – (*Pause*) I love you very much too.

   He goes to FLORA, meaning to hug her.

FLORA (*pushing him away*). Weren't you going to be sick?

JUAN. Go to hell.

   BERTHA *opens the door. She stands looking at them.*
   JUAN *notices and looks at her.*

FLORA (*to* BERTHA). What are you looking at?

   BERTHA *does not reply.*

   What are you looking at? We just need to sign the papers and we're off. (*Pause. To* JUAN.) We're not having the wake here, are we?

BERTHA (*to* FLORA). Does the girl's father already know?

JUAN (*to* FLORA). Why are you talking to her like that?

FLORA. That she died? Yes, he knows. Could you leave us alone?

BERTHA (*comes into the room*). I was looking for him . . .

FLORA. He's already here, many thanks.

JUAN. Did you know my daughter?

FLORA. She was her Spanish teacher. Now, if you could leave us alone.

BERTHA (*to* JUAN). I have a letter for you. (*To* FLORA.) Speak to the gentleman . . . Tell him . . . He'll find out anyway.

JUAN. Sister, I already know that she didn't just die . . . I already know.

BERTHA (*to* JUAN). Could I see you afterwards?

FLORA. What letter have you got for him?

BERTHA (*to* JUAN). I'll see you afterwards.

BERTHA *goes*.

JUAN. Strange . . . the nuns. Want a cigarette?

FLORA. Yes, please.

JUAN (*pause*). Why here, Flora?

FLORA. What?

JUAN. Why did Eva Alicia have to be here?

FLORA. Because I didn't have anyone to . . .

JUAN. No, don't lie.

FLORA. I thought she'd be safer here.

JUAN. I don't understand.

FLORA. I thought nothing would happen to her here!

JUAN. I don't understand.

FLORA. I was terrified of something happening . . .

JUAN. What?

FLORA. I wanted to protect her.

Pause.

JUAN. You never let me anywhere near her.

FLORA. That's not true.

JUAN. I'm not . . .

FLORA. Are you giving me that cigarette?

JUAN. Flora . . .

FLORA. It terrified me . . .

JUAN. I adored her, I think I adored her . . .

FLORA. You caressed the girl too much.

JUAN. What?!

FLORA. You caressed the girl too much.

JUAN. Are you mad? What did you say?!

FLORA. Bloody nun, she's mad . . . We've got to sign some papers . . . did they tell you?

JUAN. I'm not like that!

FLORA. It's still raining, they've got us in here . . . I just want to . . . I want to go to sleep . . .

JUAN. I didn't do anything to you, Flora! You didn't want anything, you didn't want anything . . .

FLORA. You left.

JUAN. What do you mean, I 'caressed the girl too much'?

FLORA. Enough, forget it, Eva Alicia has already . . .

JUAN. I never did anything . . .

FLORA. Maybe that's why she . . . Maybe.

JUAN (*grabs her shoulders*). Do you hear? I never, ever . . . ! That's why . . . You're a stupid . . . You're mad . . . That's it . . . Better here . . . better far away from you . . .

FLORA (*after a pause*). Yes . . . better . . .

JUAN. I . . . bloody hell, Flora . . . Bloody hell, Flora . . . I never knew why . . . never.

Long silence.

FLORA. I'm going to see about these papers.

JUAN. Never. (*Pause.*) The girl would never come near me. I couldn't be on my own with her. I never sat her on my lap. She never laughed with me. She didn't talk to me. It's not fair. It isn't fair.

FLORA. What do we have to sign?

JUAN. Her little neck all black and blue. It's not fair, Flora. What did you say to her? I could never even talk to her.

FLORA. You left.

JUAN. You threw me out.

FLORA. It's the same thing. You went far away.

JUAN. I couldn't . . . figure you out . . . work you out.

FLORA. Come off it!

JUAN. What?

FLORA. Don't talk shit!

JUAN. Don't shout!

FLORA. You knew where I'd come from . . . You knew.

JUAN. Yes.

FLORA. Don't talk shit.

JUAN. OK.

FLORA *goes to the door.*

Really, Flora, I never did . . .

FLORA. Don't talk shit . . . I'd better . . . I'm going for a smoke, outside, in the garden.

JUAN. It's raining.

FLORA. I don't bloody care.

FLORA *opens the door and bumps into the nun,* BERTHA, *in the doorway.*

(*To* BERTHA.) Are you still at it?

Looks at BERTHA *and exits.*

BERTHA. Mr Sánchez?

JUAN. Yes, that's me. At your service.

Silence. They look at one another.

You had a letter, didn't you?

BERTHA *nods.*

I've only just arrived. I came as soon as I heard. You taught her?

BERTHA *nods.*

I hadn't seen her for a long time, not since she was so high. (*Demonstrates.*) I had to go and work, a long way away . . . You know . . . it just gets worse and worse back here. I haven't been able to cry . . . I was looking at the blackboard . . . seeing her name . . . I sent money whenever I could . . . A girl . . . How did she behave with you?

BERTHA. She was a straight 'A' student.

JUAN. So they said . . . it's difficult, I still don't understand. (*Pause.*) What time do the girls come out? Will they be long? I wanted to ask one of them if . . .

BERTHA. The headmistress is thinking about it . . . she doesn't want to unsettle them any more . . .

JUAN. This is happening all over the place, isn't it?

Silence.

Everyone thinks those of us who leave have a great time . . .

BERTHA. Out of sight, out of mind . . .

JUAN. That's not true! Sorry . . . Sometimes you just have to leave because it's impossible to stay. With all due respect, you haven't lived in the outside world, you don't know . . .

BERTHA. What?

JUAN. How complicated it all is. It's asphyxiating. The girl used to cry all the time, the jealousy . . . Her mother . . . her mother and that life they lived, her mother's mother . . . Have you seen her sister?

BERTHA. I find it somewhat disrespectful that, given the situation, she's walking around wearing that make-up . . .

JUAN. And their history, both of them, their history. Flora . . . sorry . . . my daughter's mother . . . she hired a detective . . . She needed to find somebody . . .

BERTHA. You?

JUAN. No, no, I always called and sent money whenever I could.

BERTHA. So you think I don't know anything . . .

JUAN. That was it, that was when it all started . . . Her mother hired a detective, I'd already noticed something . . .

BERTHA. Why didn't your daughter want to go on living?

JUAN. I may not have been around but I never hurt her, I wanted to talk to her and I couldn't . . . !

BERTHA. Have you collected her things together?

JUAN. No. There they are.

BERTHA. The prettiest exercise books I've ever seen. She was going to study a lot, work hard, go and study medicine. She was never going to become a nun, she'd never be scared of getting out of bed at night . . . She had such promise . . . Never, she wanted to get ahead, she was going to follow her star and grab life with both hands. (*Cries.*)

JUAN. You're very shaken . . . Were you fond of her?

BERTHA. She was going to study medicine, she was going to walk along university corridors chatting with her friends, she was never going to have a bad word to say about anyone.

She dries her tears. Looks at JUAN.

Are you happy?

JUAN. What?

BERTHA. She didn't need us, she was on a long, thin thread that could be cut at any moment, she never spoke . . . She used to look at us as if we were stupid . . . (*Cries more.*) Do you know what? I sent messages, reports to her mother, reproaching her. I wanted her mother to come here, I wanted to see her, I wanted to see her and to see the stupid face that I saw her daughter saw, I wanted to spit in her face . . . I sent those messages. Maybe that was why . . . no, I don't think so, her mother never came, nor did anyone else . . . but she managed. (*Pause.*) She never wanted to study medicine. She never wanted to go to university . . .

JUAN. Can I get you anything?

BERTHA. The girls used to look at her; a straight 'A' student, exercise books full of colour, perfect, faultless, tireless, there she was, looking at us, nothing ever hurt her, we didn't matter to her, she came here and didn't teach us a thing. She didn't heal us, did she? I was annoyed by . . . her kind of indifference . . . The girl's mother.

JUAN. Would you like a glass of water?

BERTHA. I got tired of asking her questions, she never answered me, she never cared about answering, there she was, twelve years old, looking us all up and down . . . I don't mean 'this kid is judging me', no, I don't mean that, she just didn't need us . . .

JUAN. Study, be someone . . .

BERTHA. As if she was blaming us for I don't know what . . . I don't know . . .

JUAN. Getting out once and for all. Want a cigarette?

BERTHA. Yes.

JUAN *takes a packet out, gives one to* BERTHA *and lights one for himself. They both sit in silence on the edge of the platform.*

BERTHA. So you haven't been able to cry?

JUAN (*pause*). At dawn, I was on the point of crying, terribly, like when . . . A little boy . . . he'd been raped . . . I was sick, but only afterwards, but I couldn't cry, no.

BERTHA. I don't really do smoking.

JUAN. I don't really do school.

They both laugh.

BERTHA. This is all horrible. (*Pause.*) Where do you live?

JUAN. As far away as possible from this hellhole . . .

BERTHA *laughs*.

But having done that, I came to realise the world is round and you end up coming back, even if you are far away . . .

BERTHA (*laughs*). I don't believe you, I don't believe what you're saying . . .

JUAN. When a person leaves . . .

BERTHA. I get that bit, but I don't believe . . . How old are you?

JUAN. Forty-eight . . .

BERTHA. I'm forty-five . . . Isn't it dreadful!

JUAN. I didn't think people became nuns these days . . .

BERTHA. We all want to escape, don't we? The trick is to find a good cage to disappear into . . .

JUAN. And here's me saying you haven't lived . . .

The door opens. BEATRÍZ *leans in*.

BEATRÍZ. I'm going to . . . I was . . . And my sister?

BEATRÍZ *closes the door.*

BERTHA. I'm thinking: 'Where does he come from? Why is he here when there's no point any more?'

JUAN. Who?

BERTHA. Nobody . . . I'm sorry . . . Everything's confused. When you sit here, like this, day in, day out, seeing the girls coming and going . . . growing . . . and then nothing happens . . . Your daughter was a being . . .

JUAN. When there's no point any more . . . (*Pause.*) Do you know any jokes? Any at all?

BERTHA. It's boring, isn't it? We all get bored and try to distract ourselves . . . That's where praying comes in useful, it wards off the boredom. The girls get bored all the time . . . as soon as they stop playing . . . They grow up and start getting bored . . . But your daughter . . . you know?

JUAN. My daughter . . . what else should I know?

At this moment, recorders are heard playing Beethoven's 'Ode to Joy'.

My country . . . it's strange!

BERTHA. Everything's horrible . . . Will you leave me some cigarettes?

JUAN *takes out some cigarettes and gives them to her.* BERTHA *takes them and puts them into the pocket of her jumper. She looks at him for a long time.*

Your sister-in-law was hitting you, wasn't she? Blame . . .

JUAN. My stomach aches, doesn't yours? It's like vertigo . . . I feel empty, somehow. Here we are . . . Do you always smoke?

BERTHA. Behind closed doors.

JUAN. Why's that?

BERTHA. What?

JUAN. Behind closed doors . . .

BERTHA. It's against the rules.

JUAN. It's all so ridiculous.

BERTHA. I like it . . .

JUAN. Doing things behind closed doors?

BERTHA (*laughs*). Smoking.

Silence.

JUAN. I want to go now.

BERTHA. Run away.

JUAN (*laughs*). Yes.

BERTHA. I keep shuddering . . .

Silence.

Nobody cries for real any more . . .

JUAN. Better to pretend than not at all . . .

BERTHA. Same thing. (*Pause.*) It makes no sense. Do you understand?

JUAN. No. I try. But no. (*Pause.*) I was a long way away. Distant. I could never . . . They were all there, with their history . . . (*Pause.*) Why did my sister-in-law's red lipstick bother you so much?

BERTHA. I don't know . . . Strange . . .

JUAN. We carry so much baggage around with us . . . My stomach hurts . . . Where's the toilet?

BERTHA. On the way to the headmistress's office . . . there's just toilets for the girls here. (*Pause.*) Are you going to be sick?

JUAN. No. I felt like you do when you're going to sneeze, something like that.

BERTHA. Go, I'll wait for you here.

JUAN. It's OK now.

Long silence. BERTHA *looks at him.*

BERTHA. Were you about to say something? You were about to say something to me, weren't you?

JUAN. Everything's already in enough of a mess. Lies. Why am I telling you these things?

BERTHA. You're not telling me anything!

JUAN. No . . . What about the letter?

BERTHA. It was a lie. It wasn't true.

JUAN. So?

BERTHA. I wanted to upset the girl's mother.

JUAN. You're mad . . . Don't you have any compassion?

BERTHA. No. (*Pause.*) Doesn't matter now, you finding out.

JUAN. What?

BERTHA. The girl was . . .

JUAN. Yes. I know.

BERTHA. I did what I could. Strange. Eva Alicia . . . couldn't bear to be touched.

JUAN. Yes . . . like her mother.

FLORA *opens the door. They both fall silent.*

FLORA (*to* BERTHA). What were you saying? What stories are you making up now? You too, you too . . .

BERTHA. Forgive me. I'm sorry. I don't understand. It hurts. I'm trying. I'm sorry. (*To* FLORA.) Does the gentleman know that your daughter used to cut herself?

FLORA. You're mad. Bloody stark raving mad . . . and you just say it, just like that, heartless . . .

JUAN *goes up to her.*

Leave me alone, fool! Get off me!

BERTHA. I'll fetch the Mother Superior . . .

FLORA. No, no, we're going . . .

BERTHA. So you haven't told him.

FLORA. All of you . . . (*To* JUAN.) You . . . the lot of you. You never understood me, you made fun of me, you bastard, idiot, evil sodding swine . . .

JUAN. She cut herself? How? (*To* BERTHA.) Why didn't you tell me?

FLORA. It's a lie, Juan . . .

BERTHA. Did you have a proper look at her?

Silence.

You didn't look at her properly . . . Well. (*To both of them.*) Why? Eh?

Silence. Neither parent answers.

FLORA. That's enough. Leave us in peace . . . Eva Alicia's gone.

BERTHA. Gone . . .

FLORA (*to* BERTHA). You've no shame. You'd better get out. Now go away. Leave me with the girl's father. (*Pause.*) Please. I beg you.

BERTHA *heads for the door. Stops before going out.*

BERTHA. It won't stop raining. (*Goes out.*)

Long silence.

JUAN. Did you have a good look at her?

FLORA. No. Did you see her?

JUAN. Yes, but I didn't examine her.

FLORA. I saw her. It was my . . . I had to identify her.

JUAN. Has the forensics doctor said anything to you?

FLORA. No, not yet.

Silence.

JUAN. Flora . . .

FLORA. We'll see . . . ?

JUAN. This could get worse.

FLORA. How?

JUAN. I don't know.

At this moment, BEATRÍZ *enters, furious. She goes straight up to* FLORA, *takes her by the arm and leads her to a corner. She whispers.*

BEATRÍZ. Why didn't you do anything?!

FLORA. About what?

BEATRÍZ. Why didn't you save the girl?

FLORA. From what?

BEATRÍZ. I saw the reports! They called you a thousand times . . .

FLORA. When?

BEATRÍZ. I went in to see her . . . Have you seen her?

FLORA. Stop. Calm down.

BEATRÍZ. Have you seen what she was doing to herself?

FLORA. She killed herself.

BEATRÍZ. Why was she doing that to herself?

FLORA. What?

BEATRÍZ (*to* JUAN, *speaking more loudly*). Have you seen your daughter? Have you seen her, the pair of you?

JUAN. No.

BEATRÍZ (*to* FLORA). Another girl you didn't help.

FLORA. What's wrong with you, you idiot?

BEATRÍZ. What would it have cost you?

FLORA. What? As well as fulfilling . . .

BEATRÍZ. Remember . . .

FLORA. I'm very tired, Beatríz, leave me in peace.

BEATRÍZ. I'm still on my own . . . You're on your own . . . Rebecca and her crisis . . . Don't you remember anything?

FLORA. What are you talking about?

BEATRÍZ. Why don't you remember anything?

FLORA. Is this why you came here? My daughter has just . . .

BEATRÍZ. She was cutting herself . . .

FLORA. Leave me alone!

BEATRÍZ. You're covered . . . You don't feel . . . You don't see anything . . .

JUAN. Beatríz . . .

BEATRÍZ. You never want to talk. I want you . . . to talk.

FLORA. I can't.

JUAN. Beatríz . . .

BEATRÍZ. How old were you when they started on you? I don't remember any more . . . You too?

FLORA. No one did anything to me! No one. No one did anything to me. No one hit me. No one raped me. No one shouted at me. No one.

BEATRÍZ. Think back: the football commentary, the TV . . . always on full blast . . . over and over again. Did they put lipstick on you too?

FLORA. Leave me alone! Shut up!

FLORA gets into the cupboard beside the teacher's desk. She shuts herself in.

BEATRÍZ. Why do you never remember anything?

She goes to the cupboard and sits beside the door.

I used to say: 'Don't do it to me. Don't do it . . . please . . . It's for tarts. Girls who have lipstick put on them are fucked.'

JUAN goes to the door and looks out.

Then the lock turns and they beat them. They put their finger in and then they fuck them.

FLORA can be heard whining like a small animal.

My whole body used to hurt afterwards . . . You can't bear it either . . . ?

Silence.

FLORA (*from inside*). 'Dad, not now. Not you any more . . . ' I don't feel well. I don't move. I'm cold. My feet. I can't see. 'I can hear you doing it! I can hear you whistling! I can feel your greasy hands . . . ' Who are you? You touch me lovingly . . . There's no light . . . I can feel something over my eyelids.

BEATRÍZ *cries, dries her tears and covers her ears.*

You used to say to me: 'So little and so stupid. Stupid little runt.' 'Not my mouth. Please.'

BEATRÍZ *sits in a corner.*

I can feel you. You're warm. Don't hug me!

JUAN *goes to the door, opens it, looks for someone. Closes the door.*

I've got a hole in my head. No more . . . I'm not moving any more . . . I don't feel anything . . . You're not doing anything to me . . . I'm not here any more. I don't feel anything. You're not doing anything to me . . . I'm not here any more. I don't feel anything.

BEATRÍZ *rocks gently.*

I'm dead now.

BEATRÍZ (*trying to hug* FLORA). I used to say: 'Don't make me up, don't make me pretty. Leave me looking horrible.'

FLORA *hugs her tightly.*

FLORA. 'Leave me looking horrible with my hole in my head.'

BEATRÍZ *hugs* FLORA *and cries with her. They seem like terrified little girls.*

JUAN (*to* FLORA). Come on, it's over now . . . come back . . .

BEATRÍZ (*to* FLORA). They used to put lipstick on us . . . They grabbed you . . . She was silent, the bitch, the evil cow . . . They did the same thing to you . . . Evil bloody people, they used to lock the kitchen, right in there, over and over, and her with her stupid face, just keeping quiet . . . and us, enduring it, us . . . To me, they . . . and to you, too . . . and to Rebecca as well . . . it can't be . . . I can't . . . I'm sorry . . .

JUAN. Flora . . . I never . . . never did anything to Evita . . . nothing.

FLORA *nods*.

(*To* BEATRÍZ.) Let her rest. Don't talk about it . . .

He goes out. Long silence.

BEATRÍZ (*sings very softly*).
When God gave names to all the flowers,
One with blue eyes ran up to Him
And, stopping at God's feet . . .

FLORA *joins in, also very softly. The two of them sing, barely audible:*

FLORA *and* BEATRÍZ.
She asked very softly:
'I forgot the name you gave me, Sir,'
And the Father answered, lovingly
'Forget-me-not' . . .

The sisters hug each other tightly and for a long time cry like two little girls. They look one another in the eyes and hug.

Long silence. Holding hands, they both look silently into the distance.

FLORA. He grabbed his cases and left. And Mother running after him as if someone were about to . . . After he left us, something was stuck inside me, like a blockage, for years. (*Laughs.*) It's still there . . .

BEATRÍZ. Always so quiet, like little ghosts . . .

FLORA. I just wanted to get out of there. To escape. (*Laughs.*) So I got married.

BEATRÍZ. We never talked . . . We never told each other, did we? (*As she wipes the lipstick from her mouth.*) Bloody Mother. Bloody bitch . . . Bitch, bitch . . .

FLORA. I ran away like an idiot, just like an idiot. (*Pause.*) Another hell but a different one.

BEATRÍZ. And for what?

FLORA. We never heard from him again. (*Pause. Looks at* BEATRÍZ.) You wanted to know. Now you know. (*Hugs her.*)

BEATRÍZ. We're like pieces of paper, tearing ourselves apart strip by strip. (*Pause. Laughs.*) I can't be with anyone.

FLORA (*pause*). I wanted to know. I searched for him.

BEATRÍZ. You were so much fun.

FLORA. A fortune on that detective. Years.

BEATRÍZ. You used to sing. You never gave back change and then you used to blame me . . .

FLORA. They found him in a backwater town. My father. They found my father in a backwater town.

BEATRÍZ. You used to dance all the time, no one could follow your steps.

FLORA takes a carrier bag out of her bag and begins to put in it the contents of the desk.

FLORA. I left the girl with someone and got on a coach. I thought, 'I'm going to beat the living daylights out of him, I'm going to throw acid in his face, I'm going to kick him, I'm going to kill him . . . ' I took a taxi from the bus station, on the outskirts of town. I arrived, I got out of the taxi, and I saw him across this dry, dusty street, sitting beside the door. I saw him. I walked up to him . . . He was an old man . . . The widest street I've ever crossed . . . and when I'd almost, when I'd almost reached him . . . to throw up on him, to curse him, to finish him off . . . I froze . . . I froze . . . I couldn't . . . I turned round and . . .

She gets up, goes to the blackboard and looks at Eva Alicia's name.

BEATRÍZ. I never knew.

FLORA. Just so you do know. You have a spineless sister.

BEATRÍZ (*laughing*). Spineless sister? Brave sister! (*Pause.*) I'm the spineless one, the coward. The stupid one. (*Pause.*) I did nothing, I didn't even complain. Nothing. Struck dumb.

Long silence.

All the nuns here are mad . . .

FLORA (*after a pause*). She's right.

BEATRÍZ. Who?

FLORA. No one.

BEATRÍZ. How long is it since we last saw each other? (*Silence.*) So you just froze?

FLORA. What?

BEATRÍZ. So, when you saw him, you just froze?

FLORA. Let's go and see if . . .

BEATRÍZ. Have you told Rebecca?

FLORA. Shall I take her exercise books?

BEATRÍZ. Have the two of you talked about it? They did the same to her and she never said anything, did she?

FLORA. I don't think these bags will last the walk to the car . . . and since it won't stop raining. It won't stop raining.

BEATRÍZ. Who paid for the detective? Where did you get the money?

FLORA. But leaving like this, without saying goodbye . . . no way.

BEATRÍZ (*after a pause*). Did he recognise you? (*Pause.*) Did he know it was you? (*Pause.*) Was he suffering? Did he look like someone who was suffering?

FLORA (*pause*). He's dead now . . . Dad . . .

BEATRÍZ *collapses as if struck by lightning. Long silence. She gets up bit by bit until, finally, she sits on the dais, as if hypnotised.*

Shall we go?

BEATRÍZ. He's dead. (*Pause.*) My dad's dead. (*Pause. To* FLORA.) How long ago did he die? (*Pause.*) I don't know what I feel, I don't know what I feel. How long ago did my dad die? (*Pause.*) Is it true he died? I can't believe it . . . I really don't believe it . . . and does Rebecca know? Did you tell her? (*Pause.*) Did she care when she heard? Have you already told her? My dad, dead . . . (*Laughs.*) I thought he was going to live for ever . . .

FLORA. Shall we go?

BEATRÍZ. When did my dad die? Who told you? How did you hear?

FLORA. Let's go. Please.

BEATRÍZ. How long ago was it?

FLORA. I don't want to be here any more.

She takes the carrier bags containing the exercise books and heads for the door.

BEATRÍZ. Where's he buried?

FLORA (*points to her own heart*). Here. (*Laughs.*) Come on, let's go now, I've got to sign some papers.

BEATRÍZ *goes up to* FLORA *and takes her arm to stop her.*

BEATRÍZ. No, seriously . . . Did he really die?

FLORA. What do you want?

BEATRÍZ. What?

FLORA. Do you want him to be dead or not dead? What do you want?

Silence.

BEATRÍZ. I'd like . . . I want . . . I want to have a father.

FLORA. Fine! Well, he's alive then! Let's go!

BEATRÍZ. You're bloody cruel, you are. You've no . . .

FLORA (*exploding*). You couldn't care less! Could you?

BEATRÍZ. About what?

FLORA. Look, fool, look at me, look at me, see me. Can't you see anything?

BEATRÍZ. Just tell me.

FLORA (*pause*). These bags aren't going to last. (*Pause.*) What would you do with these exercise books? Where would you put them? What use are they to anyone?

BEATRÍZ (*pause*). I'm sorry . . .

FLORA sits with her back against the door with the carrier bags in her hands.

FLORA. It's not fair, it's not fair.

At this moment, the MOTHER SUPERIOR *tries to come in but* FLORA *stops her by blocking the door.*

MOTHER SUPERIOR. Could you open the door? I have the papers here for . . . (*Knocks.*) Mrs Sánchez Huerta, could you open the door?

BEATRÍZ. My sister isn't married any more!

MOTHER SUPERIOR. I can't open the door . . . Could you open it for me, please? (*Pause.*) Is there something wrong?

FLORA and BEATRÍZ *look at each other. Pause. They do not answer.*

Are you all right? Mrs Sánchez Huerta . . . Mrs Huerta?

BEATRÍZ *and* FLORA *laugh very quietly. They agree through gestures not to open the door.*

FLORA (*through the door*). Tell me something about my daughter . . .

MOTHER SUPERIOR. Open it.

FLORA. What did Eva do yesterday?

MOTHER SUPERIOR. Look, Mrs Huerta, open the door . . . This is an educational establishment, not a . . . ! Open this door!

FLORA. What do you remember about my daughter?

MOTHER SUPERIOR. What?

FLORA. Tell me something about my daughter and I'll open the door . . .

JUAN's voice is heard, also on the other side of the door.

JUAN. Open up!

MOTHER SUPERIOR. Look, I know what you're going through is very painful . . .

BEATRÍZ. You've no idea how painful what we're going through is! You don't have a clue!

MOTHER SUPERIOR. The girls are coming to . . .

BEATRÍZ. Let them come!

MOTHER SUPERIOR (*to* JUAN). This really is very bad timing. (*Knocks.*) Do you want me to call the caretaker to break down the door?

JUAN (*shouting as he bangs on the door*). Open the door!

MOTHER SUPERIOR. Mr Sánchez Huerta, would you please stop shouting?!

JUAN. My surname is not Huerta!

At this moment, the bell for the next period rings very loudly. Doors open and close, GIRLS *run and shout.*

MOTHER SUPERIOR (*towards the classroom*). Here come the girls. I'm not joking, open the door, I insist.

BEATRÍZ (*quietly, to* FLORA). Lupine brothers, white-washed sepulchres, Judas Iscariots, fallen angels . . . !

FLORA (*to her sister*). Come on, let's open the door . . .

A group of GIRLS *is heard stopping outside the door.*

MOTHER SUPERIOR (*to the girls*). Go to the chapel . . .

The GIRLS *protest, muted whistles. Questions, the* GIRLS *commenting.*

Did you hear me? Go directly to the chapel, wait there until further notice.

Footsteps, singing, whistling, moving away. The MOTHER SUPERIOR *knocks insistently.*

It's getting late now, the girls aren't to blame for any of this . . . Please open up . . .

FLORA (*to the* MOTHER SUPERIOR). Tell me something about my daughter . . .

MOTHER SUPERIOR (*interrupts*). Please, Mrs Huerta, for the love of God, don't make me tell lies, don't make me . . . You never once set foot inside this school . . . Now what's done is done, for the love of God . . . This really is very bad timing.

FLORA. Anything, tell me anything . . .

MOTHER SUPERIOR. That she had warts all over her hands?

FLORA *covers her ears*.

That you could tell that her mother didn't love her? Will that do?

BEATRÍZ *throws herself furiously at the door and bangs on it hard as she shouts*:

BEATRÍZ. We can't love anybody!

She collapses beside FLORA. *Whispers:*

We've nothing to love anybody with . . .

FLORA *holds her tightly and helps her stand up. They open the door. They see the* MOTHER SUPERIOR, JUAN *and* BERTHA. *The two sisters go for their things. Silence. The* MOTHER SUPERIOR *enters the room, followed by* BERTHA *and* JUAN. *The* MOTHER SUPERIOR *sits at one of the desks.* JUAN *is at a loss; he goes to* FLORA.

JUAN (*to* FLORA). Forgive me.

BERTHA *stands in the doorway with her arms folded*.

MOTHER SUPERIOR (*to* FLORA). I'm so dreadfully sorry, but . . .

BERTHA (*interrupts*). Is that the truth or not?

FLORA (*very quietly*). Yes.

MOTHER SUPERIOR (*to* JUAN *and* BERTHA). Mr Sánchez, Sister, be so kind as to sit down.

BERTHA *and* JUAN *sit down at desks without knowing why.* FLORA *walks towards the door and* BEATRÍZ *follows her.*

FLORA (*leaving*). I have to go outside . . . I'm suffocating . . .

BEATRÍZ (*following her*). I'll go with you . . .

MOTHER SUPERIOR. Mrs Huerta . . . Mrs Huerta, please . . . Please . . .

FLORA. What?

MOTHER SUPERIOR. The papers you have to . . .

FLORA. What papers?

MOTHER SUPERIOR. These, the ones I've brought . . .

FLORA. Ah. It's just that I would like to . . . What about them?

JUAN. They're here, Flora . . .

FLORA *and* JUAN *go to the teacher's desk and the* MOTHER SUPERIOR *holds out some papers to them. After going over them,* JUAN *cries, hugging* FLORA.

Long silence. JUAN *hands the papers to the* MOTHER SUPERIOR.

MOTHER SUPERIOR. You have to keep –

FLORA. A copy. All right.

Silence.

MOTHER SUPERIOR. What did you want to ask the girls? What were you going to ask the girls?

FLORA *does not speak.*

BERTHA (*strained*). Excuse me, Mother, could I go?

MOTHER SUPERIOR. Stay right where you are . . .

BERTHA. I have things to . . .

JUAN (*to* BERTHA). A cigarette?

BERTHA *looks furiously at* JUAN.

FLORA (*after a silence*). You were saying?

MOTHER SUPERIOR. What did you want to ask the girls?

FLORA. To know . . . I don't know . . . I was going to tell them that . . . that I am, that I was Eva Alicia Sánchez Huerta's mother . . . that if any of them, one day, wanted to come to the house . . . for lunch . . .

MOTHER SUPERIOR. Mrs Huerta . . . Mrs Huerta . . . What did you want to ask them? What did you want to ask the girls?

FLORA (*after a pause*). Nothing . . . Nothing. (*Pause.*) I wanted to see if my daughter was with them . . . that's all . . . Maybe . . .

Long silence.

MOTHER SUPERIOR. Very well. (*Looks at* BERTHA.) We must go to the chapel. Have you collected your daughter's belongings?

FLORA. Yes. They're there. (*Points to the carrier bags.*) We're going.

MOTHER SUPERIOR. There's no hurry.

FLORA. We're going.

The MOTHER SUPERIOR *leaves, followed by* BERTHA, *who is stopped by* FLORA *just before going out.*

BERTHA. I don't like you.

FLORA. Why?

BERTHA. Why don't I like you?

FLORA. No. Why my daughter . . . ? (*Pause.*) Thank you for everything.

BERTHA *exits.* JUAN *takes the bags as if to help carry them.* FLORA *takes them from him.*

No. No.

JUAN. Sorry. I . . . well, I just . . . we have to sort out the rest.

FLORA (*looks at him*). I thought you didn't remember any more . . .

JUAN. It's not remembering it's . . . (*Smiles.*) I'm going to the chapel.

FLORA. I'm coming.

They look at each other for a long time. JUAN *gives* FLORA *a paternal caress. She takes his hand.*

Thank you. I hope . . . No . . .

JUAN *turns and leaves. Silence.*

She . . . (*Pause.*) I never taught her to love life . . .

BEATRÍZ. I love you very much. I love you very much. I love you very much. (*Pause.*) I'll go on ahead. (*Smiles.*) I'll wait for you outside.

FLORA *gets up, opens the door. She sees her daughter's desk and goes to it. She hugs it.*

FLORA. I always loved you very much, I always loved you very much. I always loved you very much. (*Pause.*) You were such a good girl, so obedient. You looked on the evenings with wonder. (*Pause.*) You didn't obey me. You always had your fists clenched . . . Your emptiness scared me . . . You liked to be hugged . . . You counted your little fingers. You looked at me and you loved me . . . You scampered away, running. (*Pause.*) You answered back. And shouted. You wanted to engage with life and I didn't help you. You obeyed me. They sent reports from the school. About you. All about you. (*Pause.*) Your idiotic smile. I'm sorry. I would shout at you and it made me feel alive. I wanted to kill you. I enjoyed rejecting you. I could hurt you. I liked knowing that I could hurt you. I'm sorry. I . . . tried. Tried to treat you well. I NEVER COULD! I never could. I never understood you. I never wanted to understand you. I didn't understand you . . . I hoped . . . I don't know. I got tired of . . . I'm sorry. I always . . . I don't know. (*Pause.*) Thank you, Eva Alicia. (*Looks at the little window.*) It's raining again.

FLORA *remains still for a long time. She looks around. At this moment, a* GIRL *walks very cautiously into the room and walks up to her desk,* FLORA *looks at her. The* GIRL *is looking for something.*

FLORA. What's your name?

> *The* GIRL *does not answer. Pause.*

Have you had your breakfast? Was it a nice breakfast?

> *The* GIRL *does not answer.*

What's your best friend's name?

> *The* GIRL *does not answer.*

How are you getting on at school?

> *The* GIRL *finds her recorder and walks to the door.*

Are you happy?

> *The* GIRL *stops and looks at her. Pause.*

It won't stop raining.

Final blackout.

USED BLOOD JUNKYARD

(*Staging a Stain*)

Road-Building Programme and Theatrical Monster*

ALBERTO VILLARREAL

translated by

SIMON SCARDIFIELD

*Nothing endures except what has been
written in blood, to be heard by blood.*

Pablo Neruda

---

* 'Monster' is the name given to the unexpected congruity
of dissonant elements: To spell it out, the Centaur,
the Chimera are defined as such. I call a monster any oddity
whose beauty is inexhaustible.

Alfred Jarry, *Ymages No. 2* (1898)

Used Blood Junkyard (*Deshuesadero de sangre basura*) was first performed in English as a rehearsed reading as part of the *Arena Mexico* season in the Jerwood Theatre Upstairs, Royal Court Theatre, London, on 14 January 2006 with the following cast:

LÁZARO	Andrew Scott
SANTIAGO	Jonathan Cullen
FRANCESCO	Tom Brooke
PABLO	Alex Avery
FATHER	Richard Hope
MOTHER	Louise Gold
MAKE-UP GIRL/REBECCA	Kellie Bright
MARIANA/MERCI	Anna Francolini

Other characters were played by members of the company.

Director Tiffany Watt-Smith

Preamble

This play is a textual object that can be dismantled and put back together. The rules which traditionally tie the author to his/her work don't apply here. The text is intended as a fuse to ignite the stage action. The result should be a theatrical event whose main stage is the imagination, and which is sparked off by the throwing together of these assembled spare parts and broken bits and pieces. The order of the scenes can and should be changed; they should be taken apart, reassembled, given a respray, transformed. In a junkyard, everything is both rubbish and at the same time the seed of some future hybrid, monstrous and half-finished, physically, spiritually and politically incorrect.

The production should also include characters who haven't been invented yet. Dead people. Victims. Millionaires. People who have yet to be born. People without a name. Because, although no dialogue has been written for them, they are part of that diversion in the road called humanity and belong in that lane of the carriageway which is sealed off with bollards and signposted: 'This is theatre. We are working for you. We regret any inconvenience.'

During the play a running tally is kept of all the deaths. Every time a death occurs, one of the actors notches it up with a chalk mark on the upstage wall. In scenes with multiple deaths, the actor keeps chalking up the strokes for the duration of the scene.

Prologue: in Heaven

In the Great Bureaucrat's diary is the following entry:

> 'Remind all the temporary residents of earth that I exist. The ones who voted for me. The ones who didn't. The ones who are sickened by democracy. Divert the traffic, put up rusty road signs, reverse the traffic flow on one-way streets. Cover the lamp posts in posters again, like in the good old campaigning days when my innocent smile was over all the earth and I walked on the waters of pedestrian voters. Making your taxes work for you, for better public services. "Taxpayers, enjoy. Drink Democracy. Enjoy Democracy ice cold. Democracy should be part of a balanced diet."'

The Great Bureaucrat doesn't feel alone. Down there, in the underworld under the streets (his streets), under the drains of the government offices, nine high floors of offices away, the temporary residents might just be thinking of him. They might even stink like him.

The Great Bureaucrat went through all the paperwork, and signed it. His work was finished. He realised it was seven o'clock in the morning, and he rested.

ACT ONE

A TV commercial with a very, very big budget. A football player with the moon at his feet. He's about to take a penalty. Artificial pitch. Big stadium floodlights. The goalkeeper steadies himself.

We never got to the moon. It was all staged.

I can't be sure of that, but then I can't be sure of anything. When I say 'we' I mean us as a species.

As a nation, I reckon it'll take us years to get there.

And just me as an individual, I'll never get there.

It's odd, isn't it?

Our species has only managed to be sure it can stay on earth by learning to leave. Conquering space for the species. Everyone knows this, they've all thought about it, they all watch the news, they're all well-informed, they all claim to lead ecologically sound and neurotically low-cal lives.

Don't get me wrong, I'm not protesting, I'm not trying to touch your hearts. I've got no reason to think that the world or your hearts can be made any better, or even made to feel any better.

They are what they are. That's just how they are. Like inflation and undiagnosed cancer, like dirt under your fingernails. But the moon, that natty little brooch on the lapels of our skyscrapers, gets further and further away all the time (and by the way, what's the point of the moon in countries that don't have skyscrapers?).

All the time it's less and less about green cheese, and more and more a stop-off on the way to Mars, a military base.

But we're due some extra time, a few extra minutes. We should make someone take the penalty. Take the ultimate punishment.

The player takes the penalty. The moon, a ball with a manufacturer's logo, turns to dust the moment the boot makes contact. The goalie leaps into the air. The flashes from the cameras, like artificial stars, capture the lunar explosion.

Back door

The room where corpses are prepared for burial, in the most exclusive funeral parlour in the capital.

The LITTLE MAKE-UP GIRL *is working on the* OLD MAN's *yellow, naked and bloated body.* LÁZARO *points a revolver at her head.*

LÁZARO. No one, not even the President, or the Pope, not even the Pope's Mexican daughters are getting in here. I'm serious. Our people stay exactly where they are and they keep their guns trained on the mourners. Give the paparazzi all the shots they like of our boys abusing their authority, just so long as nobody comes in until I say so.

BODYGUARD 1. Don't worry, sir.

LÁZARO. I expect the loyalty of a friend, not some civil servant yes-man, understand?

BODYGUARD 1. You've got it.

BODYGUARD 1 *goes*.

LÁZARO. Sorry, what was it again?

THE LITTLE MAKE-UP GIRL. Guadalupe . . .

LÁZARO. Guadalupe, I'm not going to kill you. Are you a mother?

THE LITTLE MAKE-UP GIRL. I will be in a few months.

LÁZARO *aims his gun at her belly*.

LÁZARO. Have you had the scan?

THE LITTLE MAKE-UP GIRL. Yes.

LÁZARO. The first contact our parents have with us is a short but boring black-and-white television programme. And their first question is always whether we're a boy or a girl. They need to know because that decides who'll teach us how and what to wash in the bath, and then everything follows on from that. What's yours, a boy or a girl?

THE LITTLE MAKE-UP GIRL. I don't know. I didn't want to.

LÁZARO. There's national planning for you. We don't want to know. Best to buy yellow clothes. Buy blue and it'll be a girl, buy pink and it'll be a boy. Sod's law. There'll be a lot of shit whatever it is; whatever it is you'll have to clean it up, and whatever it is this won't be the last time someone points a gun at it.

THE LITTLE MAKE-UP GIRL. If it's born at all.

LÁZARO. I won't be stopping it, in fact I'm going to do you a favour. You're poor, which means that this country, which couldn't give a shit about its future mothers, will be completely ignoring your medical and mental needs. But it shouldn't, because you're the motherland made flesh – look at you. Our country respects corpses, looks up to them. Our national anthem has us all aspire to be corpses, and the motherland will do the make-up in the funeral parlour. Just like you. Remember the history books they gave you in primary school. All those heads of the martyrs of independence, like mascots, singing hymns to our liberty while they rot. And every single one of them has had a touch-up, a little facial from the motherland. The nation's first make-up girl. And get this – you and I, we both make a living doing dead people.

THE LITTLE MAKE-UP GIRL. I haven't killed anyone.

LÁZARO. You don't understand. And that's as it should be. When you begin to understand, that's when your problems will start. It's the people who want to understand who are always the first to die when the police start shooting in the streets. When you don't understand and you've got nothing anyone else wants, then you can live in peace. That big yellow fish of a body you're working on: not a day went by but hordes of barefoot pedestrians didn't long for him to die, while he just drove on past with his Brahms and the air-con turned up full. That's a great man for you. In this city the only ones who pay any attention to the traffic lights and the crowds of pedestrians are the mediocre ones in the little driving-school cars, the ones who try to understand, the ones who end up with their heads through the windscreens. The others get in their cars every day and drive until their hands are worn hard from the steering wheel and everyone else just has to watch out. Stop staring at the pistol, your eyes are tired enough as it is, just listen and learn. No one else is going to come here and tell you this, and you've got to pass it on to your son or your daughter or whatever it is that comes out of you. OK, so this is the deal, Guadalupe, my little morgue-petal: from tomorrow there'll be two kinds of waste meat passing through your hands. Some of them will be the routine ones, but most of them will be cattle branded by me. Well, fat as cattle, but smaller. Sort of like dogs. Those ones get special treatment. Not funeral make-up. Something burlesque, grotesque, clown make-up, make-up like a cross-dressing politician. Whatever takes your fancy, get creative, but I want everyone to see them for who they are. The police already know about this so don't make a fool of yourself by running to them. Remember that whenever people ask our police why they didn't answer a call for help from a rape victim, they say they thought it was just a bit of harmless fun. Difficult times for you lot. Of course you'll get commission for every client. From the moment this idea popped into my head, you became as guilty as me. Sorry about that. You can put it down to the idle life people of my class lead. Any questions?

THE LITTLE MAKE-UP GIRL. How will I know which ones are yours?

LÁZARO. I'll let you know. You'll be hearing from me. I hang out with the boss of this place and our other self-indulgent wastrel friends. And I promise that on the day your child is born I'll come to find out whether it's a boy or a girl.

THE LITTLE MAKE-UP GIRL. What's your name?

LÁZARO. Lázaro.

THE LITTLE MAKE-UP GIRL. Can I have a look at your gun, Lázaro?

LÁZARO *gives her the revolver.*

BODYGUARD 1. Sir, your mother's trying to get in.

LÁZARO. She's trying to get into a funeral parlour? Tell her not to be so impatient. Tell her her time will come, she'll see a tunnel of light and feel an inexplicable peace, the grandmother she loved so much will come to her and her life will flash before her eyes like it's a film. Tell her to remember all those yoga and reiki classes. She'll be reincarnated as a tortoise and live to a hundred, dragging herself along on her stomach. Just like now but without the surgery.

BODYGUARD 1. Remember your mother pays my wages, sir.

LÁZARO. Then this is your big chance. Your pay's terrible. Make a stand. Take the body hostage. Go and barricade the front door. Everything's for sale, you can take control of anything and everything. It's called good citizenship.

BODYGUARD 1. I'll hold her off for as long as I can, sir.

LÁZARO. A man should never have to hear that from his bodyguard. Or his lover. Go on then, let her in. Her kidneys aren't what they were and you've got lots of mouths to feed with your little pistol. Let her in. Alone.

Enter the MOTHER, *elegantly dressed for a funeral.*

MOTHER. You cretin, what do you think you're doing? The press and the cameras are . . .

LÁZARO. You're such a bad, bad mother. Why do I have this feeling of revulsion all the time? It's all the rotten flesh you've released into the world. And all those books, that travel, all that art. Go shopping, Mum. You're terrified of all the bacteria running around on these corpses, you know you are. Just go shopping.

MOTHER. I don't recognise you.

LÁZARO. That's because you're looking for Lázaro. Look for your son instead. He's the horror-show with the twisted face that's talking to you, he's sort of got your mouth and eyes. Aren't you so ashamed you just want to drop everything and run to a plastic surgeon? You don't understand, Mother. You don't understand and you never will. All you know is how to keep yourself amused. That's why you're crying. Just go shopping.

MOTHER. I will not stand by while you destroy the good name of our family, and your grandfather's.

LÁZARO. That's right, Mother. 'Your grandfather.' You're right not to say 'my father' because you've got none of his dignity. You can hear the old man in me, though, can't you? All you can think about is letting the cameras in, the reporters, you want to be seen by thousands of starving people. They'll all be delighted there's one more fat-cat dead. This nation of idiots gets up every day at six just to scratch their arses and watch the news to see if there's any more politicians caught on video, taking brown envelopes in a hotel room. Gives them the horn. Be corrupt, Mother, defend our western culture from the Chinese you hate so much, preserve our cultural heritage for future generations. Go and do some shopping. In Europe.

MOTHER. That's enough. Shut up. As of now my responsibilities to you as a mother are over. You will go right now and let in the people who have come for my father's funeral. You will take those men off the door immediately and you will tell them to put their guns away. Then you will go out through the back door and you will come back in through the front door and you will behave in a way worthy of your family name. Otherwise all these people, who I may remind you are my staff, will either throw you out or shoot you like a dog.

LÁZARO. When my mother speaks with tears in her eyes, what she says gets done. You will always have a mother's responsibilities to me, this scrap of your flesh that fell from your plate. As long as I'm on the earth or under it. You are responsible as my mother for everything I do and everyone I kill. And you should never have given up yoga.

MOTHER. Get him out of here now.

LÁZARO *takes his gun and aims it at* BODYGUARD 1.

Get him out. He's not going to do anything to you, go on, get him out.

LÁZARO *shoots.* BODYGUARD 1 *falls, wounded.*

LÁZARO. You never get me right, do you? I'm going to do more than you think. Call the police now, or the rest of the seven dwarves, and you can watch me killing my way through them until they kill me.

A group of BODYGUARDS *enters. They disarm* LÁZARO.

MOTHER. You're a dog dying for a beating, aren't you? This is for giving me the misfortune to be your mother.

The MOTHER *hits him three times. She breaks a fingernail.*

Shit.

LÁZARO. Hey, guys, anyone can become president, our country has a great future. Ten minutes ago you worked for me, and now you work for my mother. And all for a tip that a pizza delivery boy would sniff at.

MOTHER. Think very carefully about what you're doing. Look how many pairs of eyes your mother has to watch you with, and ropes to muzzle you.

LÁZARO. What's your money going to buy you, Mother? Another bodyguard, maybe? This one's leaking raspberry jam. No, your choice is this: you can use your cash to save either me, or another village church for the gringo tourists to coo over. Do you want a son who's free or one who's banged up? Which is it, Mother: do you want to be the woman there was all that scandal about because she sent her own flesh and blood to prison, or the woman who lives at peace with herself while her son is killing off the plague that's eating away at our country?

MOTHER. My motherly love doesn't stretch to this. Listen to this, pig: if you're not at church tomorrow to convert to the true faith I'll take away your share of the company, and then see how many friends you've got left. You'll have to learn how to beg. You've made me suffer enough. Faith isn't something you play around with. It's much worse to be cursed in the eyes of Him who sees everything than in the eyes of your mother, and that's bad enough. Let him go.

LÁZARO. I'll leave you to think about it. If you need me, I'm with the rest of your guests putting a pained face on, buying them a round of patriotic tequila and generally being a fraud, Mother. An emotional fraud. Out through the back door. Good citizenship, see? (*To the* LITTLE MAKE-UP GIRL.) This is the world you're bringing your child into. Ooh, a good idea for a christening gift: a godfather with friends abroad.

LÁZARO *leaves. His nose is bleeding and he has a scar on his face.*

MOTHER. Don't look at me like that, girl. If it goes on like this you won't reach my age. And your son won't reach the age when every son turns into a bastard.

Leave him, I'll look after him – you lot go.

The BODYGUARDS *go.* BODYGUARD 1 *is bleeding on the floor.*

(*To the* LITTLE MAKE-UP GIRL.) He's all yours. Don't move him. Any more trouble and you'll end up the same way. If he dies, get rid of the body. Say a prayer for him, though. Hide him somewhere, you'll think of something. Don't forget the prayer. This man was my father. Just as handsome as he was last Sunday.

THE LITTLE MAKE-UP GIRL. I was reading about the most famous magazine article ever. Hiroshima. They filled the whole magazine with a single article by one writer. Einstein ordered a thousand copies. I read about the faces of the bomb victims, completely burned, their eye-sockets hollow, and how those two white planets that they watched the fire burn their eyes out with melted into a liquid like semen, and ran down their cheeks. I read about the kimono patterns traced out on the women's skin by the heat. Beautiful twentieth-century tattoos. I read how at the moment of the blast the bomb left shadows behind. Beautiful twentieth-century flash photography. Vaguely human shadows were found imprinted on the walls and pavements. Twentieth-century photocopies. A hundred and fifty thousand photocopies of people who lost the war. At primary school a kid in my class brought in a book called *Let's Play at Nuclear Disasters*. On the cover there was a little boy in a bunker, wearing an oxygen mask and playing with a little aeroplane. Next to him was a girl playing with a doll. Falling towards the bunker was a nuclear bomb, drawn in crayon. Inside the book there were all these games meant to prepare kids' imaginations for nuclear disaster. Let's play at measuring radioactivity. Let's play at decorating our oxygen masks. Let's play at counting missing fingers. Before, in the first year of primary school, a teacher had taught us what the H-bomb was. And I used to imagine my little world, my house, the two blocks between there and school, my friends' houses, all desolate, empty. We'd all disappeared with the H-bomb. There was nothing left of me, of my body, at all. In two years I'll be a citizen of this country, I'll have official documentation, I'll pay taxes. And the statistics say that I'll disappear one night in a black car. They'll find my remains, and human rights groups, groups whose bread and butter are murders like mine, will demand justice for my killers. Being a citizen of this country scares me, being a citizen of this world scares me, even more because I'm poor and the poor aren't really citizens of this world. They should declare us items of world heritage instead. Then they'd dedicate vast sums of money to restoring us and conserving us for future generations. A heritage for the world: a bunch of unclassifiable non-citizens, scared, heading for extinction, starved to death, a heritage for their own world.

Penthouse

Party. Opulence and excess. Pool. Bar. Bikinis. Very classy drinks. Top floor of the most modern building in the city. Everything oozes wealth and beauty. As they drink multivitamin energy drinks, dance and talk, drugged up on vitamins and natural health-food garbage, they throw ice cubes over the edge. To one side of the group, their BODYGUARDS *play table football.*

SANTIAGO. I can't believe he missed that penalty. What kind of donkey misses a penalty like that? We get fucked all over again because once again wonder-boy Herrera misses a penalty. And with his left, again. Why does he insist on using his left? He hasn't got a left.

FRANCESCO. I don't know. I didn't see the match, I went to see that new production at the National.

PABLO. Me too. The play might as well have started with a big sign saying: 'Please, no one get up, don't put your coats on, it's absolutely clear to us that you are all honourable people and none of you bear any resemblance to our characters. It's just a story. It's made up. None of it is true. Please don't put your coats on.'

SANTIAGO. Writers like that look at the world through the eyes of a cleaning lady. As far as they're concerned, if you can't run a duster over it, it doesn't exist. Realism bores me in real life, let alone in a script. You can stick your nicely turned phrases in the dishwasher. Our world isn't mediocre like that.

MARIANA. There's a guy who's sort of a friend of mine who's always winning those big arts prizes. But I can't remember his name.

SANTIAGO *gets out some cocaine.*

PABLO. What's that?

SANTIAGO. Just a little something to help the party swing.

PABLO. You can keep it, you won't find any of us putting that shit inside us. Get rid of it.

SANTIAGO. Calm down, Mother Teresa, it's just for me, if you don't appreciate the revelatory power of this stuff you needn't have any. Those health drinks of yours are no different, it's all just pouring the same crap into your system. Drugs are the only holy thing we have left. That and making sure that when the time comes there's a sniper there to put a bullet between our eyes. Anything rather than end up a cripple.

He snorts a line.

PABLO. We're the snipers. The cannon fodder, the excess fat, are the artists, and the suits in the Arts Ministry.

SANTIAGO. It's not the bureaucrats' fault. They're just the symptom, the bad smell that tells you there's a problem. The infection is underneath, and it's the artists. We shouldn't be killing the pen-pushers, they only take the jobs because they need to eat.

FRANCESCO. Listen to you, coming over all peace-loving. Is that what your little something does to you?

PABLO. We've been over this. When we flush the chain, down they go. Artists and government ministers, they can all share the worms' budgets out between them in their graves. That's not so different from what they do now anyway.

REBECA. What I think we *should* talk about again is, why start with the theatre people? The theatre's dead, no one's interested, no one goes. We should start with the cinema, that's where it's at, that's what carries the country's image abroad.

MARIANA. Can't we talk about something fun instead. Everyone seems a bit crabby.

SANTIAGO. OK, important stuff: when the Martians take over the earth, what will they like, and what'll they really hate?

MARIANA. They'll hate you.

PABLO. They'd like the reality shows that Lázaro's grandfather makes – well, used to. Especially the one with the people who lead a double life for six months, and the one with the impossible mission, or that one on terrestrial, *Don't Tell a Soul*.

REBECA. That is such a banal heap of shit.

PABLO. Look, Rebeca, junk culture and trash art are precisely the things that'll still be around in a few hundred years. There's more and more demand for stuff like . . . like paintings by serial killers. It's the highbrow theatres and the museums that are full of crap.

FRANCESCO. I'll tell you who'll rub Martians up the wrong way – fucking Gandhi.

SANTIAGO. They won't like pornography either.

FRANCESCO. If there are people who like watching sex between animals, why shouldn't Martians enjoy watching a guy with antennae and a big green dick shagging a fat black woman with blue-tinted contact lenses and her hair dyed blonde? Bad taste is universal.

PABLO. Fucking racist.

MARIANA. Some pornography's really beautiful. But sex with animals is for scum.

BODYGUARD 2. Let's finish the list. Your go.

BODYGUARD 3. Julius Caesar. Roman dictator. March 15, 44 BC. In the Roman senate, at the hands of a conspiracy of senators led by Brutus, Cassius, Cimber and Casca.

Claudio I. Roman Emperor. 54 AD. Poisoned by Agripina his fourth wife.

St Thomas Becket, Archbishop of Canterbury. 1170. At the foot of the altar in the cathedral by followers of Henry II.

BODYGUARD 2. Christopher Marlowe. English poet and playwright. 1593, in a tavern brawl.

Gustav III. King of Sweden. 1792. At a masked ball by a bunch of nobles.

BODYGUARD 3. Abraham Lincoln. 1865. President of the USA. With a shot from a pistol fired by John Wilkes in a theatre in Washington.

BODYGUARD 2. Mariano Melgajero. 1872. Bolivian tyrant who whacked President Belzú and was in turn killed by his in-laws.

Emiliano Zapata. Mexican peasant leader. 1919. Chinameca.

Ernst Roehm National Socialist leader, rival to Hitler. 1934. In Hitler's Night of the Long Knives.

BODYGUARD 3. All right, you win. My round.

BODYGUARD 2. Look how yellow the clouds are.

SANTIAGO. At least I haven't been trotting along to the polling station like a docile little calf. You and all those other arse-licking dolts in the herd who believe in democracy.

PABLO. I don't believe in it either. No one with any intelligence does. But given the choice what would a calf prefer? Starving to death or . . . starving to death.

FRANCESCO. 'Make up your own mind. No one else can . . . '

SANTIAGO. Don't spew those slogans at me. You know who dreamed up that fucking campaign? That tosser Turtleface, Turtleface and the Vampire, I was with them when they got the idea for that 'If you don't decide for yourself' thing, we were speeding our tits off, so don't give me that shit. If anyone knows what cretins those adverts take people for, it's us publicists. You remember that campaign with the . . .

MARIANA. Ah, Lázaro's here.

PABLO. How do you know?

MARIANA. I've just seen him. I'll go and get him.

She runs off.

REBECA. How did that woman get to be so stupid?

SANTIAGO. She isn't stupid. She's just got a different kind of talent. She can sing and dance like no one else I know. She's a genius, but with her body. A thousand times better than being a genius with your brain.

REBECA. She's a porn actress. If it weren't for Lázaro she'd never be doing all that theatre and dance stuff.

FRANCESCO. Well, I use her website.

REBECA. That's disgusting.

SANTIAGO. It's doing her a favour. It's good for her self-esteem. That's why she does it.

FRANCESCO. To me it's very simple. The girl has a waistline like a cool glass of beer. When I go to the cinema and the theatre and her website, that's what I'm there to see. I also think it's crazy to be talking about the same crap we always talk about when we're surrounded by so many girls – look at this.

SANTIAGO. Aah, we've a poet amongst us.

FRANCESCO. I've told you, all that art stuff of yours bores me, I'm only here because you're my friends and I'm dying to put all those weapons I've got to some use. No point them going rusty at home. Everyone's got a hobby.

Enter LÁZARO.

PABLO. How are you feeling, Lázaro?

LÁZARO. God, what is this? Got a card for me, have you? Flowers? Let's get down to business. We have to get moving on this now. No more meetings, we start doing the first ones after the weekend.

FRANCESCO. That's more like it.

REBECA. We wanted to talk about starting with the cinema people. There are so few of the theatre ones and nobody cares about them. We have to start big.

LÁZARO. We start with the theatre – it's purer junk than any other art form, it's the only one we can't recycle into something else. Everything's planned, it'll only take us three weeks, then the other arts and so on until our name is tattooed on the backs of porn actresses the world over. Cheers!

ANYONE WHO HAPPENS TO FEEL LIKE IT. Cheers!

SANTIAGO. I can't help thinking you always need a few wankers around the place. Besides, we have to watch out or we'll just look like a bunch of whackos.

LÁZARO. Don't talk such crap, people will think you're a politician. They'll start asking you to tarmac their roads and give them late bar licences.

PABLO. Francesco and I have been putting a plan together. To hide the weapons we can use some old cameras I've got lying around in the studio, there's everything from Polaroid to movie cameras. We can put them together in his factories. Advantage number one: none of these jerks runs away from a camera. Advantage number two: everyone dies saying 'cheese'.

LÁZARO. The police have got their bung already, all I have to do is get in touch with a few hit men today, people who deal with this kind of stuff. The first thing is to make sure that the killings at the theatre where they're doing *Don Juan* go smoothly – the individual killings and especially the Minister for Culture and the Arts.

PABLO. I'll put my toys together on Sunday.

LÁZARO. So we start on Monday.

PABLO. By Monday we'll have three stills cameras, three movie cameras and one steadycam for a bit of variety.

SANTIAGO. Come on, guys, that's enough now, it's all right as a game, but I think you're all taking it too seriously. Sometimes you make me think you might actually be serious.

LÁZARO. We are serious, Santiago, we're going to kill people. We're going to rid art of these cankers and warts.

SANTIAGO. I'm serious.

LÁZARO. We are, too, and I thought you were on board.

SANTIAGO. I can't do that. I can't kill people.

PABLO. Don't start cocking around. You're in this now and you'll do your bit. Or are your drugs turning you into a coward?

LÁZARO. He doesn't have to do it if he doesn't want to, this isn't the Mafia. Or a political party.

PABLO. He'll grass on us.

SANTIAGO. I won't say anything, you're my friends, but I can't do this. I thought it was a game.

FRANCESCO. Tomorrow you wake up dead.

LÁZARO. No one's going to kill anyone, boys.

FRANCESCO. I'm not letting a snitch like this ruin the whole project.

LÁZARO. Go on, Santiago, we'll talk about this tomorrow.

FRANCESCO. You're not going anywhere, scum.

FRANCESCO aims at SANTIAGO. The BODYGUARDS aim at FRANCESCO.

LÁZARO. Come on, children, put your guns away. (*To the* BODYGUARDS.) And who the hell do you think you are? You point a gun at one of my guests and you don't leave this building alive.

Wrong-footed, the BODYGUARDS *put their guns away.*

PABLO. You can't let him go, he'll go straight to the police.

LÁZARO. I already told you, the police are happy, they've had their cash. Go on, Santiago, we'll talk later. Calm down, Francesco.

SANTIAGO. I swear I won't say anything, but this is going to land you guys in deep shit, think about it.

FRANCESCO. Take one step and I put holes in you, you fucking pansy.

LÁZARO. Why are you so afraid of him?

FRANCESCO. I'm not afraid. Traitors make me sick, that's all.

LÁZARO. OK, but not like this, Francesco.

SANTIAGO. You have my word, I won't say anything, but I can't be in on it. I can't. I've got my beliefs.

MARIANA. Fucking Buddhist.

LÁZARO. Go on – nobody will touch you, we'll meet up and have a chat. He won't try anything.

LÁZARO *puts his finger in the barrel of* FRANCESCO*'s gun and at the same time aims at him with his.* SANTIAGO *runs off with his* BODYGUARDS.

FRANCESCO. All right, people, let's get drunk. Only love and leisure are worth anything in this turncoat world. You just made your first mistake, boss.

REBECA. You will kill him, won't you?

LÁZARO. I said I wouldn't.

REBECA. He'll ruin everything.

LÁZARO. Come on, let's dance.

REBECA. I don't like traitors and I like the people who put up with them even less.

FRANCESCO *and* REBECA *leave.*

PABLO. We don't need them.

LÁZARO. They'll be back.

MARIANA. Dance with me, Lázaro.

LÁZARO. Bastard penalties. They turn decent people into dogs. Cheers.

LÁZARO *downs his vitamin drink in one.*

The federal laws as they pertain to authorised violence in the Republic of Mexico

Free and indiscriminate violence may be exercised with the full approbation and to the acclaim of the whole of society, and entirely in keeping with our most cherished national traditions, by anyone acting with one or more of the following motives:

When a baby in the womb senses that its mother is being attacked, the aforementioned baby may take his or her revenge after his or her birth in whatever way he or she likes.

When a foreigner says that in *his* country, maize is fed to pigs.

When a group of foreigners attacks a lap-dancer or a prostitute born within the borders of our heroic nation.

When a man discovers his wife in bed with another man.

When a man discovers his man in bed with another man.

When a woman behaves in too masculine a way.

When a man behaves in too feminine a way.

When a prisoner flirts with or whistles at the sister of a fellow inmate.

When said violence is perpetrated against hooligans, skinheads, or anyone else who considers themselves to be more violent than we are.

When members of the police forces are found to have kidnapped children or when they are discovered doing anything to children which we wouldn't let our neighbours do.

When poor people are contracted to kill rich people. Better still if those engaged under the terms of the contract are young people from gangs in deprived neighbourhoods of the capital and will have the chance to get to know the most exclusive areas of the city centre when they go there with their false ID in their pockets to kill their victims; better still if those contracted are illiterate and ignorant and before opening fire will have the chance to take in the best that the arts have to offer, see an opera, a play, go to an exhibition, have a few sips of a cocktail, eat something they've never tried before and never will again, to have something to tell their girlfriend or the hooker they happen to be with that day or their mother when they're at home and there's another power cut and they can't watch television, to be able to stand up and applaud in theatres and then pull the trigger with their eyes still filled with tears from the emotion of having seen something beautiful or perhaps still yawning after having not understood a word. Better still if they have a chance to gorge their eyes on the faces of beautiful women, so many that they won't be able to choose which one to dedicate the final moment of their rough and orgiastic happiness to, and better still if they, from the world of popular art, graffiti, rock bands and tattoos, can stand up in the middle of a theatre and put a bullet in the head of the director or the lead soprano, interrupting their hectic schedules of European tours and international festivals. Under these circumstances we would all be obliged not only to forgive them, but indeed applaud them with patriotic fervour.

When a player misses a penalty.

Anyone who is the perpetrator of violence under one or more of the above-mentioned circumstances will receive the full endorsement of the public and will further be allowed to relapse into violence whenever they fancy it.

Confession with Diego in the Alameda

LÁZARO *is chatting to* DIEGO RIVERA. *All the figures in the mural, 'Dream of a Sunday Afternoon in the Alameda', are looking at them.* DIEGO *has a brush in his hand.* LÁZARO *has a section of wall hung from wires. He moves it in and out of* DIEGO*'s reach, as* DIEGO *tries to paint on it.* LÁZARO*'s* BODYGUARDS *play table football in silence.*

LÁZARO. Killing someone is always personal, Diego. Juarez was a great revolutionary but he lied about that. 'It's the ideas I'm killing, not the people behind them,' he said. But he did kill people, it's always people that do the dying, not ideas, and the blood you choke on in the end is always yours. Ideas don't exist, only bodies that are, to varying degrees, decomposed, dismembered, or just unrecognisable by the time they make it to autopsy. I like you, Diego, you're like a big doughnut filled with jam. Your paintings remind me of the faces of our people. Flat, in dull, ochre colours, like rockets without a fuse. They're never going to explode, no matter what you do to them. Our powder's wet. I don't think you really mind about dying. Your murals will survive as pieces of art, that dead whore we used to call art, and that we now restore like a stuffed bear to give the tourist guides something to go on about. The buildings you painted will be destroyed by earthquakes. The textbooks in our schools will have new illustrations to replace yours, something with a Japanese sort of look, our heroes drawn with big eyes, our heroines with perfect bodies. And then all that's left for you is death, and that's dead easy to portray. A pushover. I'm tired of you, Diego, of what you represent, and that's why I have to kill you. But before I do, there are a few things I have to confess to you. I know I'm about to kill you, but there are some things that only you understand. Like what it means to be a corpse in this desert corner of the planet.

So this is my confession, Diego: I'm afraid. I'm alone. There's no one I can call a friend. Not a single person I would call a kindred spirit. All I want is for life to grab me and crush me between its teeth like bones. But I don't know how, it's impossible to know how. These are bad times, Diego. It's the comfortable and the happy ones who are in the driving seat. The future of our country is with those women with careful hair who go out doing the soup-run in their shiny

SUVs. Everything has to be a free gift, or at a knock-down price. We know our pathologies too well and we're proud of them. Forgive me for telling you all this, but these days, which aren't your days any more, if it's not a spectacle, if it's not a show, if the audience aren't enjoying themselves, if the spectators don't clap at the end, then the whole thing is just considered masturbation. Bad times, Diego, when everything has to be entertainment.

Look at you, just staring at the wall. Like the mouse and the lump of cheese, the donkey and the carrot, the artist and his work. But that's enough speeches. Back to work.

LÁZARO *lets* DIEGO *paint a red stripe on the wall. He shoots* DIEGO *in the head. Black blood like Chinese ink spurts from his body. The figures from the mural look at each other in horror, some of them splashed with* DIEGO*'s blood.*

The Massacre of the Holy Innocents-Schminnocents

A television studio set. The whole thing – a nineteenth-century battlefield with trenches, nineteenth-century armies and weapons and tattered Mexican and US flags – is being dismantled, pieces of it being moved around. In its place, a cave with rock paintings is being assembled. Production assistants help the actors put on Neanderthal costumes while the actors chat and joke on their mobiles. Huge panels from the Kama Sutra *go by upstage on their way from one set to another.* LÁZARO*'s* BODYGUARDS *play with a spinning top.*

LÁZARO. Heroes from history, don't go yet, I want a word with you.

An actor dressed as EMILIANO ZAPATA, *another one looking like* EINSTEIN *with a primitive bomb in his hands, and a third dressed in black carrying a skull, all sit down.*

OK, let's be clear about this. The only reason we're making these programmes is because the President of the Republic wants us to. If it was down to me, we'd broadcast beauty contests and cookery programmes all day, but the powers that be want these programmes done. Having said that, what they really don't want on a public TV channel is any kind of exposé of our national heroes, their private lives laid bare, and they certainly don't want us saying that they're not heroes at all, got that?

THE MAN WHO LOOKS LIKE EINSTEIN. We think it's time to tell the country the truth.

LÁZARO. You don't say. I'll tell you the truth. The truth is that the national side, the team that represents this nation forged by heroes and saints, rich in virtues and glory, lost two–nil to the US yesterday.

Enter Lázaro's FATHER. *The others leave.*

FATHER. How is the new chief exec on his first day? Putting the world to rights?

LÁZARO. As far as I know the world is unrightable, the best thing to do is run it into the ground. We've run out of victims now so we might as well just throw the prison gates open. But have a seat, Father, you may as well relax for a minute, we've got millions of years to kill yet until we're extinct.

FATHER. The worst of it is, you actually believe what you're saying.

LÁZARO. Don't you? You should be a politician.

FATHER. You despise them.

LÁZARO. I don't like people who never manage to wean themselves off breastfeeding from the poor.

FATHER. I'll have to remember that one.

LÁZARO. No, just remember what you came here for. Tell me what you want.

FATHER. I've come to give you some advice, and to ask you a favour.

LÁZARO. If it has anything to do with women . . .

FATHER. Is there anything else?

LÁZARO. Of course – there are monsters, freaks and torturers, like the one I'm sure you're dying to introduce me to.

FATHER. I don't care what your girlfriend does with her life, I've long since stopped wondering why you seem to like the idea of her displaying herself to the world like that. No, I wanted to ask you to do something for me.

LÁZARO. Ah, you must be cheating on Mother.

FATHER. No, actually, I want to do something for her, because I love her very much, and since you've been such a shit you should be ready to do anything for me if it means making up to her.

LÁZARO. There's the emotional blackmail.

FATHER. This is something very close to my heart. You're my son. I need your respect and your help on this one.

LÁZARO. And there's the heartfelt bit. I'm listening.

FATHER. Your mother has always thought that I'm a coward, a bit of a fool. At our age, with so much water under the bridge, it's too late to change much, least of all what your wife thinks of you. But I just want to show her how wrong she is. She's not going to like it, of course, but at least she'll know that I'm good for something. Otherwise I have to spend my last years next to someone who doesn't know what it means to be afraid of me. That's no kind of way to go. So anyway, what I want is for you to let me be part of this project to clean up art.

LÁZARO. Oh, so you found out. The police have an entertainments division do they?

FATHER. Mendoza told me about it. He also assured me that they'd make sure nothing happened to you – in exchange for a few tweaks in their pay and conditions, of course, and I thought I could look after those as a little thank you to you. All I want is for you to let me kill someone, an actor, with the whole funeral-home thing, the full works. Just the one actor. Your mother and him write to each other, I found out about them yesterday.

LÁZARO. I'm not doing this as some kind of therapy service for broken-hearted fathers and husbands. This isn't a business, this is for real, it's serious.

FATHER. I'm a man who needs revenge. I'll do anything to win back your mother's respect. Help me out here.

LÁZARO. Then put your money where your mouth is.

LÁZARO *gives him his gun.*

Kill me. You'll solve Mum's problems and yours all in one go. I'm the one who's getting in the way. If you want to prove your manhood do what God's chosen ones traditionally do when they want to start a good strong family line: kill your son. Maybe the angel will turn up to stop you and maybe he won't.

FATHER. Don't get God mixed up in this. If I didn't live my life by his laws I'd have done it ages ago.

LÁZARO. Done what? Been a proper man for your wife or killed me? Mum wasn't wrong, you are a coward. And a father who shows himself a coward in front of his son is a waste of skin. Run along and consult some managers or whatever it is you do. Mum's bound to need more money for her foundation, they've got no end of things to restore, this country's full of ruins.

FATHER. Life comes around, you'll see.

LÁZARO. That's our whole problem: the advice you presume to give me is stuff that I could have said to you years ago. And talking of women: go to your future daughter-in-law's website, click in the top right-hand corner where it says 'Write to me, sweetheart,' and ask her what it means to be a man. You'll be surprised. You can learn something every day. And yet some people don't learn anything in their whole lifetimes.

FATHER. You're a disgrace.

LÁZARO. No, no, I'm not. We've got special eyedrops we use for actors who can't do tears. Do you want to see what you look like when you cry, Father?

FATHER. We'll soon see who's crying, in the mud.

LÁZARO. I really hope I remember to set the video on the day they expose your frauds and scams on television. Everything's a joke, Father, you have to treat life like a game. Smile, your son loves you.

The FATHER *leaves.*

Gaby.

LÁZARO'S PA *arrives.*

We'll do the Neanderthals next, and then the giant in the big Mexican hat roaring over New York, OK? Thanks.

The lights go out. Upstage, the Neanderthals paint the walls of their cave. They find a bone and fight over it. One of them kills the other.

This space is reserved for our sponsors

MARKETING WOMAN. This is a chance for all of you, potential sponsors, to get involved in the marketing opportunity that this production represents. We are making one minute of the show available to you as a kind of shop-window, if you will, for you to harness the publicity potential locked up here in the audience.

She looks at her watch, timing the minute, and steps into the audience. No one volunteers. She reappears on the stage.

Failing that, we could turn to the theatre management for a few words about other events here at the theatre?

No response.

Or maybe the actors would like to talk about any other projects they're involved in . . .

They shake their heads. At the last moment one of them speaks up:

ACTOR. Actually, me and a few friends have been working on a sort of . . .

MARKETING WOMAN (*interrupting*). Well, I'll be in the bar afterwards if anyone wants to come and find me there.

Posthumous interview with the corrupt Minister for Culture and the Arts

In the conference room a sign reads:

'Please, no one get up, don't put your coats on, it's absolutely clear to us that you are all honourable people and none of you bear any resemblance to our characters. It's just a story. None of it is true. Please don't put your coats on.'

The MINISTER *is sitting at a table behind a plaque with his name on it. He is wearing a suit that is covered in blood from a wound to his head.* REPORTERS *fill the room.*

REPORTERS. Do you hold a grudge against them?

MINISTER. No, all I'm holding are the two bullets that lodged in my cranium. Hardly a groundbreaking way of killing someone, is it? Little shits.

REPORTERS. Can you tell us what happened that day?

MINISTER. Mariana came to my office with a file on a project. It was called, well it *is* called, because she still has it, 'Two things a bastard should think about before leaving his government post.' I didn't think it was aimed at me. She kicked me twice and punched me once in the head, then she shot me. I think I died immediately, although I should add, for those of you who have sometimes wondered about this: it really hurts, you don't stop feeling. The police didn't give me an autopsy. Natural causes, they said. They were bribed, I saw it from the black tunnel that stretches out in front of you when you die. As my relatives came towards me, I felt an inexplicable peace, and then in the funeral parlour a young pregnant woman made up my body so that nobody would notice anything.

REPORTERS. Why do you think they killed you?

MINISTER. They're people who think the world owes them something. None of them has ever won any grants or prizes, I mean, they're nobodies. They say we only give them out to our cronies, but they're wrong, we choose – I mean we used to choose – the best projects. I wasn't corrupt.

Revenge, I want revenge. I want to speak to the President, he owes me a few favours.

REPORTERS. What was the project about?

MINISTER. I never read the file, so I don't know anything about her proposal. I was going to read it but the bitch shot me before I got the chance.

REPORTERS. Was no one there with you?

MINISTER. When she killed me we were in a rehearsal room. There's always people around, and you hear all kinds of things when people are rehearsing plays, so everyone thought it was just a rehearsal. It was only when I started to stink that they realised I was there.

Laughter.

REPORTERS. Was there a lot of sex in your life?

MINISTER. No, no one could accuse me of that, not even back when I was an actor. I did what everyone does, I gave jobs to my friends, but only to the intelligent ones, I cheated on my wife with secretaries, but it was for love and not the kind of thing that you can really blame anyone for.

REPORTERS. Nothing else?

MINISTER. Well, the odd thing that you'd have to say was worse than that, but generally I was drunk and I let myself get carried away by my baser instincts.

REPORTERS. One of the people who plotted your death knew you before you were a government minister, and said that you were a sensitive man, but that power had corrupted you. That only a good and sensitive person such as yourself could be corrupted to such a degree. What's your response to that?

MINISTER. I think I know why they targeted me. Lázaro and I once went to the airport to pick up some English people who'd come to lead some workshop or other. You know what it's like in International Arrivals, all those blondes, those dark girls with their perfectly cut features. I said to Lázaro, 'I can't help feeling inferior, they've got centuries of good breeding over us.' Lázaro looked at me and said, 'Which of your eyes has the weaker prescription?' I told him my right one. So they bullet through my good eye. To leave me more blind. More blind and dead.

REPORTERS. What do you have to say to your killers, who'll be reading all about you tomorrow in the papers as they eat breakfast on the terrace by the pool?

MINISTER. That I wasn't corrupt and that they should stand up and say that I was to my face. Even though I'm dead. What's more, I didn't have anything against anyone, but my job makes, well, made, certain demands on me. I had the country's artistic future in my hands, that's a weighty responsibility. And that they're a bunch of *beep*. They can go *beep* themselves.

REPORTERS. Tell us about your life now that you're dead.

MINISTER. Well, I'm resting in peace but things carry on pretty much as normal. I didn't commit any mortal sins. But I think you might be interested to know that I'm going to come back as a close relative of Lázaro's. I can't tell you who. Let's just say, what goes around . . . Karma, I think they call it.

REPORTERS. What advice would you give young civil servants just starting out?

MINISTER. Have integrity, really get into your work, make fast and effective contacts and set out to make things happen with the money that you have to allocate here. That's the polite way of putting it. Alternatively: everyone will envy you, everyone will ask you favours but deep down they'll hate you. Kill them first, pull their guts out before they do it to you, don't trust anyone. This is politics, not art, this is about getting power: kill your enemy, show him no mercy, make him suffer as he dies, it feels really good. Your bosses are all a bunch of dogs, and your colleagues and the people under you all hate them. Use power for what it is, use it to kill other people, kill them.

REPORTERS. Anything you want to add?

MINISTER. All these people envied me. I'm the victim here. History will vindicate me.

REPORTERS. Can we take a few photos?

MINISTER. Of course, but promise me you'll run a tribute, and soon.

REPORTERS. Of course. Thanks.

The MINISTER *lies on the floor and gets into the position his body was found in. Lots of flashes, other government employees kneel down and weep for him, some leave flowers, others leave personal items for him, a photo of him in his early career as an actor. Everyone wants to be photographed next to him. When the session is over the government people and the photographers take their leave. The* MINISTER *is left alone in the darkness, dead.*

Romance of the porn actress (pornography's salvation)

A beautiful old church. Light pours in through the windows.
LÁZARO'S BODYGUARDS *and* MARIANA *are praying.*

MARIANA. I don't like coming here. I hate places where it's all about goodies and baddies. Cowboys and Indians, dogs and cats. Cookery. People are cookery and shit and that's it.

LÁZARO. We won't be long, I've just come to tell them yes, and we're done.

MARIANA. Are you going to convert?

LÁZARO. Does that worry you?

MARIANA. You know it doesn't.

LÁZARO. It's just a nice bit of PR. It's the packet that's being sold, not the contents. I need my mother to be less stressed, and I've already cut a good deal with my old man.

MARIANA. They had an item on the news about your grandfather's funeral. They made you out to be this eccentric millionaire artist who'd staged it all in his honour like some huge performance installation. Twats.

LÁZARO. Two magazines tipped me as the future businessman of the year. They had the whole country to choose from, the whole den of iniquity, and they picked me. TV news is for the poor, magazines are for the rich, that's the only difference. Here come the wrinklies. Look virginal.

Enter LÁZARO'S MOTHER *and* FATHER, *followed by five* BODYGUARDS.

MOTHER. Ah, Mariana, sweetheart, you look absolutely gorgeous. Next time I see you here I want it to be in a wedding dress. This man doesn't know how to appreciate you, all he cares about is all that strange art of his.

LÁZARO. Don't suffocate her, Mother, we just came to say that I'll convert, that's all.

FATHER. Good decision, son.

Awkward pause.

MARIANA. Is this one of the churches you restored, Señora?

MOTHER. Yes, dear. Well, my foundation did. It's back to exactly how it was in the sixteenth century. We've restored about twenty churches now, with this one. Could I have a quick word, just the two of us?

MARIANA. Of course.

The women move to one side.

FATHER. Times really do change. At your age I was going to the cinema with your mother to see smoochy films and canoodle in cars. The worst thing we ever did was lie to our parents. Have you got me down on the list for killing my little actor?

LÁZARO. I've already told you who you can kill, and Mum should be grateful.

FATHER. My little actor.

LÁZARO. I'll gift-wrap him for you, and send him to you in the post so you can drown him in the bath, what do you think?

FATHER. Do it. I'll rub him with your mother's loofah till he bleeds. I've got a present for you.

LÁZARO *opens it. It's a pipe.*

LÁZARO. A pipe.

MARIANA. I don't have to take that from anyone.

MOTHER. Don't be like that, I'm only telling you for your own good.

MARIANA. Look, I'm not a tart, I do serious work, it's art, I'm not a whore. My work saves more lives than your shitty religion does.

LÁZARO. Father, keep your hands off her.

MOTHER. Lázaro has converted now, you're going to have to accept certain things I say.

LÁZARO. You want a conversion? Watch this then, Mother.

LÁZARO *goes up to an* OLD MAN *who's selling religious pictures by the entrance to the church, drags him back by the hair, and plonks him in front of one of the statues that his* MOTHER *has restored. A* MAN *tries to come to his aid and the* BODYGUARDS *beat him and pull out their to weapons to warn off anyone else.*

Have you got any pictures of this monster?

MOTHER. You are cursed.

LÁZARO. Have you or not? You know, little postcards for the tourists?

OLD MAN. Yes, yes.

LÁZARO. Many?

OLD MAN. A boxful, don't hurt me.

LÁZARO. By the way, this is the woman who restored this place, it turned out 'beautiful' like she said, didn't it? Tell me, did it or didn't it?

OLD MAN. Yes, for God's sake.

LÁZARO. All right, Mother, since we've got so many reproductions we don't need the original any more.

LÁZARO lets the OLD MAN *go and fires two shots at the effigy.*

I declare the superiority of the porn actress over your restoration work, Mother, I declare as holy all the women who have tattoos on their breasts, on their hips, between their legs, everything that sets itself against pain and martyrdom, against the corruption of everything, and I declare the porn actress to be our goddess. Why shouldn't I be able to start a new cult? Everyone's doing it, for God's sake, everyone's doing it.

The parents' BODYGUARDS *approach* LÁZARO.

Stay right there. You know how I love killing cockroaches. But of course I'd have my work cut out – you'll be crawling out of the woodwork after a nuclear disaster, or the next elections, whichever is worse. We're in a time of war, Father.

MOTHER. Watch what you're saying. This is blasphemy.

LÁZARO. The new faith, where the lion will lie down with the lamb and then eat it.

He takes the clothes off an effigy and puts them on MARIANA.

MOTHER. You're a devil.

LÁZARO. I've checked the script. I don't have any more dialogue with you, Mother. Or you, Father.

LÁZARO *leaves, with his* BODYGUARDS *and* MARIANA. *A* PAPARAZZO *follows them.*

FATHER. I'll avenge you, my love.

MOTHER. Shut up, just shut up. Take everything away from him, leave him with nothing.

ACT TWO

Lap-dancing. The BODYGUARDS *have the* PAPARAZZO *tied up. Each of the* BODYGUARDS *has a stripper to himself, and they've paid for one for the* PAPARAZZO *too.*

BODYGUARD 2. Now this is what I call a very, very positive market indicator. Princesses dancing on us. That's got to bode well.

BODYGUARD 3. I've always said it: business deals only really last when they're made between two people cross-eyed from looking at so much ass.

BODYGUARD 2. I was never a *true* bodyguard, you know. The occasion didn't arise, but if it had ever come down to a choice, him or me, then I'd have left him to his own good death. Goes without saying.

BODYGUARD 4. Nobody has a good death. We all have a bad one.

BODYGUARD 2. Felipe had a fucking bad one, then it got worse. He woke up inside his coffin. What I heard.

BODYGUARD 4. I'm worried about my mum, I'm not sure she's going to have a good death. Twice now I've thought she was dead, but she wasn't, she was alive. You can't tell if she's dead or alive.

BODYGUARD 3. I'm taking you to see Toño.

BODYGUARD 4. Is she a lap-dancer?

BODYGUARD 3. No, Toño's my dog. He's trained to sniff for drugs, but he can find dead people too. Some Germans taught him to sniff for drugs, but somehow he picked up this sniffing for stiffs thing too.

BODYGUARD 4. No, sounds like it'd be dangerous for Mum.

BODYGUARD 3. He doesn't bite, he only barks. If she's alive

he'll bark, if she's dead he won't do anything, just scratch himself. Or slobber.

BODYGUARD 4. Mum's lived with cats all her life, he'll think she *is* a cat and bite her.

BODYGUARD 2. Guys, we have to go kill our bosses.

BODYGUARD 4. Can you just hang on for a minute? We're talking about my mum. I'm worried about this cat thing.

BODYGUARD 3. Dogs don't eat cats, only in cartoons. Toño doesn't slobber when he sees a cat. He slobbers when he sees a nice piece of meat, but not a cat. He's incredible, he's like a person. He's watching TV and some bigmouth artist comes on and it gets on his tits. And he can't stand those women who've had too much plastic surgery. Wanna know how I can tell?

BODYGUARD 4. He likes a nice piece of meat, not plastic.

BODYGUARD 3. He pisses on the floor. He never does that, only when there's arty types mouthing off or actresses who've had their faces done. He likes football, of course, he's a bloke. And Pedro Infante films.

BODYGUARD 2. Drink up, we've got to go and kill Lázaro.

BODYGUARD 4. We're talking about my mother.

BODYGUARD 2. I know.

BODYGUARD 3. Do you know what peromones are?

BODYGUARD 4. No.

BODYGUARD 3. They're smells that make you horny. It's an instinctive thing. My dog's got a good sense of smell, right? Pedro Infante had peromones, more than most, that's why people fancy him, and I think my dog can sense, when he sees a Pedro Infante film, that this guy had like loads of peromones, and that's why he barks at him. If you smell them on someone you can't help yourself. You'll fall in love with a transvestite if you smell peromones on her. If you don't, you won't.

BODYGUARD 4. How can you avoid them?

BODYGUARD 3. You can't. You smell them and – bam, you're in love, that's it. Terrifying isn't it? Think about it, you smell someone and you're fucked. Everything else, if you like her, if she's hot, if it's a man or a woman, none of that matters, just if what you smell turns you on or not.

BODYGUARD 2. What's this got to do with your dog and his mum?

BODYGUARD 3. I'm giving you a little bit of background on the subject. I went to school and I've read a few books, and you . . .

BODYGUARD 2. Come on, guys, we have to go and kill Lázaro. Turtleface is face-down in his own blood thanks to him and we're sat here talking about whether your pits smell or not.

BODYGUARD 4. Hold on, I want to know about this, it's important. I've always thought my wife snared me with some kind of witchcraft. Put spells on me and stuff. But no, turns out it was her sodding peromones turned my brain to mush and now I'm fucked.

BODYGUARD 3. Exactly. It's all in the smells.

BODYGUARD 4. That's it. From now on she's having a bath every day.

BODYGUARD 3. Might be a good idea.

BODYGUARD 2. Can we go now? We have to kill him today. We won't have time tomorrow.

BODYGUARD 3. All right, mate, dry your eyes. Come on then, God's sake.

At another table the HIT MEN *are with the two ugliest women in the place.*

HIT MAN 1. Think of a number.

HIT MAN 2. OK.

HIT MAN 1. Add ten, multiply it by two, take away seven, divide it by two, and take away the number you first thought of.

HIT MAN 2. OK.

HIT MAN 1. Your number is seven.

HIT MAN 2. Yes.

HIT MAN 1. It's always seven.

HIT MAN 2. That's incredible.

HIT MAN 1. I know. And if it isn't seven, it means something really terrible's going to happen. What do you think's the worst thing they can do to you?

HIT MAN 2. Got to be the penalty.

HIT MAN 1. The ball-base is worse. More humiliating.

HIT MAN 2. If it's humiliating you're after, the knockout is a real fucker.

HIT MAN 1. Have you ever had a knockout?

HIT MAN 2. Only penalties.

HIT MAN 1. That's not so bad.

A WOMAN *comes up to* HIT MAN 1 *and whispers something in his ear.* HIT MAN 1 *replies with a kiss on her cheek. The* WOMAN *goes.*

HIT MAN 2. Those four pansies are off.

As the BODYGUARDS *are getting up, the* HIT MEN *shoot at them. Only* BODYGUARD 2 *is left alive, wounded, on the floor.*

HIT MAN 1. Think of a number.

BODYGUARD 2. Please.

HIT MAN 1. Sorry. Please think of a number. If you get it right I'll let you go. Think of a number. Add ten, multiply by two, take away six, divide it by two.

BODYGUARD 2. Hold on. OK.

HIT MAN 1. Take away the number you first thought of. What do you get?

BODYGUARD 2. Eight.

HIT MAN 1. You can't even add up, you twat.

BODYGUARD 2. I had to divide and take away as well.

   HIT MAN 1 *kills him.*

HIT MAN 1. Couldn't even fucking add up.

Trailer for a feature film

The camera gives big panoramas of various Mexican tourist spots, in the style of a tourist-board promo film. Beautiful photography and women in bikinis. A few shots of Acapulco in the seventies and Cancún in the nineties.

VOICE-OVER. Believe it, foreigner. Mexico isn't just a country of poor people and picture-book beaches. Its territory is peppered with volcanoes and they're about to explode, sending ashes raining down all over the earth.

   Sequence in which a vast, stereotypical Mexican in a wide-brimmed hat roars over New York like King Kong or Godzilla. A giant Mariachi appears, pissing over Paris. In Tokyo a classic figure from the Mexican revolution gathers up women and stuffs them down his flies.

   All you non-Mexicans out there had better get used to the sound of these word. C*hingar*: that's Mexican for 'fuck you'. And *chingón*: that's 'you bastard'.

The screen fades to black, and then we see a huge sculpture of a stereotypical Mexican charro in wide-brimmed hat, in Rio de Janeiro, face to face with the famous statue of the open-armed Christ.

Space for our sponsors

The MARKETING WOMAN *steps forward to resume her spiel. She is immediately interrupted by the next scene, and sits down again.*

Don Juan distributing alms

The set of a postmodern staging of Don Juan. *Important figures from the arts world cram the auditorium.*

ACTOR PLAYING DON JUAN. This is as far as I'm paid to act, Mephistopheles, so it's time for the real money-spinner. I haven't got any books to burn, so I'm going to burn my friends. The people who know what we're like as people. We've had enough of being people.

All the ACTORS *on stage, who in reality are hired killers, shoot into the audience. Others open fire from the auditorium. Others, stationed in the aisles, slam the exit doors shut. Others all over the theatre kill the* SECURITY PERSONNEL. *The beautiful theatre. Temple of the Fine Arts. In every home that has a television people watch it burn.*

Virtual circle of Hell (the one for artists)

The fire burns, bombs are still going off. Shots. All the characters from the play are caught in the flames; they're all burning up. Bodies plummet from the flies.

ACTRESS/DÕNA INÉS. By the time I find you, everyone will be dead. They've been hurling themselves out of the boxes. I never imagined a human body could find so many different positions to fall in. Some of them are quite surprising, like cycling face up, walking face down, looking at the soles of your feet, walking with your legs bending the wrong way like a dog's. One guy looked like he was cleaning a window and waving at the people inside. And all that while they burn up and die. It's horrible.

SHADOW. Don't be afraid, everything's going to be OK.

SANTIAGO. No, no, it's not going to be OK, nothing is going to be OK. Stop pretending you're just doing the bastard gardening, nothing is going to be OK.

SHADOW. We're lucky, we really are. We're victims, we'll always be the ones who did nothing wrong. No matter what a cock-up you were making of your life, people will always talk about us as that terrible, irreparable loss. We're victims. For mortals who weren't up to much, that's the best ending we could have hoped for.

SANTIAGO. Rubbish, I was an artist, I deserved a better send-off than this. An obituary, seminars, anthologies, a monograph, tributes.

SHADOW. You're better off dying as a victim, I promise. No one will dare say a word against you, no one will dare suggest you're anything other than pure as the driven snow. You should be grateful to whoever it was who saw to it that we finish up like this. Sure, it hurts, yes, but not as much as cancer. Old age. Clotted arteries.

SANTIAGO. I don't care about that, I want revenge, I want . . .

MINISTER. Wretched soul, I am the angel sent to console you, hear my celestial voice . . .

SANTIAGO. You always were a shitty actor.

MINISTER. Yes, but I'm dead, I don't have to worry about reviews now.

ACTRESS/DÕNA INÉS. Look how we're burning, I never imagined a body could burn in so many different ways, look at our bones, they're going all wrinkly, like your skin does when you've been in the water for a long time.

SANTIAGO. She should listen to herself.

SHADOW. She can say what she likes, she's a victim, they'll forgive her everything. Everyone'll just say how beautiful and sad it all is.

MINISTER. I've been forgiven for everything I did and everything I didn't do. Now I've come over to the celestial side I intend to help people, make miracles happen for them. It's high time there was a patron saint of 'people who aren't quite getting it together to make the most of their potential'. There's a real gap in the market, I could do some really good work in that field, and that way when I reincarnate I'll be born into a good family, a family that spends its time, I don't know, saving endangered species, and all my childhood I'll play with wild animals as if they were kittens. That's how I'll redeem myself from being a relative of Lázaro's, because with all this junk in flames . . .

SANTIAGO. Junk, what do you mean, junk?

MINISTER. Oh all right then, people, whatever. The point is it's not exactly brilliant karma, is it, setting light to them all? I, on the other hand, am ready to follow the Tao.

SANTIAGO. I think you're getting your religions crossed there, mate.

MINISTER. I'm not getting anything crossed. Now that I'm dead I can see perfectly clearly what happens to us when we depart the world.

SHADOW. Victims are poetic and adorable.

SANTIAGO. Stop being so flippant, you wanker.

Trying to land a punch on the SHADOW, SANTIAGO starts to disintegrate and mingle with the remains of the MINISTER's shadow and the ACTRESS/DÕNA INÉS; the remains of other people join the mix.

ACTRESS/DÕNA INÉS. How beautiful to cease to be a thing, a recognisable thing like a little boat or a glove, to have your body turned to paste, to smoke, and to have nothing to say, or to say things that don't make any sense but which I've always liked the sound of like recipient flannel raincoat dorsal bulb gouda concoction with three c's navigate marsupial shhh shhh shhh.

The building collapses.

Angels descend to sow justice in the world

Rubble and fire from the building, sirens and helicopters and all the spectacle of a big catastrophe. RESCUE WORKER 1 *is* HIT MAN 1.

RESCUE WORKER 1. There's one over here.

RESCUE WORKER 2. Careful, don't tear his coat.

RESCUE WORKER 1. He's moaning.

RESCUE WORKER 2. A live turd.

SURVIVOR 1. It's a miracle, I'm alive, oh thank you, God. You don't know what happened. There are more survivors underneath me. I'm seeing the light of day again, I'm breathing, it's air. God, this air is so beautiful . . .

RESCUE WORKER 2. A dead turd.

> RESCUE WORKER 1 *takes out a pistol and kills the* SURVIVOR.

You numpty, you put a hole in the coat, can't sell it now. I think it was your size, too.

RESCUE WORKER 2 *takes the watch and valuables from* SURVIVOR 1 *as he lies dying*.

RESCUE WORKER 1. I don't care, I get paid anyway. Whatever you think you can use you can keep. Where are your friends?

RESCUE WORKER 2. I don't know, we have to get a move on before they cordon off the area.

RESCUE WORKER 1. I need more uniforms for my mates. We could pair up with you guys, we'll finish them off and you keep what you want, but I need those uniforms now.

RESCUE WORKER 2. I told them already, they're on their way. He's still not dead.

RESCUE WORKER 1. I'm not going to shoot him again. I'm not made of bullets.

> RESCUE WORKER 2 *takes a rock and hits him*.

SURVIVORS. Hey, we're down here, there are five of us.

RESCUE WORKER 2. I hate doing this.

RESCUE WORKER 3. Where are you from? Which NGO?

RESCUE WORKER 1. We're volunteers.

RESCUE WORKER 3. You have to go and register at that hut over there, there are some people going around killing survivors.

RESCUE WORKER 1. So I've heard. You identify yourself first.

RESCUE WORKER 3 *shows him an ID card.*

I can't see it.

RESCUE WORKER 3 *comes closer,* RESCUE WORKER 1 *hits him and shoots him.* HIT MAN 2 *comes running up, salutes* RESCUE WORKER 1 *and puts on* RESCUE WORKER 3*'s uniform.*

RESCUE WORKER 2. Come on, wristwatch, come to daddy.

Elsewhere in the rubble:

FIREMAN 1. I saw them last night. It's true.

FIREMAN 2. Are they like they said?

FIREMAN 1. No, but they do want revenge.

FIREMAN 2. But not on us, right? They know we wanted to save them.

FIREMAN 1. Have you heard of a writer called Chessbeer?

FIREMAN 2. No.

FIREMAN 1. There's this play of his about a man who breaks his leg. They sack him from his job, and then they put the wrong sort of pin in the joint so he ends up disabled. He has to beg for a living, but nobody believes him about the pin because you can't see it, it's inside his leg, so he gets an X-ray done and he hangs it round his neck, to show why he can't walk, but nobody believes it's his leg in the picture and they don't give him any money. Then these three witches turn up and I can't remember the rest, but what he says is, that people who want revenge just want revenge full stop, they couldn't care less who they get it from. That's how revenge gets spread through the world.

FIREMAN 2. Doesn't mean to say it's true, just because he said it.

FIREMAN 1. You don't have to be afraid. There's some really good self-help literature out there you could read. Your fear is a reflection of your insecurities.

FIREMAN 2 *hears something.*

I heard that too – over here, quick, get all these tiles out of the way.

SURVIVOR 2. Please don't move me any more. Let me die like this, I know I'll have to go back under the earth in a moment, but I just wanted to come up to the surface to die. Please, laugh, I'm trying to do this with a sense of humour, leave the world with an appreciative smile, mocking the life that mocked me. Life, you don't owe me anything. Ahhh. We're nothing more than actors who are taking the place of other actors who didn't make it through the audition, that was rigged anyway, to get into this world that's a stage, laugh with me, *I want to wake up in the city that never sleeps* . . . It hurts, I'm afraid, smile for me . . . My . . . God . . .

FIREMAN 1. Half-boiled idiot clown. As Chessbeer might have said.

REBECA *and* LÁZARO *appear on a different part of the stage.*

REBECA. Tell me you love me, tell me here, on top of what we've created together.

LÁZARO. I love you.

REBECA. Can you feel it?

LÁZARO. No, but I'd like to be able to. I'd like to be a whale and destroy tourist boats, we'd swim together in their blood, I'd collect their wet clothes and give them to you like bunches of flowers.

REBECA. Stop your profanities and kiss me.

PABLO *and* FRANCESCO *enter a small tent where* SURVIVORS *of the fire and the collapsing buildings are being kept. They are armed.*

PABLO. Everyone who can, run for it.

Those who can, run. With burlesque choreography, they beat and kill the rest.

Some events which did not occur but which were imagined by the characters

PABLO. Darkness. A sports car's headlights appear. Expensive, deluxe, beautiful. A coward crouching in the lights begs for mercy, saying things like 'Please, no,' those soft pleas a person makes when they're definitely doomed. The car's bonnet pops open. 'Unscrew the oil cap. See if it's full. Is it? Right, then drink some.'

I get out of the car. I'm wearing a beautiful navy blue jacket. I get the man to follow me, and make him lick the dipstick. And then I slam down the bonnet.

The car reverses away with the man's tongue hanging off the bumper.

A beautiful scene, backlit.

FRANCESCO. Open it, you animal, or I'll blow your cock off. Open your e-mail. Now, you are going to send this message to all the contacts you sent your little joke to. Write: 'I am a dog, an envious dog, I sent the last e-mail out of pure envy, because I was wetting myself with jealousy.'

Once the writer has sent the e-mail, I close the laptop and smash it against the writer's head. He falls to the floor. The computer is wrecked. I pick up some of the letters that have come off the keyboard and jam them into the writer's mouth as he breathes his last.

Eat your words, feed on yourself, dog, swallow your slobber, swallow yourself.

I leave the man dying slowly on the floor.

REBECA. I drag a woman in, give her two very precise blows and the woman falls to the floor clutching her stomach. I bring over a fan with metal blades. I put the woman's hand in it, and the woman screams. I bring over a double bass case and put the woman inside. It's difficult and I have to use force. The case moves desperately and screams. I sit on it. I shoot into it. The case stops moving.

FRANCESCO. Nice.

Simple version of the same story

MARIANA (*reads and remembers*).

'Dear Mariana,

I'm sorry that I took so long to get as far as being carnal with you. We deserved something better. But you can consider it a compliment, or just a funny little quirk, your female instincts will tell you how best to take it. At least we split up before it was too late. The secret of success in relationships is finding the right moment to split up. Dawn is best. I suspect we've already forgotten our best moment together. And we'd never agree which one it was. When lovers row there's always a third party involved, and it's subjectivity. You'll say: our anniversary night. Our first night together, I'll say. For you it's all about completing things, for me it's about starting them in the first place. Since we've got down to intimacies let me tell you something, to show you that my leaving you makes some sense. Don't turn it into the vulgar idea that there are other women apart from you, of course there are other women, the others are all the women that aren't you, the possibility of the infinite compared to the limited space you take up with your body. Do you remember the day we bought those secretly recorded videos? From hotels all over the city, remember? We were curious what it would be like to see couples copulating in hotels, recorded without their knowledge. You thought it was disgusting, I found it boring, everyone doing the same thing, going over the same old ground without any sense of creativity or instinct. I hope what we saw then inspires you to go on being yourself, to open your mouth and say: "This is all lies," or "This guy is mad." "I believe in love and happiness." If you're honest, though, if you ask your body, it will agree with me. The pornography you make has saved me from you. From your kind. From needing you. Please, don't start any home-grown psychology on this. Just repeat my name until you get bored of it. An instinctive and natural method familiar to lovers through the ages. Repeat the name until it loses all meaning, until you think it might be the word for some kind of cheese, or a bodily organ. It's such a pity to live in an age when clothes let you see everything. Remember? When the paintings on the walls of people's houses were of the Greek gods in flagrant acts of vice and lechery, drowning in our gorgeous human flaws. All those paintings, those sculptures, made for the walls of public buildings and civic spaces. Now they're hanging in museums, and they see all kinds of idiots walking by talking about art and the aesthetic project, with their cheap cameras, being tourists instead of doing something worthy of the species. All those portraits, those harpsichord concertos, those tapestries were made for one thing, for lust. Now they're stuck in those freezer cabinets of humanity, museums.'

Two of the other ACTORS *have started fidgeting and chatting at the edge of the stage.* MARIANA *drops her Latino accent.*

Could you just shut the fuck up? It's hard enough doing this accent without you two cocking around.

Back with the accent.

'When did art stop being all about copulation, about tricks and ruses to seduce a woman? It was a truly sorry day and a terrible shame when some artist first had the idea that art wasn't about seducing women, a sorry, sorry day, and nothing good has come of it. What does art mean to most people nowadays? Auctions. And the occasional robbery on the front page. Art used to be the son of lechery, of greed, of unbounded pleasure, but that's all history, we're superfluous now, we produce diversions for people who need something to do before they go back to the hotel to be filmed in secret. When did art part company with copulation? When did it part company with flesh? There I go, talking about my stuff again. I never get round to talking about you. No one can see the point any more and it's going to come crashing down on us.

With zombified scraps of love,

Lázaro.'

The urinal pacts between a businessman and an ex-president

A huge public toilet. Noises of a party going on outside drift in. The FATHER *and the* EX-PRESIDENT *are talking. Upstage we glimpse a dead man with his head in a toilet bowl.*

FATHER. I've splashed myself.

EX-PRESIDENT. Doesn't matter.

FATHER. Yes it does. They'll think I've wet my pants.

EX-PRESIDENT. Nobody will think that.

FATHER. They'll all think that.

EX-PRESIDENT. We've all done it.

FATHER. Let's wait until it dries, please. Please.

EX-PRESIDENT. If you want.

FATHER. I'm very grateful for this.

EX-PRESIDENT. There's no need.

FATHER. Nobody chooses their children.

EX-PRESIDENT. You don't have to feel guilty. *You* didn't fry those people like so much popcorn.

FATHER. I feel as though I did. My wife's ill. Has been since the day of the funeral.

EX-PRESIDENT. I spoke to Aaron yesterday. He said to me, 'Do you know what the worst thing about having a son is? It's like having a dim-witted enemy who you have to dig out of all the scrapes he gets himself into, just so that he can start fighting you again.'

FATHER. It's always about war with Aaron. His office is covered in scale models of all the planes in 201 Squadron.

EX-PRESIDENT. He's not governor for nothing. He's got a scale model of his state, with everything – the capital, little towns, roads, drugs plantations, the brothels operating out of hairdressing salons. He pores over it at breakfast and mends the broken pieces, tweaking this and that. Every day he makes some little adjustment or other. That church your wife had restored, he restored it on his model too. You should go and have a look one day. Stunning thing. I don't mean your wife, of course.

FATHER. I didn't think you did.

EX-PRESIDENT. And he's got a model of that drug rehabilitation centre in Chiapas, he's got his eyes on the governorship there, too. It's beautiful. When you go and visit your son you'll want to stay. It's right on the edge of the national park. Beats any prison I've ever seen. He should be in high security for what he's done, but no, he's got a river view, fruit straight off the tree and day trips every Sunday, from what I can gather.

FATHER. How many inmates are there?

EX-PRESIDENT. None. Your son will be the only one there. Like something out of *Arabian Nights*. That won't be coming cheap.

FATHER. The money's not a problem. I've just bought up all the factories in the entire Central American division.

EX-PRESIDENT. Oh, congratulations, very wise purchase.

FATHER. I never imagined my son would be capable of something like that.

EX-PRESIDENT. It wasn't pretty, there were people running around the streets still on fire. Like sparklers on legs. But let it go, it was just as if it had been an accident in the end. You have to let things go. If you get into the right mindset, things that have already happened don't exist any more. The past doesn't exist.

FATHER. It's a shame about the building, it was beautiful.

EX-PRESIDENT. Why doesn't your wife restore it?

FATHER. I told you, she's not well.

EX-PRESIDENT. That doesn't matter, she can put a tender out, get the building done up and the matter's closed, not even any tax to pay, job done.

FATHER. I feel responsible.

EX-PRESIDENT. You can't see it any more, come on.

FATHER. Are you sure? There's still a bit of a dark patch.

EX-PRESIDENT. Only if someone's looking really hard. And who's going to be scrutinising your groin?

FATHER. What does it feel like to be an ex-president?

EX-PRESIDENT. It doesn't feel like anything. Well, all right, it feels good. Like with this, for example, because I can help you out. I've learned a lot. Come on.

FATHER. Not yet, you can still see it a bit. Have you ever seen Federico Fellini's *Orchestra Rehearsal*?

EX-PRESIDENT. What's that?

FATHER. A Fellini film.

EX-PRESIDENT. I don't like special effects, I'm a man of action. Practical. If you've got a computer the world seems simple, but life's not like that. Young people don't understand that. They should be made to understand.

FATHER. In this film the members of an orchestra go on strike, but the union won't support them so they paint a fifteenth-century building.

EX-PRESIDENT. Sport is important. It instils competitiveness. The strongest, the weakest, the also-ran. That's what life is like.

FATHER. You should see the film.

EX-PRESIDENT. I don't like special effects.

FATHER. There aren't any.

EX-PRESIDENT. Oh, a low-budget thing is it? Can't see it now.

FATHER. I'll pull my shirt out.

EX-PRESIDENT. Not such a great look.

FATHER. Better than them thinking I wet my trousers.

EX-PRESIDENT. Do you really want to know what I learned as president?

FATHER. Yes.

EX-PRESIDENT. That the only important thing, the only thing that counts, is love. It's love that makes the world go round. Aaron makes his models out of love, your wife restores buildings out of love, you save your son out of love, just like any father would. Everything happens out of love. If you relax you can feel it, flowing through you, infinite, eternal.

FATHER. And all those regrets you had, about what happened with . . . the people who died . . .

EX-PRESIDENT. I realised that I was living a mistake. Universal love forgave me, why shouldn't I forgive myself? Like I was saying just now, if you think about it carefully, none of that exists, we live in the eternal present, not in the past, in love's present. I feel much better since I've been thinking like this. I'm getting younger. I've opened my heart to you. I hope you appreciate that.

FATHER. Of course, don't worry.

EX-PRESIDENT. Poor sod. Wasn't he a friend of your wife's?

The FATHER *closes the toilet door.*

Diversion

LÁZARO. Forget the whole idea of home. Being static stunts the emotions. Go. Learn to go. Like chewed meat goes down our throats. Like your body goes towards the windscreen in a car crash. Like the old man's body goes towards its bed. Like the handicapped person's body goes towards its wheelchair. Like the newborn child goes towards the doctor's sterilised hands. Learn to go. Like cultured viruses go through the syringe. Like damp and cracks go over walls. To go. Go along the broken line in the middle of the road. The white line which goes past one point above the tarmac and another one below it, underneath the tarmac, where the dead people are. Go without using your legs. Let things go past you. Let the trees go past. Let the grass go past. Let shops, signposts, railway sidings go past. On the road, it's all about going, letting things go past. Of all the things that men build, the road is the only one which urges us to go. The others all teach us, badly, to stay where we are. And it's best to go in the passenger seat or in the back, not to drive, not to have the correct angle for the rear-view mirrors, your feet nowhere near any pedals, if possible not to see the little spots of blood on the windscreen from the insects that die as you drive. Being static stunts the emotions.

The flow of blood towards the ground and the fields

A donkey is dying in the road. It has been hit by a car. Its broken body is blocking both carriageways, its blood is all over them. A dog and an OLD MAN *are keeping it company. A wooden cart carrying cactuses has been abandoned in the middle of the road.* LÁZARO *arrives.*

LÁZARO. Was it yours?

OLD MAN. It's not dead yet, son. Best not touch him, he's dying, this is when they can turn on you.

LÁZARO. Did you see who hit him?

OLD MAN. A lorry. And they're all the same.

The OLD MAN *goes to his cactus cart and starts pulling it away.*

LÁZARO. You can't go.

OLD MAN. You keep him, if he's any use to you.

LÁZARO. He was yours.

OLD MAN. He wasn't mine. I just looked after him. You stay, if you want.

LÁZARO. You miserable old bugger, I thought you might have learned something by your age.

OLD MAN. I've learned that when there's nothing to be done, you don't do anything. If you can do a miracle and save him, you're welcome to him.

LÁZARO. I will.

LÁZARO *approaches the animal cautiously. He strokes it. The animal stirs, but lets* LÁZARO *stroke it.*

OLD MAN. Great miracle.

The OLD MAN *goes back to his cart and starts pulling it.* SANTA CLAUS *enters where the* OLD MAN *is about to leave. The donkey dies.*

SANTA CLAUS. Afternoon, gentlemen. Anyone hurt?

LÁZARO. It's more serious. There's a dead animal.

OLD MAN. You killed it.

LÁZARO. He died.

SANTA CLAUS. I can help you move him to one side.

LÁZARO. What makes you think we want to move him? Besides, you'll get blood all over your white bits.

OLD MAN. Don't talk to him, he's a killer. You can smell it on him.

SANTA CLAUS. Shit. I have to get to the village and I'm late already.

LÁZARO. Funny time of year for it.

OLD MAN. You want my advice? Don't talk to him.

SANTA CLAUS. Old Fernandez's son has fallen very ill, they think he won't last the night. His father's asked me to take his toys round to him before he dies, he wants him to see me before he goes so that he dies believing that I exist. That Santa exists. So I have to look the part. The kid's five.

OLD MAN. He won't understand, he doesn't understand anything, he must be from the capital.

LÁZARO. I'll help you move him.

SANTA CLAUS. Where are you headed?

LÁZARO. To the hostel by the national park.

SANTA CLAUS. Oh, very nice. That's a beautiful place. Foreigners, mostly. They say they've turned it into a rehab place for drug addicts, but I don't believe it. It's gorgeous there. I was a taxi driver before this, I went there a few times, very smart. Holiday, is it?

LÁZARO. Yes.

SANTA CLAUS. Can we try pushing him out of the way?

While SANTA CLAUS *starts taking off his clothes,* LÁZARO *waves offstage, and two* BODYGUARDS *armed with pistols in their belts, enter.*

LÁZARO. They're with me.

SANTA CLAUS, LÁZARO *and the two* BODYGUARDS *push the mule to one side of the road. They get covered in blood. The* WISE MEN *put their costumes back on over their dirty clothes.* SANTA CLAUS*'s mobile rings.*

SANTA CLAUS. Hello? . . . Yes señor . . . Oh no. All right . . . That's fine . . . Yes . . . No, don't worry . . . No, really, don't worry . . . Our prayers are with you . . . Goodbye. He says the kid's dead, there's no point us coming now, he'll send the cheque first thing.

OLD MAN. May God receive him into his glory.

LÁZARO. Who, the kid or the mule?

OLD MAN. I told you he was with Satan.

SANTA CLAUS. You don't joke about stuff like this.

LÁZARO. Cigarette?

SANTA CLAUS. Thanks

One of the BODYGUARDS *offers* SANTA CLAUS *a cigarette and exits. The* OLD MAN *takes his cart and pulls it in the opposite direction to where he was going before.*

LÁZARO. Weren't you going the other way?

OLD MAN. I'm going into the village to pray for the kid's soul. Little children are dying and people like you are still alive. Makes me sick.

SANTA CLAUS. Are you his father?

LÁZARO. No. Does he look like he is?

SANTA CLAUS. I thought hatred like that only existed between fathers and sons.

LÁZARO. No. As long as there are similarities.

SANTA CLAUS. What do you do for a living?

LÁZARO. I'm an aesthetic terrorist. My job is to provoke terror and compassion. Art is dead and terrorism is alive. Terrorism is the art of our times. The radical staging, the ultimate realism, the dismantling of the system, the deconstruction of humanity. The only things I believe in are terrorism and pornography. The salvation of the pornographic muse. And everything I say is a lie. That's what an artist is, that's what I do.

SANTA CLAUS. Wow. Well, as you can see, I'm a Santa.

LÁZARO. Yes. We're in the same business.

The OLD MAN leaves with his cactuses. People from the village start to arrive with machetes. The first ones chop the mule up into bits, then more come and argue over its meat. Fights break out. The villagers get covered in blood. LÁZARO and SANTA CLAUS smoke in silence.

Front door

Funeral parlour. All the mourners. The REPORTERS fire off their flashes in LÁZARO's face. News cameras, the mass media. The interview with LÁZARO is over.

LÁZARO. That's what I have to say about the death of my grandfather. I have nothing to add.

The photographers come closer to photograph the OLD MAN in the coffin, and ask for shots of the young, well-dressed women who are there in their short dresses.

MERCI. Hi, you're Lázaro.

LÁZARO. I don't know you.

MERCI. I'm Merci, your grandfather's partner.

LÁZARO. If my mother sees you, she'll kill you, she thinks you poisoned the old man.

MERCI. And what do you think?

LÁZARO. I don't care what the old man spent his money on.

MERCI. I want to tell you how he died.

LÁZARO. I'm not interested.

MERCI. It will help you to make decisions about –

LÁZARO. I told you, I'm not interested.

MERCI. Lázaro, I –

LÁZARO. Get out.

MERCI. I'm a man, I deceived your grandfather all his life.

LÁZARO. You're lying.

MERCI. Touch me here. And your stupid old man never realised. Let's go somewhere private where I can tell you the whole story, it'll help you decide things.

LÁZARO. Follow me.

LÁZARO and MERCI go into a side room.

So you're a man and you deceived Grandpa.

MERCI. Actually no, the fact is . . .

LÁZARO hits MERCI, a few kicks and punches. She can't defend herself. Once she's on the ground, LÁZARO checks that her body is that of a woman.

LÁZARO. Shit, you're a woman.

MERCI. Yes.

LÁZARO. Why did you tell me you were a man? What the fuck was that all about? You don't cock around with me like that.

MERCI. Don't kill me.

LÁZARO. I'm not going to kill you, I wouldn't have touched you if you hadn't told me –

MERCI. I didn't kill your grandfather, I loved him.

LÁZARO. You didn't love him, you wanted his money.

MERCI. Your grandfather was the most beautiful person I have ever –

LÁZARO. Quiet, someone's coming, this place is crawling with my mother's bodyguards.

He covers MERCI*'s mouth and drags her into the room where the* LITTLE MAKE-UP GIRL *is looking after the injured* BODYGUARD 1.

THE LITTLE MAKE-UP GIRL. Do you want me to do her?

LÁZARO. No, not this one. You look after that one.

BODYGUARD 1. Please, call a doctor.

LÁZARO. We will if you shut up.

BODYGUARD 1. How can you do this to me? I worked for you for five years.

MERCI. Don't kill me.

LÁZARO. We'll see you get better.

MERCI. I didn't kill your grandfather, it was the woman who tried to sort him out.

LÁZARO. What, and she sorted him out once and for all?

BODYGUARD 1. Have pity on me.

LÁZARO. If you don't shut up we'll leave you there to croak. How did the old man die?

MERCI. We went to the Texas desert with some friends of mine, to hunt emigrants.

LÁZARO. Shit, it's always so twisted with you people.

MERCI. Your grandfather's rifle went off in his hands, he was wounded, we had to take him back to Mexico through a hole in the border fence so that no one would see us, and we bumped into some emigrants, one of the women said she could cure him if we gave her dollars, I gave her some and she put some herbs on the wound, it soothed his pain, but he was dead within a couple of hours. They gave me some kind of tea, and then in the hospital they had to pump my stomach out or I'd have died too.

LÁZARO. Why didn't you take him to a hospital?

MERCI. Because we'd killed two emigrants and they were in the back of the truck.

LÁZARO. How can I have come from such shit?

MERCI. It's the truth.

BODYGUARD 1. Please, in the name of God.

LÁZARO *kicks him in the wound.*

LÁZARO. Shut up. When my mother finds out about this . . .

MERCI. I wanted you to tell her. I loved your grandfather.

LÁZARO. Why did you tell me you were a man?

MERCI. I don't know. I wanted to talk to you alone.

LÁZARO *drags her over to where* BODYGUARD 1 *is. He says something to the* LITTLE MAKE-UP GIRL *and leaves.*

BODYGUARD 1. Who are you?

MERCI. The dead man's wife.

BODYGUARD 1. Señora Merci, it's me, Alejandro.

MERCI. I don't remember you, leave me alone, get away from me.

BODYGUARD 1. I can't move, I'm dying. Will you hear my confession.

MERCI. I'm not a priest. I'm not even Catholic.

BODYGUARD 1. God will understand, all you have to do is when I've finished say that I'm forgiven, please, I'm dying.

MERCI. Shut up. Get away.

BODYGUARD 1. I killed three people, but they were all thieves and I've repented. The guilt has been a living hell. I cheated on my wife, I said bad things, I lied, I wished bad things on other people, I've arrested innocent people and said they were guilty, I've tortured, I've tried to rape girls . . .

MERCI. Shut up, I'm not a Catholic, I don't care about your life. As for what you've done, I hope you rot in some hell or other. You, child, get me out of here, I've got lots of money, have pity.

BODYGUARD 1. I have a son, I never acknowledged him as my own, but he's sixteen years old, I know where he lives, I'd like to send him something. Let me write something to him.

MERCI. For God's sake, I've got money, do you believe in God?

BODYGUARD 1. Don't listen to her, she's a monster, she just told me that she's not Catholic and now she's talking about God.

MERCI. You won't get out of this, I will, I've got people looking for me.

The MAN IN CHARGE *of the funeral home enters.*

MAN IN CHARGE. God above.

MERCI. Señor, help, please.

THE LITTLE MAKE-UP GIRL. Señor, I don't know anything about this . . .

The MAN IN CHARGE *takes out a pistol and shoots* MERCI *and* BODYGUARD 1.

MAN IN CHARGE. That's how problems get solved, sweetheart. While you work for me in this funeral home you have to learn to solve problems. Understood?

A state of rights and its obverse

LÁZARO *and* SANTA CLAUS *are next to the skeleton of the mule in the road, smoking.* SOLDIERS *appear. When* SANTA CLAUS *and* LÁZARO *see them, they get up.*

SOLDIER 1. This is them. These are the guys from the rebels.

LÁZARO. No, we're not.

SOLDIER 2. Shut it. If they are, they are, and that's that.

SOLDIER 1. They're not only traitors, they're poofs, look at the clothes on this one.

SANTA CLAUS. I work as a –

SOLDIER 1. Shut up, you fucking queer.

He hits him with his rifle butt. SANTA CLAUS *falls to the ground. He's bleeding.*

SOLDIER 2. Right, let's play a little game. Who's got the camera? Take some photos of me. You have to guess who I am. Come on, bark like a dog, you bastard.

He puts a rope round SANTA*'s neck while the other* SOLDIER *takes a photo of him.*

Now make like an elephant. Look at the little elephant. Have you guessed what I am? A gringo soldier in Iraq. We'll be like them one of these days, just like them and we'll invade the rest of the world. Now make like . . . like . . . what do you think? Oh yes, look at him on his knees worshipping me, I'm a star.

SOLDIER 1. Quick, officers coming.

SOLDIER 2. Stand up, you pansies.

LÁZARO, *the* BODYGUARDS *and* SANTA *line up. The soldier with a machine gun opens fire on them.*

Fucking traitors.

Finally . . . a miracle

Dusk. A junkyard in the desert, near the border between Mexico and the US. A truck pulls up and EMILIO, MERCI *and two* BLONDES *get out. The* BLONDES *are drunk and hold each other up, giggling.*

EMILIO. You're going to love this, it only happens every few thousand years when the earth's polarity changes. It's to do with magnetism.

MERCI. Isn't it dangerous?

EMILIO. No. I just want you to see this and then we'll go and hunt us some emigrants, I promise.

MERCI. All right.

The BLONDES *laugh and fall over. They talk in English, but we can't hear what they're saying.*

EMILIO. Can you be quiet for a moment, just for one moment?

MERCI. Shut up, *fucking bitches.*

The BLONDES *laugh.*

EMILIO. See that? It's a miracle of nature. See?

The junk metal is starting to lift off the ground, banging together. It makes a riotous concert of metal sounds. The BLONDES *scream, terrified. The junk metal spirals higher, whole chunks of car, spare parts, only the tyres stay on the ground.*

This is a miracle. And no one to see it.

The metal carries on flying. Old EMILIO *shoots at it with a rifle,* MERCI *laughs.* EMILIO *blasts the junk apart with his gun, the* BLONDES *are crying with fear. The moon gets covered in bullet holes. Craters, if you like.*

MERCI. It's beautiful, it's beautiful, I want to cry, it exists, it does exist.

Awkwardness

Military post by the road. SOLDIER 1 *and* SOLDIER 2 *are playing cards. Shots in the distance.*

I hope this world forgets me, like someone who signs for
  someone else's parcel.
But you can't ask so much of anyone

Born under the only rule that the creator cares about us
   not forgetting:
Survive for as long as you can. Survive.
I have been boring.
I'm writing it because I don't have anyone to say it to:
I have been boring.
We should finish before we get boring,
Before the yawning and the nodding of heads from those
   who have loved us,
But I outstayed my welcome.
I have been boring.
A few lines more, a few lines less. It doesn't matter
I am guilty.

And the Great Bureaucrat keeps a silence as cold as the
   hook they hang cattle on.
Over all of us.

The SOLDIERS *carry on playing, bored. The distant shots get more frequent.*